Arizona
Real Estate
License
Exam Prep

2nd Edition

All-in-One Review and Testing to Pass Arizona's Pearson VUE Real Estate Exam

Stephen Mettling
David Cusic
Ryan Mettling
Kurt Wildermuth

Performance Programs Company
502 S. Fremont Ave., Ste. # 724
Tampa, FL, 33606
www.performanceprogramscompany.com

Material in this book is not intended to represent legal advice and should not be so construed. Readers should consult legal counsel for advice regarding points of law.

© 2017 by Performance Programs Company
502 S. Fremont Ave. Suite #724,Tampa, FL 33606
info@performanceprogramscompany.com
www.performanceprogramscompany.com

ISBN 978-0915777044

Contents

Introduction

Welcome licensee candidates and future real estate professionals!

We know you have worked hard just to get here – you've completed or nearly completed your prelicense curricula, and now all you have to do is pass the state license exam. But easier said than done – and that's where we come in. We know the exam can be tough, and very nerve-wracking to prepare for. That's why we created the Arizona Real Estate License Exam Prep (AZ-RELEP) the way we did. Since we have been managing real estate schools and developing curriculum for forty years, we know how all this works – or fails to work. Let us assure you – you made the right decision buying this publication to prepare for your Arizona exam. Here's why.

First, AZ-RELEP is comprehensive in that it contains both key content review and testing practice. And the text review is AZ-specific – not just simplistic national content, but terse, relevant and accurate state laws and regulations presented as a well-organized set of state 'key point reviews' ideal for pre-test memorization. But let's not dismiss the importance of the national content either. AZ-RELEP's national key point reviews are a succinct compression of tested national principles and practices that comprise the national portion of state license exams from coast to coast. Our content is drawn from our own national textbook, Principles of Real Estate Practice – one of the most widely used principles textbooks in the country. Finally, our national content, as well as our question selection, is further tailored to the state testing outline promulgated by Pearson VUE for Arizona. Thus the breadth and depth of the law reviews and test questions reflect the topic emphasis of your state's testing service and your AZ license exam.

A word about the test questions… AZ-RELEP's testing practice section consists of ten national practice tests, six state practice tests, and one state exam sample test. The test questions are designed to cover the content covered by the law reviews – which reinforces your learning of the total body of information tested by your state exam. The questions are direct, to the point, and designed to test your understanding. When you have completed a given test, you can check your answers against the answer key in the appendix. You may also note that each question's answer is accompanied by a brief explanation, or "rationale" to further reinforce your understanding.

Your particular study and testing practice strategy using AZ-RELEP is up to you. But to fully exploit its comprehensive content coverage, you should try to review and memorize the key point reviews as much as possible. Then you should make every effort to take each exam, review your mistakes, and re-read the key point reviews that cover your weaker areas.

In the end, as you know, it's all up to you. Unlike other publications, we are not going to tell you that using this book will guarantee that you pass your state exam. It still takes hard work and study to pass. But we have done our best here to get you ready. Following that, the most we can do is wish you the best of success in taking and passing your state exam. So good luck!!

About the authors

For over forty five years, Stephen Mettling and David Cusic, PhD, have operated Performance Programs Company, one of the nation's most successful training organizations specializing in real estate program development. Mr. Mettling and Dr. Cusic have jointly written over 100 books, courses, and custom programs in all facets of real estate for some of the country's largest real estate schools, associations and organizations.

Mr. Mettling has also served as vice president and author for the country's largest real estate training and publishing organization. Under various capacities, he has managed the acquisition, development, and sale of national real estate textbooks and publications, as well as directed the country's largest affiliated group of real estate schools.

Dr. Cusic, an author and educator with international real estate training experience, has been engaged in vocation-oriented education since 1966. Specializing in real estate training since 1983, he has developed numerous real estate training programs for corporate and institutional clients around the country.

Ryan Mettling, junior partner and currently general manager and marketing director of Performance Programs, is an accomplished online curriculum designer, author and course developer. His other principal publication is Real Estate Math Express. Mr. Mettling graduated Valedictorian from the University of Central Florida's College of Business Administration.

Kurt Wildermuth is an Arizona Department of Real Estate Certified School Administrator, Certified Instructor, and Associate Broker. He is the owner and director of the Arizona Mountain School of Real Estate in Flagstaff, and has been teaching real estate salesperson and broker pre-licensing courses as well as continuing education classes since 2005.

In addition to his real estate education expertise, Kurt has taught marketing and communication courses on the university level for more than 25 years. His business experience includes serving as a former vice president of an internationally affiliated public relations counseling firm. As a member of the Real Estate Educator's Association, Kurt has conducted numerous workshops and seminars in various real estate education subjects, including curriculum development.

Section I: National Principles & Law Key Point Review

Note: in the following pages, salespersons are sometimes distinguished from brokers. For broker-only states, the reader should substitute "broker" for "salesperson" and "managing broker" or similar title for "broker" as appropriate.

Rights

Land / Real Estate / Real Property

Land:	surface, all ***natural things*** attached to it, subsurface, and air above the surface
Real estate:	land + **manmade** permanent attachments
Real property:	real estate + bundle of rights

Bundle of Rights

"PUTEE":	***P*** ossess
	U se
	T ransfer
	E xclude
	E ncumber

Physical Characteristics of Real Estate

Physical characteristics
- Immobility; indestructibility; heterogeneity. (*uniqueness*)

Immobility
- Land cannot be moved from one site to another; its location is forever fixed

Indestructibility
- Land is permanent and cannot be destroyed since by definition it extends below ground and into the sky
- Since land is permanent, it does not depreciate
- Only improvements depreciate and are insurable

Non-homogeneity
- Land is non-homogeneous; no two parcels of land are exactly the same since they have a different location

Physical aspects of real estate

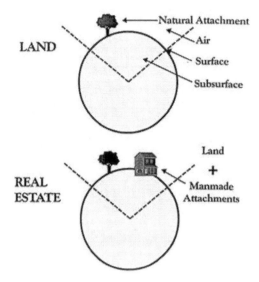

Legal Title v. Equitable title

Legal title

- Full legal ownership of property and the bundle of rights as they apply to it. Contrasts with equitable title.

Equitable title

- An interest that gives a lienholder or buyer the right to acquire legal title to a property if certain contractual conditions occur

---

Riparian / Littoral

Riparian Rights (Rivers and Streams)

- navigable: own land to water's edge
- *not navigable*: own underlying land to midpoint of stream

Littoral Rights (Lakes and Seas)

- own to high water mark

Memory Tip: R : River Riparian   L: Lake Littoral

Real / Personal / Fixture

Real Property:
- land
- fixtures
- attachments

Personal Property:
- chattels
- trade fixtures
- emblements

Differentiation criteria:
- intention; adaptation; functionality; relationship of parties; contract provisions

Conversion:
- real to personal property-- severance personal to real property-- affixing

Emblements:
- plants or crops considered personal property

Trade fixtures:
- personal property items temporarily attached to real estate in order to conduct business

Interests & Estates

Interests

Possession	Non-possession
• Estate	• Encumbrance • Public interest

Estates

Freehold (Own)	Leasehold (Lease)

• Fee simple
  - Absolute
  - Defeasible
 	
• Life Estates
  - Conventional
  - Legal
	• Estate for years
	• Periodic
	• Estate at Will
	• Estate at Sufferance

Freeholds

Fee simple — Highest
- *not limited* by one's lifetime
- absolute: *highest* form of ownership interest
- defeasible: *reverts* to previous owner per conditions

Life estate
- passes *to another* upon death of a named party
- remainder: *named party* to receive estate
- reversion: *previous owner* to receive estate

Conventional life estate
- *limited* to lifetime of life tenant or named party
- pur autre vie: limited to lifetime of another,

9

passes to remainderman or previous owner

Legal life estate
- created by operation of state law as opposed to a property owner's agreement
- designed to protect family survivors
- homestead:
  - rights to one's *principal residence*
  - laws protect homestead from creditors
  - family must occupy the homestead
  - cannot be conveyed by one spouse
  - endures over life of head of household
  - interests extinguished if property destroyed

Leaseholds

Estate for years
- specific, *stated duration*, per lease

Periodic
- lease term *renews automatically* upon acceptance of rent

Estate at Will
- for *indefinite period* subject to rent payment; cancelable with notice

Estate at Sufferance
- tenancy *against landlord's will* and without an agreement *Don't mule at*

Ownership

Forms of Ownership

Tenancy in severalty
- *sole* ownership

Tenancy in common
- co-tenants individually own undivided interests
- *any ownership share possible*
- no survivorship
- can convey to outside parties

Joint tenancy = 1 S PiTI
- equal undivided interest jointly owned
- *survivorship*
- requires *four unities* to create: time, title, interest, possession

Tenancy by the entireties
- *husband and wife* own equal undivided interest
- Now applies to same-sex couples in some states

Community property *Spouse*
- *joint property ownership* by spouses as opposed to separate property

Joint Tenancy & Four Unities

Unity of ownership
- owners hold single title jointly

Equal ownership
- owners always hold equal shares

Transfer
- may transfer to new owner as a tenancy in common interest with remaining joint tenants

Survivorship
- on death, interests and rights pass to other joint tenants

Creation
- requires "four unities," *PITT*:

  1. *P*ossession: acquire same possessory rights
  2. *I*nterest: acquire equal, undivided interests
  3. *T*ime: acquire interests at same time
  4. *T*itle: acquire interests with same deed

Community Property

Separate

- acquired *before marriage*
- acquired by *gift or inheritance*
- acquired with *separate-property funds*
- *income* derived from *separate property*

Community

- all other property earned or acquired during the marriage

Estates in Trust

- *Trustor* gives title, deed, trust agreement to trustee
- *Trustee* renders fiduciary duties to trustor and beneficiary ℝℯ𝒞
- *Beneficiary* receives ownership benefits

Condominiums   Airspace / common elements Shared

- ownership of a *unit of airspace* plus an *undivided interes*t in the *common elements* as tenant in common with other owners
- may be sold, encumbered or foreclosed *without affecting other unit owners*
- creation: by developer's declaration

Cooperatives /Corporation

- ownership of *shares in owning corporation*, plus *proprietary lease* in a unit
- corporation has sole, undivided ownership

nant

sw/land [handwritten]

- *attaches* to the estate
- *dominant* tenement's *right to use* or restrict adjacent *servient* tenement
- *by necessity*, to *landlocked* owners
- party wall easement in a shared structure: to not damage or destroy

in Gross

-not transffered
- not attached [handwritten]

- *does not attach* to the estate
- **Personal**-- not transferrable, ends upon death of easement holder
- **Commercial**-- transferrable, granted to a business

by Prescription

Squatter [handwritten]

- obtainable through *continuous, open, adverse use* over a period

License

Can use property [handwritten]

- *personal* right to use a property
- *does not attach*
- *non-transferrable*
- *revocable*

Lien Types

Examples

voluntary / involuntary:
general / specific:
superior / junior:

- mortgage lien / tax lien
- against any & all assets / against car or house
- paid before juniors / paid after superiors by date of recording

---

Lien vs. Title Theory State

- **lien theory state** -- lender of mortgaged property holds equitable title rather than legal title; borrower holds legal title.

- **title theory state** – lender holds legal title to the mortgaged property until the mortgagor satisfies the terms and obligations of the loan.

Lien Priority

- Order in which liens against a property are satisfied
- The highest priority lien is paid by foreclosure proceeds before any other lien

Superior Liens by rank

- Real estate tax liens
- Special assessment liens

Junior Liens by date of recording

- Federal income tax liens
- Judgment liens

- Federal estate tax liens
- State inheritance tax liens

- Mortgage liens
- Vendor's liens
- Mechanics liens (priority by date work performed)

Foreclosure

Mortgage lien foreclosure:
- liquidation of collateral property by *judicial, non-judicial,* or *strict* foreclosure

Judicial foreclosure:
- lawsuit and court-ordered public sale; *deficiency judgments, redemption rights*

Non-judicial foreclosure:
- *"power of sale"* granted to lender; no suit; *no deficiency* judgment; *no redemption* period after sale

Strict foreclosure:
- court orders *legal transfer of title directly to lender* without public sale

Deed in lieu of foreclosure:
- defaulted *borrower deeds property to lender* to avoid foreclosure

Transferring & Recording Title

Notice

Notice:
- how ownership is evidenced to the public

Actual notice:
- *knowledge acquired directly* through demonstrable evidence, e.g., presenting or inspecting a deed, visiting a party in possession

Constructive notice:
- *knowledge one could have obtained*, as presumed by law; imparted by recording in public records "for all to see"

Voluntary / Involuntary

Voluntary transfer
- deed
- will
- public grant

Involuntary transfer
- descent (without will, with heirs)
- escheat (without will nor heirs)
- foreclosure (loan default)
- eminent domain (public good)
- adverse possession (hostile, open use)

Deed Validity

Requirements:
1. grantor
2. grantee
3. in writing
4. legal description
5. granting clause
6. consideration
7. grantor's signature
8. acknowledgement
9. delivery and acceptance

Deed Clauses

Premises:	granting
Habendum:	type of estate
Reddendum:	restrictions
Tenendum:	other property included

Deed Types

Bargain and sale: "I own but won't defend"
General warranty: "I own and will defend"
Special warranty: "I own and warrant myself only"
Quitclaim: "I may or may not own, and won't defend"

Special purpose deeds: Used for different purposes, interests conveyed, or by different parties

---

Deed Restrictions

Deed restriction
- single-property use restriction as stipulated in a deed; may not be discriminatory

- examples: minimum area of a residence; setbacks; limits on other structures; conducting commercial activities

Declaration restriction
- use restriction in multiple-property declarations; enforced by court injunction

Deed condition
- usage restriction that can trigger repossession by a previous owner if violated

---

Transfer Tax

- **Documentary stamp tax:** tax on conveyance of real property based on price of property conveyed
- Facilitates ad valorem assessment
- Payment evidenced on deed

14

Testate / Intestate

Order of Title Transfer

Dies testate with heirs:
- first to creditors
- then to homestead
- then **to heirs by will**

Dies intestate with heirs:
- first to creditors
- then to homestead *no will*
- then *to heirs by laws of descent*

Dies intestate, no heirs:
- first to creditors
- then **to state by escheat** *no will*

Evidence of Title

Forms of evidence to prove marketable title and ownership:

- title insurance
- attorney's opinion of abstract
- title certificates
- Torrens registration

Leases

Estate Types

Gross lease
- landlord pays expenses; tenant pays higher rent than net

Net lease
- tenant pays some or all expenses; rent is less than gross

Percentage lease *Company*
- landlord receives rent minimum plus percentage of retailer's sales *Company*

Residential lease
- gross lease hybrid; short term; uniform terms reflect landlord-tenant standards

Ground lease
- landlord owns and leases ground but does not own improvements

Proprietary lease
- for cooperative unit owners; indefinite term; assigned to new unit owner on sale

Leasing of rights *(Air, mineral, water)*
- leasehold transfer of rights for limited use; examples: air, mineral, water rights

URLTA

Leases:
- clear lease terms
- fair market rent
- cannot waive rights

Deposits:	• limits on amounts • tenant's right to interest • rules and deadlines for returning
Landlord Obligations:	• bargain in good faith • provide maintenance and repairs • comply with building codes • provide safety and access • procedure for delivery of notices
Tenant Obligations:	• maintain condition • abide by rules and regulations • no damage or abuse • abide by approved uses • no disturbance of other tenants

Lease Termination

Causes

- default
- notice
- property destruction
- death

- term expiration
- voluntary agreement
- condemnation
- abandonment under certain conditions

Land Use

Planning and Zoning Definitions

Building code: A standard of construction of an improved property established by local government officials

Certificate of occupancy: A document confirming that a newly constructed or renovated property has fully complied with all building codes and is ready for occupancy

Concurrency: A planning policy that requires developers to correct foreseen negative impacts of a development during the construction period of the project itself rather than afterwards

Condemnation: 1. A decree that a parcel of private property is to be taken for public use under the power of eminent domain. 2. A government order that a is no longer fit for use and must be demolished.

Deed restriction: A provision in a deed that limits or places rules on how the deeded property may be used or improved

Eminent domain: A power of a government entity to force the sale of private property for subsequent public use

Land use control: Regulation of how individual owners use property in a municipality or planning district. Control patterns are in accordance with a master plan

Master plan: An amalgamated land use plan for a municipality, county, or region which incorporates community opinion, the results of intensive research, and the various land use guidelines and regulations of the state. Acts as a blueprint for subsequent zoning ordinances and rulings

Non-conforming use : A legal or illegal land use that is not consistent with the current zoning ordinance

Police power: A government's legal authority to create, regulate, tax, and condemn real property in the interest of the public's health, safety, and welfare

Restriction: A limitation on the use of a property imposed by deed, zoning, state statute, or public regulation

Special exception: A land use in conflict with current zoning that is authorized because of its perceived benefit to the public welfare

Variance: A land use that conflicts with current zoning but is authorized for certain reasons, including undue hardship to comply and minimal negative impact to leave it alone

Zoning ordinance: A municipal land use regulation

Land Use Planning

Goals of land use control
- preserve property values; promote highest and best use; safeguard public health, safety and welfare; control growth; incorporate community consensus
- process: develop plan; create administration; authorize controls

puble per

The master plan
- long term growth and usage strategies; often required by state law
- local plans fuse municipal goals and needs with state and regional laws

Planning objectives
- control growth rates: how much growth will occur and at what rate
- control growth patterns: type of growth desired, where it should be located
- accommodate demand for services and infrastructure

Plan development
- research trends and conditions; blend local and state objectives into master plan

Planning management
- commission makes rules, approves permits, codes, and development plans

Public Land Use Controls

Zoning
- "police power" granted by state-level enabling acts; zoning ordinance: creates zones, usage restrictions, regulations, requirements
- Enables urban land managers to create separate land uses that do not conflict with one another nor create incompatible adjacencies

Types of zone
- residential, commercial, industrial, agricultural, public, PUD
- residential zoning regulates *density*, or number of dwellings in an area
- commercial zoning regulates *intensity*, or how much commercial activity is permitted in relation to size of the site

Zoning administration
- Zoning Board of Adjustment oversees rule administration and appeals

Zoning Appeals
- **Nonconforming use:** legal if use existed prior to zone creation, illegal otherwise
- **Variance:** use exception granted based on hardship
- **Special exception:** based on public interest
- **Amendment:** change of zones; rezoning

Eminent Domain
- allows a government entity to purchase a fee or easement interest in privately owned real property for the **public good** and for **public use** in exchange for "just compensation"

Planned Unit Development (PUD)
- PUD zoning designed to regulate use of whole tracts of land with a singular design
- Design purposes are to achieve optimum space efficiency and open space

Subdivision Regulation
- plat of subdivision and relevant requirements must be met and approved; must meet FHA requirements for insured financing
- location, grading, alignment, surfacing, street width, highways
- sewers and water mains
- lot and block dimensions
- building and setback lines
- public use dedications
- utility easements
- ground percolation

Building Codes
- comprehensive onsite and offsite construction and materials standards; must be met to receive certificate of occupancy

Environmental Restrictions
- flood control; solid waste disposal; air quality; water quality; marine protection; noise control; toxic substances controls; lead paint; CERCLA; Superfund

Zoning Appeals

Zoning Board of Adjustment: oversees rule administration and appeals.

Nonconforming use: legal if use existed prior to zone creation, illegal otherwise

Variance: use exception granted based on hardship

Special exception: based on public interest

Amendment: change of zones; rezoning

Environmental Controls

Areas of concern
- air, soil, water quality; ambient health hazards; natural hazards

Major legislation
- limits damage to environment; standards for air, land, water, materials use

Responsibilities & liabilities
- disclosure and information for practitioners; remediation for owners

Environmental Laws

Legislation	Date	Regulated
Solid Waste Disposal Act (later part of RCRA)	1965 (1976, 1999, 2002)	landfills
Air Quality Act, Clean Air Act	1967 (1970)	air quality standards
National Environmental Policy Act (NEPA)	1969 (1970)	created EPA
Flood Control Act	amended 1969	building in flood zones; flood insurance
Resource Recovery Act	1970	solid waste disposal
Water Quality Improvement Act	1970	dumping in navigable waters; wetlands
Water Pollution Control Act amendment	1972	dumping in navigable waters; wetlands
Clean Water Act	1972 (1977)	dumping in navigable waters; wetlands
Lead-based paint ban (US Consumer Product Safety Commission rule)	1978	lead-based paint in residences
PCB ban (EPA rule)	1979	polychlorinated biphenyls
RCRA amendment	1984	underground storage tanks
Comprehensive Environmental Response, Compensation and Liability Act (CERCLA)	1980	hazardous waste disposal
Superfund Amendment and Reauthorization Act	1986	hazardous waste cleanup costs
Asbestos ban (EPA rule)	1989	asbestos in building materials
Residential Lead-based Paint Hazard Reduction Act (EPA and HUD rule)	1992 (1996)	lead-based paint disclosure and treatment
Flood Insurance Reform Act	1994	flood insurance in flood zones
Brownfields legislation	2002	industrial site cleanup

Legal Descriptions

Purpose
- to accurately locate and identify the boundaries of a parcel of real property to a degree acceptable by courts of law in the state where the property is located
- general criterion is that it alone provides sufficient data for a surveyor to locate the parcel

Metes and Bounds Method

- describes perimeter by landmarks, monuments, distances, angles
- usable within rectangular survey system
- starting at point of beginning (POB), follow perimeter, **return to POB**

Lot and Block System
- used to describe properties in residential, commercial, industrial subdivisions
- tracts of land divided into lots, then grouped into blocks

Rectangular Survey System

Meridians:	• north-south lines six miles apart
Parallels:	• east-west lines six miles apart
Range:	• north-south strip between meridians
Tier:	• east-west strip of area between parallels; also called township strip
Township: ~~6 x 6 36 w~~	• the six-mile by six-mile square at the intersection of a range and a tier
Section of a township: ~~(x) = 640 w~~	• a 1 mile x 1 mile square; 1 section = 640 acres; 36 sections per township
Fractions of a section:	• going from the smallest to largest unit, indicate size and location within successively larger quarters or halves of the section: E 1/2 of the NE 1/4 of the NE 1/4 of Section 8

Economics

Supply
• the quantity of a product or service available for sale, lease, or trade at any given time

Demand
• the quantity of a product or service that is desired for purchase, lease, or trade at any given time

Supply / Demand / Price

Real Estate Supply	• property available for sale or lease; measured in dwelling units, square feet, acres
Real Estate Demand	• property buyers and tenants wishing to acquire; measured in households, square feet, acres
Interaction	• if supply increases relative to demand, price decreases; • if demand increases relative to supply, price increases

Supply-Demand Cycle

unmet demand →
    construction adds supply →
        market equilibrium →
            construction adds more supply →
                oversupply →
                    construction stops →
                        market equilibrium →
                            demand absorbs supply →
                                unmet demand →
                                  cycle repeats

Factors Influencing Supply and Demand
- cost, availability of financing
- availability of developable land
- construction costs
- capacity of infrastructure
- governmental regulation and police powers
- changes in the economic base
- in- and out-migrations of major employers
- labor availability
- land availability

Government Influences on the Real Estate Market
- local zoning power
- local control and permitting of new development
- local taxing power
- federal influence on interest rates
- environmental legislation and regulations

Market Indicators
- **Vacancy rates**
  - increases indicate buyer / tenant market & falling prices / rents
  - decreases indicate seller / landlord market & rising prices / rents

- **Building permits** – increases indicate declining vacancy; increasing prices & construction
- **Prices**
  - increases indicate rising demand or declining supply or both
  - decreases indicate falling demand or rising supply or both

Appraisal

Regulation of Appraisal Practice

FIRREA
- Financial Institutions Reform, Recovery and Enforcement Act (**FIRREA**) enacted in 1989 to regulate appraisal practices
- requires that competent individuals whose professional conduct is properly supervised perform all appraisals used in federally-related transactions
- As of January 1, 1993, federally-related appraisals must be performed only by state-certified appraisers
- **USPAP** - Uniform Standards of Professional Appraisal Practice – competency standards established by the **Appraiser Qualifications Board** of the Appraisal Foundation

Concepts and Principles of Value

Supply and demand
- When demand exceeds supply, scarcity exists, values rise.
- When supply exceeds demand, surplus exists, values decline.
- When supply and demand are, the market is in balance, values stabilize.

Utility
- A property's use in the marketplace contributes to the demand for it.

Transferability
- How readily or easily title or rights to real estate can be transferred affects the property's value.

Anticipation
- The benefits a buyer expects to derive from a property over a holding period influence what the buyer is willing to pay for it.

Substitution *Pay no more than comp*
- A buyer will pay no more for a property than the buyer ~~would have to pay for an equa~~lly desirable and available substitute property

Contribution
- the contribution to value of an improvement is equal to the change in market value that the addition of the improvement causes

Change
- Market conditions affect the benefits that can arise from the property

Highest and best use
- A property achieves its maximum value when it is put to whichever use generates the greatest income and return. The highest and best use must be legally permissible, physically possible, financially feasible, and maximally productive

Conformity
- A property's maximal value is attained when its form and use are consonant with surrounding properties and uses

Progression and regression
- The value of a property is influenced by the values of neighboring properties

Assemblage
- Conjoining adjacent properties can create a combined value in excess of the values of the unassembled properties. This excess value is called **plottage value**

Subdivision
- The division of a single property into smaller properties can result in a higher total value

Types of Value

Market value
- Market value is an estimate of the price at which a property will sell at a particular time. This type of value is the one generally sought in appraisals and used in brokers' estimates of value

Insured value
- Insured value is the face amount a casualty or hazard insurance policy will pay in case a property is rendered unusable

Reproduction value
- Reproduction value is the value based on the cost of constructing a precise duplicate of the subject property's improvements, assuming current construction costs.

Replacement value
- Replacement value is the value based on the cost of constructing a functional equivalent of the subject property's improvements, assuming current construction costs

Salvage value
- Salvage value refers to the nominal value of a property that has reached the end of its economic life. Salvage value is also an estimate of the price at which a structure will sell if it is dismantled and moved.

Assessed value
- Assessed value is the value of a property as estimated by a taxing authority as the basis for ad valorem taxation

Depreciated value
- Depreciated value is a value established by subtracting accumulated depreciation from the purchase price of a property

Book value
- Book value is the value of the property as carried on the accounts of the owner. The value is generally equal to the acquisition price plus capital improvements minus accumulated depreciation.

Investment value
- The value of an income property as indicated by the capitalized value of the cash flow the property generates

Market Value Requirements

The price willing buyer and seller would agree on given:

- a cash transaction
- reasonable market exposure
- parties have market and property use information
- there is no pressure to complete the transaction
- transaction is arm's length: parties are not related
- marketable title
- no hidden influences

Appraisal Process \

1. Identify the purpose
2. Assimilate the relevant data
3. Assess the highest and best use
4. Estimate the value of the land
5. Apply the three approaches to value
6. Reconcile the values from the approaches
7. Compile the report

Sales Comparison Approach — VACANT LAND

1. Identify comparable sales
2. Compare comps to the subject and make adjustments to the comparables
3. Weight values indicated by adjusted comparables for the final value estimate of the subject

Adjusting Comparables

Rules for selecting comparables
- must be physically similar
- in subject's vicinity
- recently sold in arm's length sale

Rules for adjusting comparables
- never adjust the subject!
- deduct from comparable if better than subject
- add to comp if worse than subject
- Remember: ("Subtract if Superior !")

Weighting adjustments
- best indicator has fewest and smallest adjustments and smallest net adjustment from the sale price

Cost Approach (LAND VALUE) churches

1. Estimate land value
2. Estimate replacement cost of improvements
3. Estimate total depreciation
4. Subtract: (improvements - depreciation) + land value
5. Add: (land value + depreciated improvements)

Depreciation, etc.

Depreciation
- **loss of value** from deterioration, functional obsolescence, or economic obsolescence

Deterioration
- **wear and tear** from use and aging

Functional Obsolescence
- **outmoded** physical or design **features**: curable or incurable

Economic Obsolescence
- loss of value due to adverse **changes in surroundings**: incurable

Curability
- curable: cost to cure is less than resulting

contribution to value

- incurable: cost to cure exceeds contribution to value

Income Approach *NOI Income - Expense ÷ cap Rate*

- Based on the principle of anticipation: the expected future income stream of a property underlies what an investor will pay for the property
- Also based on the principle of substitution: that an investor will pay no more for a subject property with a certain income stream than the investor would have to pay for another property with a similar income stream.

Steps in the Income Approach

1. Estimate potential gross income
2. Estimate effective gross income (potential - vacancy)
3. Estimate net operating income (NOI) (effective income - expenses)
4. Select and apply capitalization rate (NOI ÷ cap rate)

Gross rent multipliers
- Simplified income-based methods to estimate value
- Method consists of applying a multiplier to the estimated gross rent of the subject
- Multiplier is derived from market data on sale prices and gross rent
- Does not necessarily produce accurate value estimates

Formula
- GRM = price divided by monthly rent
- Value = GRM times monthly rent

Preparing a Comparative Market Analysis

Steps
1. Identify comparables sold, for sale properties, and expired listings
2. Compile comparison data for each comparable: price, sale date, location, age, lot size, site aspects, living area, bedrooms, etc.
3. Complete adjustments for differences; rules:
   a. Never adjust the subject
   b. Add value to the comparable if a feature is inferior to the subject
   c. Subtract value from the comp if a feature is superior to the subject
4. Derive total adjustments for each comparable
5. Reconcile all value-adjusted comps to the subject to identify a value estimate

Mortgage Transaction

Elements
- promissory note: promise to repay loan
- mortgage: pledge of property as collateral for loan

Mechanics
- borrower gives lender promissory note and mortgage
- lender gives borrower funds and records a lien

Hypothecation —6wc proper
- use of real property as collateral for a mortgage loan

Financial components
- original principal: capital amount borrowed on which interest payments are calculated
- loan balance: remaining unpaid principal at any point in the life of the loan
- interest: charge for the use of money; rate fixed or variable
- Annual Percentage Rate (APR) includes interest and all other finance charges; lender must disclose on residential properties
- point: one percent of the loan amount
- loan origination fee: charged by lender at origination to obtain required return
- term: period of time for repayment of interest and principal
- payment: the periodic payment of interest and/or principal
- down payment: borrower's cash payment applied to the purchase price
- loan-to-value ratio: the loan's share of the total value of the property
- equity: at closing, the borrower's cash invested in the property; thereafter, the difference between the market value and the loan balance

Trust Deed Transaction

Elements
- promissory note: trustor's promise to repay loan
- deed of trust: title to property as collateral for loan

Mechanics
- trust deed conveys title from the borrower/trustor to a third-party trustee
- trustee holds title on behalf of the lender/beneficiary until the debt is repaid

Promissory note
- legal instrument executed by borrower stating debt amount, loan term, method and timing of repayment, interest rate, promise to pay; may repeat other provisions from mortgage document or deed of trust; negotiable instrument assignable to a third party

Mortgage Clauses

Payment of Principal and Interest: Prepayment and Late Charges
- Borrower must make timely payments according to the terms of the note
- Late payments or early payoffs may trigger penalties

Funds for Taxes and Insurance
- Borrower must make monthly payments to cover taxes and hazard insurance
- Borrower may also have to pay flood insurance and mortgage insurance premiums

- **Escrow account**: reserve account for periodic payments of taxes and insurance.
- Real Estate Settlement Procedures Act (RESPA) limits funds the lender can require for this purpose.

PITI
- Borrower's monthly payment for principal and interest is called the P&I payment (principal and interest)
- The amount which includes the escrow payment is called PITI (principal, interest, taxes, insurance).

Charges and Liens
- Borrower is liable for paying any charges, liens, or other expenses that may have priority over the mortgage or trust instrument.

Hazard or Property Insurance
- Borrower must keep property insured as the lender requires.

Occupancy, Preservation, Maintenance and Protection of the Property
- Borrower must take and maintain occupancy as the borrower's principal residence according to requirements
- Borrower must not abuse or neglect the including use for illegal purposes, creating hazardous waste on the property, or destroying the improvements

Protection of Lender's Rights in the Property
- Lender may take actions to protect its rights in the property if the borrower jeopardizes the property's value. The costs of these actions would be charged to the borrower

Mortgage Insurance
- Lender may require private mortgage insurance, or PMI which protects the lender against loss from borrower default
- Applies to loans that are not backed by the Federal Housing Administration (FHA) or Veterans Administration (VA) and that have a down payment of less than 20% of the property value

Inspection
- Lender may inspect the property with reasonable cause to fear damage to the collateral

Condemnation
- If the property is condemned or taken by eminent domain, lender reserves a claim on any resulting proceeds

Transfer of the Property or a Beneficial Interest in Borrower
- If borrower sells the property without the lender's approval, the lender may demand immediate repayment of the loan balance. This alienation clause, aka a due-on-sale clause, allows lender to prevent unapproved loan assumptions
- The requirement to repay the loan before the scheduled due date is called **acceleration**.

Borrower's Right to Reinstate
- If lender holds borrower in default, borrower has the right to reinstatement by performing certain actions, usually paying overdue payments plus expenses the lender
- Clause is called a redemption clause
- Gives the borrower time to satisfy obligations and prevent a forced sale

Release
- Agreement to release the lien obligation when borrower has paid off the loan
- Release clause, aka **defeasance** clause, may require lender to execute a **satisfaction of mortgage**, aka **release of mortgage**

- If deed of trust, lender directs trustee to execute a **release deed** or **deed of reconveyance** to the borrower as trustor.
- Release deed or satisfaction should be recorded as necessary

Escalation Clause
- Allows lender to increase the loan's interest rate

Types of Mortgages

Conventional mortgages
- Originated by banks and private financial institutions
- No government-related insurance or guarantees as with FHA or VA
- Typically require 20% down payments; smaller down payments may require PMI
- Assumptions require approval

Government loan programs
- **FHA** – federally insured loan programs (see following)
- **VA** – federally guaranteed loan programs (see following)

Amortized fixed-rate v adjustable loans
- **Amortized:** payments include increasing increments of principal which retire loan balance over loan term
- **Fixed rate:** interest rate does not change – can have for amortized or interest-only loans
- **Adjustable loans:** interest rate fluctuates up or down with an index; payments may also vary

---

Adjustable Loan Characteristics

- **Mechanics**: rate adjusts up or down with index; payments may or may not change;
- **Negative amortization**: loan balance increases if payments are less than what is owed given the balance and rate, i.e., unpaid monthly amounts are added to the principal balance
- **Rate and payment caps**: maximum amounts the interest rate or payments can increase in a given adjustment period or over the life of the loan; protects borrower from unaffordable increases
- **Index and margin**: interest rate tied to any number of financial indices. Margin equals a fixed point spread between the index and the interest rate
- **Teaser rates:** to attract borrowers, adjustable loans may have low initial rates which increase over subsequent adjustment periods to a more permanent market level.

Custom Mortgages

- **Partially amortized with a balloon:** payments will not retire principal balance over life of the loan, thus requiring a lump-sum payment, or "balloon" payment at end of term
- **Interest-only loans:** loans where payments are interest only, and the principal balance is retired in full at maturity using a balloon payment
- **Biweekly mortgage:** loan payments are every-two weeks, a device that reduces total interest paid, but also shortens risk period for the lender
- **Package mortgage:** mortgage loans which also finance articles of personal property as part of the purchase transaction
- **Home equity loans:** funds borrowed using the homeowners equity for collateral; funds can be used for any purpose
- **Purchase money mortgage:** a seller-financed loan to the buyer of portions of the purchase price using the property as collateral. Usually accompanied by a senior underlying first mortgage
- **Reverse annuity mortgage:** a financial arrangement where the homeowner pledges equity to a lender in exchange for periodic payments of the pledged equity. In essence it is the periodic receipt of equity liquidation in exchange for an increase of debt owed on the property.

FHA Loans

Insured loans granted by approved lenders to qualified borrowers.

Loan term:	• 15, 30 years
Qualifying ratios:	• income: 31% • debt: 43%
Minimum downpayment:	• 3%
Mortgage insurance:	• required at 78% LTV or above • premium = one-time 1.75-2.25% of loan am plus annual premium
Points:	• None
Maximum loan amount:	• varies by Metropolitan Statistical Area

VA Loans

Guaranteed loans:	• granted by approved lenders to qualified veterans
Qualifying ratios:	• depends on lender
Minimum downpayment:	• None
Points:	• 1.25 - 3.3, depending on downpayment, type of loan, type of veteran

Loan Qualification

Equal Credit Opportunity Act
- lender must evaluate applicant according to applicant's own income and credit information

Income qualification
- income ratio and debt ratio qualify borrower's income; income ratio applied to gross income determines housing expense maximum; debt ratio takes revolving debt into account
- income ratios: 25-28% conventional; 29% FHA-insured
- debt ratios: 36% conventional; 41% FHA and VA

Cash qualification
- lender verifies applicant's sources of cash for down payment; extra cash enhances income qualification evaluation

Net worth
- extent to which applicant's assets exceed liabilities as a further source of reserves

Credit evaluation
- lender obtains credit reports to evaluate applicant's payment behavior

Loan commitment
- written pledge by lender to grant loan under specific terms; firm, lock-in, conditional, take-out

---

The Mortgage Market

Supply and demand for money
- relationship between supply and demand for money affects interest rates, consumer prices, availability of mortgage money; regulated by Federal Reserve

Federal Reserve control of money supply among banks
- Sells T-bills to reduce money supply and increase interest rates; buys T-bills to increase supply and decrease rates
- Sets the reserve requirement for member banks
  - increase reserves to tighten money and raise interest rates
  - decrease reserves to loosen money and lower interest rates
- sets the discount rate for member banks
  - increase rate to tighten money
  - decrease rate to increase money supply

Federal Home Loan Bank System (FHLBS)
- Counterpart to the Fed for savings and loan associations

Federal Deposit Insurance Corporation (FDIC)
- Insures deposits up to $250,000 per depositor, per insured bank, for each account ownership category

The primary mortgage market
- Originates mortgage loans directly to borrowers;
- Includes savings and loans, commercial banks, mutual savings banks, life insurance companies, mortgage bankers, credit unions

The secondary mortgage market
- Buys existing loans to provide liquidity to primary lenders; Fannie Mae, Ginnie Mae, Freddie Mac, investment firms, life insurance companies, pension funds

Role of FNMA, GNMA, and FHLMC
- FNMA buys conventional, FHA- and VA-backed loans and pooled mortgages; guarantees payment on mortgage-backed securities
- GNMA guarantees payment on certain types of loans
- FHLMC buys and pools mortgages; sells mortgage-backed securities

Mortgage loan originator v. lender/banker v. broker
- Mortgage loan originator: solicits, negotiates mortgage loans; requires MLO license
- Mortgage broker: an intermediary who brings mortgage borrowers and mortgage lenders together, but does not use its own funds to originate mortgages
- Mortgage banker: person or entity who funds or services loans for others and/or who sells mortgages to the secondary market

Investment

Investment Terminology

Appreciation
- An increase in the value of a property owing to economic forces beyond the control of the investor

Asset
- A tangible or intangible item of value

Basis
- A measurement of how much is invested in the property for tax purposes; **adjusted basis** is the original cost of the asset plus capital improvements minus depreciation

Capital gain (or loss)
- The difference between the net sales proceeds of an asset and its adjusted basis

Cash flow
- The remaining positive or negative amount of income an investment produces after subtracting all operating expenses and debt service from gross income

Equity
- That portion of a property's value owned by the legal owner, expressed as the difference between the property's market value and all loan balances outstanding on the property

Leverage
- The relationship between the yield rate of an investment and the interest rate of funds borrowed to finance the investment. If the yield rate is greater than the loan rate, positive leverage results. If the yield rate is less than the loan rate, negative leverage results

Liquidity
- The degree to which an investment is readily marketable, or convertible to another form of asset. If immediately salable, an investment is liquid; the longer it takes to sell, the more illiquid the investment. Real property is relatively illiquid in comparison with other types of investment

Tax shelter
- An investment that produces depreciation or other non-cash losses that a taxpayer can deduct from other income to reduce tax liability

Investment Characteristics

Ownership benefits
- income
- appreciation
- tax shelter: depreciation and interest deductions

Ownership risks
- relatively illiquid
- management intensive
- negative leverage and price movements

Investment Entities

Direct
- investor buys directly and manages personally

General partnership
- all members own and manage

Limited partnership
- general partner manages; limited partners own but do not manage

Real Estate Investment Trust
- investors buy trust certificates; trust invests in real estate assets
- investors share returns per ownership percent

Risk Assessment

Market risk
- Changes in the demand may cause investment to lose value and become illiquid

Business risk
- Changes in the operation of a business impacting the investment may reduce the income and appreciation capacity of the investment

Purchasing power risk
- Changes in the value of money as an exchange medium, such as through inflation, may decrease the practical value of your invested resource

Financial risk
- Changes in financial markets & interest rates may reduce the value of the investment by making it less desirable and more expensive to maintain

Business Brokerage

Licensed activity
- Business brokers must be licensed in real estate
- Involves lease or fee conveyancing or dispositions

Business enterprise v business opportunity brokers
- Business enterprise brokers – engage in corporate transactions to sell or buy businesses that sell goods or services
- Business opportunity brokers – sell or buy small businesses

Comparisons between business and real property brokerage
- Different to real estate brokerage –
  - involves non-real-estate assets
  - business valued differently than real estate
  - may include corporate stock
  - may involve assuming short- and long-term liabilities
  - business market unlimited in geographic scope

- Experience & knowledge needed beyond real estate
  - corporate finance
  - business accounting
  - business valuation
  - business laws

Taxation

Real Property Taxation

Property exemptions
- Immune property: government property
- Exempt property: religious organization and nonprofit facilities
- Partial exemption: homestead exemption

Tax lien enforcement
1. unpaid taxes →
2. tax sale ordered →
3. equitable right of redemption →
4. tax sale to pay taxes, interest, and charges →
5. statutory right of redemption →
6. tax deed to successful bidder or holder of tax certificates

Federal Income Taxes

Principal residence taxation
- Taxpayers can deduct mortgage interest, ad valorem taxes, and fees relating to mortgage loan acquisitions including points
- May also deduct portions of living area used for in-home business, with qualifications

Investment property income taxation
- Tax is payable on net income after mortgage interest, depreciation, and operating expenses
- Owners may not deduct reserves from income, nor loan principal
- Taxable income is payable at ordinary income tax rates
- Annual depreciation allowed is equal to the improvement value divided by the number of years in the depreciation term (established by IRS); cannot depreciate the land portion of total value

Capital gain taxation of income property
- Taxes are charged on the capital gain realized from the sale of income properties
- Capital gain is equal to the amount realized at closing (price – selling costs) minus the adjusted basis of the property (beginning basis + improvements – total depreciation)

Contract Law

Contract defined
- An agreement between two or more parties who have a "meeting of the minds," and have pledged to perform (or refrain from performing) some act.
- A *valid* contract is *legally enforceable* by meeting certain requirements of contract law.

- If a contract does not meet requirements, it is not valid and the parties to it cannot resort to a court of law to enforce its provisions

---

Contract Status

Valid
- meets all requirements

Valid but unenforceable
- certain oral contracts; if performed, cannot change outcome

Void
- not valid; unenforceable

Voidable
- may be rescinded due to subsequent discoveries: if performed, cannot change outcome

---

Contract validity

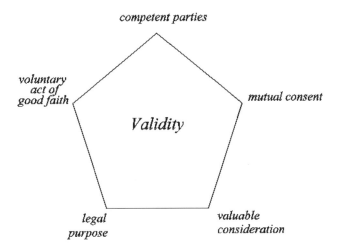

Competent parties
- legal age
- mental competency
- legitimate authority

Mutual consent
- clear and unequivocal **offer and acceptance** with an underlying **meeting of the minds**

Valuable consideration
- two-way exchange of valuable consideration for performance by the other party; not "love and affection"

Legal purpose
- promise, intent and content must be lawful; if illegal, contract is void – cannot contract to break the law

Voluntary, good faith
- no duress, coercion, fraud or misrepresentation

Offer / Counteroffer / Acceptance

Offer
- intention to enter into contract
- must contain all intended terms
- must be in writing
- expires in "reasonable time" or date and time specified

Acceptance
- unequivocal and manifest agreement to offer
- no changes to offer whatsoever
- signed, preferably dated

Completed contract
- communication of acceptance to offeror
- if by mail, offer is communicated upon mailing

Counteroffer
- new or amended terms of a received offer
- original offer is void

Revoking an offer
- may be done at any time prior to offeree's communication of acceptance

Contract Classifications

Oral vs. written
- oral, or parol, contract may not be enforceable

Express vs. implied
- express: all terms expressly agreed to
- implied: unintentional agreement deemed to exist due to terms implied by actions

Bilateral vs. Unilateral
- bilateral: both parties promise to perform
- unilateral: one party performs only if other party performs

Executed vs. Executory
- executed: fully performed
- executory: performance yet to be completed

Termination

Causes
- performance
- infeasibility
- mutual agreement
- cooling-period rescission
- revocation
- abandonment
- lapse of time
- invalidity of contract

36

Breach & Remedies

Rescission
- cancel contract; return deposits

Forfeiture
- defaulting party gives up something according to contract terms

Liquidated damages
- damages due a damaged party as stated in contract

Suit for damages
- civil suit for money damages not covered by contract

Specific performance
- suit to force party to fulfill contract promises

Agency

Universal / General / Special

Universal
- represent in all matters
- can contract for principal

General
- represent in business matters
- agent can contract for principal

Special
- represent in single business transaction
- normally agent cannot contract for principal
- characterizes the brokerage relationship

Termination

Causes

- fulfillment
- expiration
- mutual agreement
- incapacity
- abandonment or destruction of property
- renunciation
- breach
- bankruptcy
- revocation of license

Duties & Obligations

Agent's Fiduciary Duties to Client

Skill, care and diligence
- proactive; competent; act within bounds of expertise

Loyalty	• place client interest above customer and self
Obedience	• provided actions, instructions are legal
Confidentiality	• extends beyond listing term indefinitely
Full disclosure	• property condition; customers; material facts
Accounting	• proper handling of monies and documents

Obligations Owed Customers

- honesty and fair dealing
- reasonable care and skill
- proper disclosure

Misrepresentation and Fraud

Puffing – licensee boasting about property's benefits

Fraud
- misstatement or failure to disclose material fact
- knowledge that statement was false or fact should have been disclosed
- party relied on misstatement
- party was damaged by misstatement

Misrepresentation – misstatement or concealment of fact
- intentional misrepresentation: **purposeful misstatement** of material fact
- intentional omission: **purposeful concealment** of material fact
- negligent misrepresentation: **unintended misstatement** that agent should have known
- negligent omission: **unintended concealment** that agent should have known

---

Single / Dual / Sub / No Agency

Single agency	• seller or buyer agency • tenant or landlord representation
Subagency	• outside brokers and agents who help listing agent • listing broker's own agents
Dual agency	• representing both sides • potentially illegal or conflict of interest • must disclose & obtain written consent • voluntary by consent • involuntary by actions of parties (implied agency) • duties: all but full disclosure and loyalty
No agency	• "facilitator" or "transaction broker" • representing neither party in the transaction • duties to both parties: accounting; skill, care and diligence; honesty and fair dealing; disclosures affecting property value

Disclosure Rules

Objectives of disclosure
- declare
- explain
- offer choice
- obtain documented consent

Seller agent disclosures to client
- in writing
- on or before listing is executed

Seller agent disclosures to customer
- in writing
- prior to substantive contact
- oral disclosure permitted but must have written follow-up

Buyer agent disclosures to seller
- in writing
- upon first contact with listing agent or seller
- substantive contact is assumed

Dual agent disclosures
- "informed, written consent"
- may not disclose price or financing positions or motivations unless authorized

Facilitator disclosures
- on becoming transaction broker or on substantive contact, whichever is first

Listings

Parties / Duties / Contract

Parties	• listing broker-- fiduciary of buyer client or seller client • subagent-- fiduciary of listing broker's client • customer-- non-fiduciary principal in transaction
Fiduciary duties	• to client: loyalty; obedience; disclosure; care; diligence; accounting • to customer: honesty, care and disclosure
Authority	• limited agency agreement • broker may not contract for client unless specifically authorized • clients liable only for broker's acts within scope of authority
Contract law	• unilateral contract • oral listing is valid and enforceable • exclusive listing in some states must be written to be enforceable • personal service contract-- not assignable

Types

Exclusive right-to-sell
- given to one broker
- usually must be written
- must expire
- broker gets commission if property transfers during period

Exclusive agency
- exclusive excepting owner
- oral or written
- must expire
- broker gets commission unless owner sells

Open listing
- non-exclusive
- oral or written
- no stated expiration
- procuring cause gets commission
- no commission if client procures customer

Net listing
- all sale proceeds above a seller's minimum price go to the broker
- discouraged, if not illegal

Multiple listing
- listing placed in MLS
- owners consent to rules and provisions of MLS

Buyer agency agreements
- create a fiduciary relationship with the buyer
- if exclusive, buyer agrees to only work with the buyer representative in procuring a property
- must have an expiration date along with other requirements of a valid listing

Compensation / Termination

Compensation
- negotiated between agent and principal
- where disputed among agents, agent with procuring cause is owed commission
- based on results: find ready willing and able customer

Causes for termination
- performance
- infeasibility
- mutual agreement
- revocation
- abandonment
- breach
- expiration
- invalidity
- incapacitation or death
- involuntary transfer
- destruction of property

Agent's performance	• may perform only authorized tasks
	• must verify owner and property data
	• may delegate duties to salespeople and other brokers
Revoking a listing	• clients always have power to revoke during period
	• may incur liability for commission or damages

Brokerage

Who May Broker

Varies from state to state

Yes

1. sole proprietorship
2. for-profit corporation
3. general or limited partnership
4. joint venture

No

1. non-profit corporation
2. business trust
3. cooperative association

Broker-Agent Relationship

Legal relationship
- salesperson
  - is agent & fiduciary of broker
  - acts in broker's name
  - is subagent of client

- salesperson may not
  - have two employers
  - be paid by other parties
  - bind clients contractually

Salesperson's employment status
- employee or independent contractor
- defined by agreement

Obligations and responsibilities
- agent to broker:
  - obtain & sell listings
  - follow policies and employment provisions
  - promote ethics and broker's reputation
- broker to agent:
  - provide data, office support, compensation, training
  - uphold ethics, policies, and employment agreement

Agent compensation
- commissions per schedule after splits with cooperating brokers

---

Commingling & Conversion

Not allowed !!

Commingling
- mixing broker's personal or business funds with trust funds
- includes failure to deposit funds in a timely manner

Conversion
- using trust funds for personal or business purposes

Advertising Requirements

- no misleading ads
- ads must contain broker's ID
- broker is responsible for content
- no blind ads (concealed identity)
- must disclose if agent owns property

Anti-Trust Laws

no collusion:
- two or more businesses conspiring to disadvantage a competitor

no price fixing:
- two or more brokers agreeing to fix prices

no market allocation:
- colluding to restrict competition in a market segment in exchange for a competitor's reciprocal agreement

---

Ethics & Fair Housing

Professional Ethics

- apply Golden Rule
- does not have to conflict with profit
- influenced by personal code of behavior
- influenced negatively by employer's or other agents' bad behavior
- not regulated by statute
- support improved professional standards
- act can be legal but unethical
- Code of Ethics and Standards of Practice
  - developed by the National Association of Realtors (NAR)
  - promotes fair dealings with public, clients, and other brokers

Fair Housing Law

Civil Rights Act of 1866
- no discrimination in selling or leasing housing based on race

Executive Order 11063
- no race discrimination involving FHA- or VA-backed loans

Fair Housing Act of 1968 (Title VIII)
- no discrimination based on race, color, religion, national origin

- Exemptions:
  - privately owned home where no broker is used and no discriminatory advertising is used
  - rental of 1-4 unit building where owner is also an occupant; no discriminatory advertising
  - facilities owned by private clubs; leased non-commercially to members
  - facilities owned by religious organizations with non-discriminatory membership requirements

Jones v. Mayer
- no race discrimination, without exception

Housing and Community Development Act of 1974
- no discrimination based on sex

Fair Housing Amendments Act of 1988
- no discrimination based on sex or against the handicapped or familial status

Equal Opportunity Poster
- must be displayed by brokers

Prohibited Acts

Forms of illegal discrimination

discriminatory misrepresentation	• misrepresenting facts in order to discriminate
advertising	• ads that restrict availability
appraising	• may not consider protected classes as a factor adversely affecting value
unequal services	• not rendering same service to all parties
steering	• channeling buyers to or away from neighborhoods
blockbusting	• inducing sale or rent based on incoming minorities that will lower values

restricting MLS access	• MLS restriction to protected classes
redlining	• not making loans in certain areas for discriminatory reasons

Discriminatory Advertising (HUD)

Race, Color, Origin, Religion	• cannot make limitations or preferences
Sex	• no explicit preference
Familial Status	• no preference or exclusion based on family makeup
Handicap	• no exclusions based on physical capabilities

Violations & Enforcement

- File HUD complaint with Office of Fair Housing and Equal Opportunity
  - within one year
  - HUD investigates
  - attempt to resolve out of court

- May sue in court
  - within two years
  - can get restraining order, damages

- Violators are subject to criminal prosecution

Truth / Reg Z / ECOA / RESPA / Flood

Truth-in-Lending and Regulation Z	• Reg Z implements Truth-in-Lending Act & Consumer Credit Protection Act
	- lender must disclose finance charges and APR prior to closing
	- borrower has limited right of rescission
	- lender must follow advertising disclosure requirements
Equal Credit Opportunity Act	• prohibits discrimination in lending
Real Estate Settlements and Procedures Act	• standardizes settlement practices
	- lender must provide CFPB booklet, "Your Home Loan Toolkit"
	- lender must provide CFPB's H-24 Loan Estimate of settlement costs within three days of application
	- lender must use CFPB's H-25 Closing Disclosure
National Flood Insurance Act	• requires borrowers of "federally-related loans" to obtain flood insurance if property is in designated hazard area

Sale Contracts

Characteristics

- binding, bilateral contract for purchase and sale
- the enforceable "blueprint" for closing
- contract is executory, or to be fulfilled
- expires upon closing
- must be in writing
- for validity, must
  - contain valuable consideration
  - identify property
  - be signed by all

Creation / Deposit / Contingencies

Creation
- created by unqualified acceptance of an offer
- gives buyer equitable title, and power to force specific performance

Deposit, or earnest money escrow
- secures contract validity and buyer's equitable interest
- varies in amount
- deposit controlled by disinterested party who must act according to escrow instructions

Contingencies
- conditions that must be met for the contract to be enforceable
- must be clear
- have expiration date
- require diligence to satisfy

Primary Clauses

- parties
- consideration
- legal description
- price and terms
- loan approval provisions
- earnest money
- escrow
- closing and possession dates
- conveyed interest
- type of deed
- title evidence
- property condition warranty/disclosures
- closing costs
- damage and destruction
- default
- broker's agency disclosure and who pays commission
- seller's representations: property condition, marketable title

Secondary Clauses

- inspections
- owner's association disclosure
- survey
- environmental hazards, compliance with laws
- rental property tenant's rights
- FHA or VA financing condition
- flood plain and flood insurance
- condominium assessments

	• due-on-sale and seller financing disclosure	• foreign seller withholding • tax-deferred exchange • boilerplate: merger of agreements, notices, time of the essence, fax transmission, survival, dispute resolution, addenda

Options

Essentials	• optionor gives option to optionee • unilateral contract: seller must perform, buyer need not • if option is exercised, option becomes bilateral sale contract
Contract requirements	• non-refundable consideration for the option right • price and terms of the sale • option period expiration date • legal description • must be in writing • must meet contract validity requirements
Common clause provisions	• how to exercise option • terms of option money forfeiture • how option money will be applied to purchase price

Contract for Deed

Essentials	• purchase price is paid over time in installments • seller retains title, buyer takes possession • at end of period, buyer pays balance, gets legal title
Interests and rights	• seller may encumber or assign interest • seller remains liable for underlying mortgage • buyer may use, possess, or profit • buyer must make periodic payments, maintain the property, and purchase at the end of the term
Default and recourse	• buyer may sue for cancellation and damages or specific performance • seller may sue for specific performance or damages, or may need to foreclose

Closings

Settlement process
- Identify selling terms & costs
- Determine non-prorated debits and credits
- Complete prorated debits and credits
- Complete closing statement
- Disburse funds

RESPA

Applicability	• for residential property • first or second mortgage • federally-related mortgage, or • assumption modifying loan terms
Information booklet	• lender must provide CFPB booklet, "Your Home Loan Toolkit"
Loan Estimate	• lender must provide CFPB's H-24 Loan Estimate of settlement costs within three days of application
Closing Disclosure	• lender must use CFPB's H-25 Closing Disclosure
Referral fees and kickbacks	• RESPA prohibits payment of referral fees and kickbacks • business relationships between firms involved in the transaction must be disclosed

Debits & Credits

Amount buyer must produce: excess of *buyer's debits* over credits

Amount seller must receive: excess of *seller's credits* over debits

Buyer's credits
- earnest money
- loan amount
- seller's share of prorations buyer will pay

Buyer's debits
- purchase price
- expenses (per agreement or custom)
- buyer's share of prorations prepaid by seller

Seller's credits
- purchase price
- buyer's share of prorated items prepaid by seller

Seller's debits
- expenses (per agreement or custom)
- seller's share of prorated items the buyer will pay
- loan balance and other liens to be paid off

Non-prorated expenses

Buyer usually pays	Seller usually pays
Mortgage recording fees	Stamp tax on deed
Documentary stamp tax	Title insurance
Intangible tax on mortgage	Brokerage fee
Mortgage-related fees: appraisal, credit, survey, loan origination	Inspection fees
Impound reserves: insurance, taxes	Title-related expenses
Attorney fees	Attorney fees

Prorated items

	arrears	advance
real estate taxes	x	
insurance premiums		x
mortgage interest	x	
rents received by seller		x
utilities	x	

30-Day 12-Month Proration

Formula: Monthly Amount = (Annual amount ÷ 12)
Daily Amount = (Monthly amount ÷ 30)
Proration = (Monthly amount x no. of months) + (Daily amount x no. of days)

Example: An annual tax bill is $1,800. Closing is on April 10. What is the seller's share of the taxes?

1. ($1,800 ÷ 12) = $150 monthly amount
2. ($150 ÷ 30) = $5.00 daily amount
3. ($150 x 3 months) = $450 Jan - Mar; ($5 x 10) = $50 Apr 1 - Apr 10; ($450 + 50) = $500 seller's share

365-Day Method

Formula: Daily amount = Annual amount ÷ 365 days; or
Daily amount = Monthly amount ÷ no. of days in month
Proration = (Daily amount x no. of days)

Example: An annual tax bill is $1,800. Closing is on April 10. What is the seller's share of the taxes?

1.   ($1,800 ÷ 365) = $4.93 daily amount
2.   Jan 1 thru April 10 = (31 + 28 + 31 + 10) days, or 100 days
3.   ($4.93 x 100 days) = $493 seller's share

Truth-in-Lending/RESPA Integrated Disclosures Rule

Forms and Procedures
- effective since October 3, 2015
- mandatory: Your Home Loan Toolkit booklet at loan application
- Loan Estimate form: 3 business days after loan application
- Closing Disclosure: 3 business days before consummation

Good faith
- Loan Estimate costs based on best information available
- Closing Disclosure costs equal estimate costs within certain tolerances

Types of charges
- no limitation on increase over estimate
- 10% tolerance charges
- 0 tolerance charges

Applicable transactions
- most closed-end consumer mortgages, including: construction loans, loans secured by vacant land, loans to trusts
- not covered: home equity loans, reverse mortgages, loans on mobile homes, loans by small lenders (no more than 5 loans per year)

The H-25 form
- 5 pages, variable by loan type

Risk Management

Risk Management Strategies

Avoidance	• refrain from risky activity
Reduction	• reduce probability; share responsibility
Transference	• pass risk by contract; insurance
Retention	• accept risk; self-insurance

Risk Management Procedures

Education	• train in laws, forms and procedures, job performance
Disclosure	• provide information to reduce misunderstanding & lawsuits; agency, property condition, duties, personal interest
Documentation and record keeping	• maintain evidence of compliance; manuals, forms, records, contracts, accounting, other documents
Insurance	• general liability, E & O, fire and hazard, flood, casualty, workers, personal property, consequential loss, surety bond

Primary Areas Of Risk

Agency	• duties to all: honesty, fairness, care, skill, required disclosures; • duties to clients: diligence, loyalty, obedience, confidentiality, accounting, full disclosure • conflicts of interest • confidentiality duty lasts forever
Property disclosures	• property condition, lead-based paint, other conditions
Listing and selling process	• risks: listing agreement accuracy, Comparative Market Analysis results, closing cost estimates, advertising, authorizations and permissions, exceeding expertise
Contracting Process	• contracts for real estate must be in writing • risks: inaccuracy, illegal form, omitted elements, lapsed contingencies, wrong data, unauthorized practice of law
Fair Housing	• may not state preference, limitation or discrimination based on race, color, religion, national origin, sex, handicap, familial status
Antitrust	• Sherman Antitrust Act outlaws restraint of trade; Clayton Act outlaws practices that harm competition; Federal Trade Commission Act outlaws unfair methods of competition
Rules and regulations	• risks: commission of prohibited acts, practicing with an expired license, disclosure failures, earnest money mishandling
Misrepresentation	• unintentional: inaccurate information conveyed unknowingly • intentional: fraud, knowingly conveying false information

Recommending providers	• risks: consumer dissatisfaction, possible vicarious liability, undisclosed business relationship (RESPA violation as well as license violation)
Financing and closing	• risks: fair housing and ECOA violations; failure to monitor contingency period; failure to ensure proper disclosure of closing costs; RESPA violations
Trust fund handling	• risks: mishandling of earnest money deposits; commingling and conversion of trust funds; errors in use of trust accounts

Property Management

Management Functions

Types of manager	• individual, managing properties for multiple owners; building manager, employed to manage a single property; resident, employed to live and manage on site. • may specialize in a property type • manager is a fiduciary of the principal • specific functions determined by management agreement
Reporting	• monthly, quarterly, annually • annual operating budget, cash flow reports, profit and loss statements, budget comparison statements
Budgeting	• operating budget: rental rates, capital expenditures, reserves, salaries and wages; projects income based on past performance and current market • expenses, variable and fixed; capital expenditures: outlays for major renovations and construction; cash reserves set aside for variable expenses
Renting	• keep property rented and tenanted; • select compatible tenants and collect scheduled rents • legal issues: compliance with fair housing laws, Americans with Disabilities Act, and ECOA
Property maintenance	• balance costs of services, owner financial objectives, and tenant needs • routine, preventive, or corrective; staffed in-house or contracted out
Construction	• tenant alterations, renovations, expansion, environmental remediation • legal concerns: Americans with Disabilities Act;
Risk management	• risk ranges from natural disaster to personal injury, terrorism, and employee malfeasance • avoid or remove the source, install protective systems, buy insurance, self-insure

- insurance for rented properties includes casualty, liability, workers' comp, fire and hazard, flood, contents, consequential loss, surety bonds, multi-peril
- handling of trust funds is a major risk area; mishandling carries heavy penalties

---

The Management Agreement

Components

- names; description; lease term; owner's purpose; responsibilities; authority; budget; allocation of costs; reporting; compensation; Equal Opportunity statement

Rights, duties and liabilities

- landlord: receive rent; receive premises in specified condition; enter and inspect; examine books; contract, hire vendors, set rents; pay management fee; comply with laws
- manager: hire and fire; contract; perform management tasks without interference; maintain financial records, make reports, budget, collect rent, find tenants, maintain property, meet owner goals; liability for trust funds; comply with laws

---

Leasing Considerations

Lease types

- for years, periodic, at will, at sufferance, gross, net, percentage, graduated

Owned and leased inclusions

- items included or excluded in the lease; owner's insurance covers only what is included

Reversionary rights of owners

- all rights of ownership revert to

Landlord rights and responsibilities

- rights: enter premises, receive payment, retake on termination, pursue remedies
- responsibilities: provide habitable conditions; maintain heating, cooling, electrical, plumbing; keep clean and in repair

Tenant rights and responsibilities

- rights: quiet enjoyment, habitable conditions, right to sue for default
- responsibilities: pay rent, obey rules, give proper notice, return property in prescribed condition, use only for intended purpose

Evictions

- actual: legal procedure; notice, suit, judgment, taking
- constructive: tenant vacates on account of landlord failure to maintain premises

Tenant improvements

- ownership and payment according to agreement

Termination of a lease

- expiration, performance, agreement, abandonment, breach, notice, destruction of premises, condemnation, foreclosure, death of either party (tenancy at will), death of landlord (life estate)

Security deposit procedures
- determined by law, rules, and agreement

Universal Residential Landlord-Tenant Act
- model law regulating lease language and lease terms; adopted by many states

Section II: Real Estate Math Review

Basic Math

Fractions

Adding and subtracting same denominator:

      Formula: $a/c + b/c = (a + b) \div c$

      Example: $1/2 + 1/2 = (1 + 1)/2 = 2/2 = 1$

Adding and subtracting different denominators:

      Formula: $a/c + b/d = (ad + bc)/cd$

      Example: $1/2 + 1/3 = (3 + 2)/6 = 5/6$

Multiplying:

      Formula: $(a/c) \times (b/d) = ab/cd$

      Example: $(2/5) \times (4/6) = 8/30 = 4/15$

Decimals and Percents

Converting decimals to percentages

      Formula: *Decimal number x 100 = Percentage number*

      Example: $.022 \times 100 = 2.2\%$

Converting percentages to decimals

      Formula: *Percent number $\div$ 100 = Decimal number*

      Example: $2.2 \div 100 = .022$

Multiplying percents

      Formula: *1. Percent number $\div$ 100 = Decimal number*

                          2. Beginning number x Decimal number = Product

      Example: 75% of 256 (75% x 256) = ?

                       1. $75 \div 100 = .75$

                       2. $256 \times .75 = 192$

Dividing by percents

Formula: 1. *Percent number $\div$ 100 = Decimal number*

                      2. *Beginning number $\div$ Decimal = Dividend*

Example: 240 $\div$ 75% = ?

                      1. 75% $\div$ 100 = .75

                      2. 240 $\div$ .75 = 320

Decimals, Fractions, and Percentages

Converting fractions to percents

Formula: (1)   a / b or a $\div$ b = a divided by b = decimal number

                  (2)   decimal number x 100 = percent number

Example: (1)   2 / 5 = 2 divided by 5 = 0.4

                  (2)   .4 x 100 = 40%

Converting a percent to fraction and reducing it

Formula: (1)   X% = X $\div$ 100 or X / 100

                  (2) $\dfrac{X \div a}{100 \div a}$ where a is the largest number that divides evenly into both numerator and denominator

Example: (1)   40% = 40 $\div$ 100, or 40 / 100

                  (2) $\dfrac{40 \div 20}{100 \div 20} = \dfrac{2}{5}$

Converting fractions to decimals and percentages

Formula: *Decimal x 100 = Percent number*

Example: .75 x 100 = 75%

Equations

Additions and Subtractions

Formula: *if*   *a = b + c*

                then   *b = a - c (subtracting c from both sides)*

                and   *c = a - b (subtracting b from both sides)*

Example: 10   = 6 + 4

6	= 10 - 4
4	= 10 - 6

Multiplications and Divisions

Formula: *if* $a = b \times c$

        then $b = a / c$ *(dividing both sides by c)*

        and $c = a / b$ *(dividing both sides by b)*

Example: $10 = 2 \times 5$

        $2 = 10 \div 5$

        $5 = 10 \div 2$

Linear and Perimeter Measurement

Linear measure of rectangles

Formula: *Side A = Area ÷ Side B*

Example: A rectangular house has one side 40' side long and area of 1,200 SF. What is the length of the other side?

Side A = (1,200' ÷ 40') = 30'

Perimeter measurement

Formula: *Perimeter = Sum of all sides of an object*

Example: A five-sided lot has the following dimensions:

Side A = 50' Side B = 60'
Side C= 70' Side D = 100'
Side E = 30'

What is the perimeter of the lot?

P = 50' + 60' + 70' + 100' + 30' = 310'

Area Measurement

Square and rectangle

Formula: *Area = Width x Depth (Horizontal) or Width x Height (Vertical)*

Width= Depth (Height) ÷ Area

Depth (Height)= Width ÷ Area

Example: A house is 40' deep and 30' wide. What is its area?

$$\text{Area} = 40' \times 30' = 1{,}200 \text{ SF}$$

Triangle

Formula: *Area = (Height x Base) ÷ 2*

Note: Base is also sometimes referred to as "width"

Example: An A-frame house has a front facade measuring 30' across and 20' in height. What is the area of the facade?

$$\text{Area} = (30' \times 20') \div 2 = 300 \text{ Square feet (SF)}$$

Square foot-to-acre conversion

Formula: *Acres = Area SF ÷ 43,560 SF*

Example: How many acres is 196,020 SF?

$$196{,}020 \text{ SF} \div 43{,}560 \text{ SF} = 4.5 \text{ acres}$$

Acre-to-square foot conversion

Formula: *SF = Number of acres x 43,560 SF*

Example: How many square feet is .75 acres?

$$.75 \text{ acres} \times 43{,}560 \text{ SF} = 32{,}670 \text{ SF}$$

Linear and Area Conversion Chart

Linear measures

(cm = centimeter; m = meter; km = kilometer)

1 inch	=	1/12 foot	=	1/36 yard	
1 foot	=	12 inches	=	1/3 yard	
1 yard	=	36 inches	=	3 feet	
1 rod	=	16.5 feet	=	1/320 mile	
1 mile	=	5280 feet	=	1760 yards	= 320 rods
1 centimeter	=	1/100 m			
1 meter	=	100 cm	=	1/1000 km	
1 kilometer	=	1,000 m			

Area measures

1 square inch	=	1/144 sq. foot			
1 square foot	=	1/9 sq. yard	=	144 sq. inches	
1 square yard	=	9 sq. feet	=	1,296 sq. inches	
1 acre	=	1/640 sq. mi	=	43,560 SF	= 208.71 ft x 208.71 ft
1 square mile	=	640 acres	=	1 section	= 1/36 township
1 section	=	1 mi x 1 mi	=	640 acres	= 1/36 township
1 township	=	6 mi x 6 mi	=	36 sq. mi	= 36 sections

Metric conversions

(cm = centimeter; m = meter; km = kilometer)

1 inch	=	2.54 cm				
1 foot	=	30.48 cm	=	.3048 m		
1 yard	=	91.44 cm	=	.9144 m		
1 mile	=	1609.3 m	=	1.60 km		
1 centimeter	=	.3937 inch				
1 meter	=	39.37 inches	=	3.28 feet	=	1.094 yards
1 kilometer	=	3,281.5 feet	=	.621 mile		

Fractions of sections, acres, and linear dimensions

Fraction		# Acres
1 section	=	640 acres
1/2 section	=	320 acres
1/4 section	=	160 acres
1/8 section	=	80 acres
1/16 section	=	40 acres
1/32 section	=	20 acres
1/64 section	=	10 acres

Calculating Area from the Legal Description

Formula:

(1) *First multiply all the denominators of the fractions in the legal description together.*

(2) *Then divide 640 by the resulting product.*

Examples:

How many acres are in the Northern 1/2 of the Southwestern 1/4 of Section 6?

640 / (2 x 4) = 640 / 8 = 80 acres

How many acres are in the Western 1/2 of the Northwestern 1/4 of the Northeastern 1/4 of Section 8?

640 / (2 x 4 x 4) = 640 / 32 = 20 acres

Volume Measurement

Formula:

Volume = Width x Height x Depth   (assume objects with 90 degree angles)

Base = (Height x Depth) ÷ Volume

Height = (Base x Depth) ÷ Volume

Depth = (Base x Height) ÷ Volume

Example:

What is the volume of a 40' x 30' x 20' house?

40' x 30' x 20' = 24,000 cubic feet

Ownership

Condominium Assessment Calculation

Formula: *Monthly assessment = (Total annual building budget x Condo unit % of value) ÷ 12*

Example: Assume a condominium complex with a $300,000 budget and a unit that comprises 1.48% of the total value of the complex. Monthly assessment?

($300,000 x .0148) ÷ 12 = $370 monthly assessment.

Leases

Percentage Lease Rent Calculation

Formula: *Monthly percentage rent = Sales x percent of sales charged*

Example: A store generates $50,000 per month. The lease calls for 1.5% percentage rent. Monthly rent amount?

($50,000 x .015) = $750 / month

Contracts for the Sale of Real Estate

Percentage of Listing Price Calculation

Formula: *Percentage of listing price = Offer ÷ Listing price*

Example: A property listed for $150,000 receives an offer for $120,000. The offer's percentage of listing price is:

$120,000 ÷ $150,000 = 80%

Earnest Money Deposit Calculation

Formula: *Deposit = Offering price x required or market-accepted percentage*

Example: A seller requires a 2% deposit on a property listed for $320,000. The required deposit (assuming a full price offer) is:

$320,000 x 2% = $6,400

Appraisal & Value

Adjusting Comparables

Rules: 1.   Never adjust the subject!

2.   If the comparable is superior to the subject, subtract value from the

comparable.

3. If the comparable is inferior to the subject, add value to the comparable.

Example: The subject has a $10,000 pool and no porch. A comparable that sold for $250,000 has a porch ($5,000), an extra bathroom ($6,000), and no pool.

Adjustments to comp: $250,000 (+10,000 - 5,000 - 6,000) = $249,000 indicated value of subject

Gross Rent Multiplier

Formulas: *Sales price = Monthly rental income x GRM*

Monthly rental income = Sales price / Gross Rent Multiplier

Note: Gross rent multiplier is often abbreviated as GRM.

Examples:
1. What is the value of a fourplex with monthly rent of $2,800 and a GRM of 112?

   $2,800 rent x 112 GRM = $313,600

2. What is the GRM of a fourplex with monthly rent of $2,800 and a value of $313,600?

   313,600 price ÷ $2,800 rent = 112 GRM

Gross Income Multiplier

Formulas
Gross Income Multiplier = Sales price ÷ Annual income

Sales price = Annual income x Gross Income Multiplier

Annual income = Sales price ÷ Gross Income Multiplier

Note: Gross income multiplier is often abbreviated as GIM.

Examples:
1. What is the value of a commercial property with an annual income of $33,600 and a GIM of 9.3?

   $33,600 income x 9.3 GIM = $312,480

2. What is the GIM of a commercial property with annual income of $33,600 and a value of $312,480?

   $313,600 price ÷ $33,600 = 9.3 GIM

Cost Approach Formula

Formula: *Value = Land value + (Improvements + Capital additions - Depreciation)*

Example: Land value = $50,000; home replacement cost = $150,000; new garage added @ $30,000; total depreciation = $10,000

Value = $50,000 + (150,000 + 30,000 - 10,000) = $220,000

Depreciation

Formulas: *Annual depreciation = Beginning depreciable basis ÷ Depreciation term*

Depreciable basis = (Initial property value + Any capital improvements - Land value)

Note: The depreciation term is in number of years.

Example: Property value = $500,000; land value = $110,000; depreciation term = 39 years

Step 1: ($500,000 - $110,000) = $390,000 depreciable basis

Step 2: ($390,000 ÷ 39 years) = $10,000 annual depreciation

Income Capitalization Formula

Formulas: *Value = Annual Net Operating Income ÷ Capitalization rate*

Capitalization rate = Annual Net Operating Income ÷ Value

Annual Net Operating Income = Value x Capitalization rate

Examples:
1. A property generates $490,000 net income and sells at a 7% cap rate. What is its value?

   $490,000 ÷ 7% = $7,000,000 value

2. A property has a net income of $490,000 and sells for $7,000,000. What is its cap rate?

   $490,000 ÷ 7,000,000 = .07, or 7%

3. A property's value is $7,000,000 and the cap rate is 7%. What is the property's net operating income?

   $7,000,000 x .07 = $490,000

Net Operating Income (NOI, Net Income)

Formula: *NOI = Potential rent - Vacancy loss + Other income - Operating expenses*

Note: NOI does not include debt payments!

Example: A building has 10 office suites generating annual potential rent of $10,000 each. Vacancy = 10% and annual expenses are $35,000. Vending machines yield

$5,000. What is the NOI?

$100,000 rent - 10,000 vacancy + 5,000 other income - 35,000 expenses = $60,000 NOI

Finance

Points

Definition: 1 point = 1% of the loan amount or .01 x loan amount

Formulas: *Points = Fee paid ÷ Loan amount*

Fee paid = Loan amount x Points

Loan amount = Fee paid ÷ Points

Examples:
1. A borrower pays $500 for a $10,000 loan. How many points are paid?

    $500 ÷ 10,000 = .05 = 5 points

2. A borrower pays 5 points on a $10,000 loan. What is the fee paid?

    $10,000 x .05 = $500

3. A borrower pays $500 as 5 points on a loan. What is the loan amount?

    $500 ÷ .05 = $10,000

Rules of
Thumb: 1 point charged raises lender's yield by .125%

8 points charged raises lender's yield by 1%

Example: A lender wants to yield 7% on a 6.5% loan. How many points must he or she charge?

(7% - 6.5%) = .5%

.5% ÷ .125% = 4 points

Interest Rate, Principal and Payment

Caveat!

Interest rates in mortgage financing apply to the <u>annual</u> interest payment and <u>exclude</u> principal payment. Remember to convert annual payments to monthly or vice versa as the question requires, and to exclude principal payments from your calculations!

Formulas: *Payment = Principal x Rate*

Principal = Payment ÷ Rate

Rate = Payment ÷ Principal

Examples: 1.   A borrower has a $100,000 loan @ 6% interest. What are the annual and monthly payments?

Annual payment = $100,000 x .06 = $6,000
Monthly payment = $6,000 ÷ 12 = $500

2.   A borrower has a $500 monthly payment on a 6% loan. What is the loan principal?

Principal = ($500 x 12) ÷ 6% = ($6,000 ÷ .06) = $100,000

3.   A borrower has a $500 monthly payment on a $100,000 loan. What is the loan rate?

Rate = ($500 x 12) ÷ $100,000 = ($6,000 ÷ 100,000) = .06 = 6%

Total Interest, Interest Rate, and Loan Term

Formulas: *Interest-only loan:*   *Total interest = Loan amount x Rate x Term in years*

Amortized loan: *Total interest = (Monthly PI payment x 12 x term) - Loan amount*

Examples: 1.   A borrower obtains a 10-year interest only loan of $50,000 @ 6%. How much interest will he or she pay?

($50,000 x .06 x 10) = $30,000

2.   A borrower obtains a 10-year amortized loan of $50,000 @ 6% with monthly payments of $555.10. How much interest will he or she pay?

($555.10 x 12 x 10) - $50,000 = $16,612

Amortization Calculation

Formulas: *Month 1:*   *Principal paid = Monthly payment - (Loan amount x Rate ÷ 12)*

Month 2:   *New loan amount = (Previous month principal - Principal paid)*

Principal paid = Monthly payment - (New loan amount x Rate ÷ 12)

Example: A borrower obtains a 30-year $100,000 amortized loan @ 7% with a $665.31 monthly payment. What is the principal paid in the second month?

Month 1:   Principal paid = $665.31 - ($100,000 x 7% ÷ 12) = $665.31 - (583.33 interest paid) = $81.98

Month 2:   New loan amount = $100,000 previous month beginning loan amount - $81.98 principal paid = $99,918.02

Principal paid = $665.31 - ($99,918.02 x 7% ÷ 12) = $665.31 - (582.86 interest paid) = $82.45

Loan Constants

Formulas:
Monthly payment = (Loan amount x Loan constant) / 1000

Loan amount = (Monthly payment ÷ Loan constant) x 1000

Loan constant = (Monthly payment ÷ Loan amount) x 1000

Examples:
1. A borrower obtains a loan for $100,000 with a 6.3207 constant. What is the monthly payment?

   Monthly payment = ($100,000 ÷ 1,000) x 6.3207 = $632.07

2. A borrower has a monthly payment of $632.07 on a loan with a monthly constant of 6.3207. What is the loan amount?

   Loan amount = ($632.07 ÷ 6.3207) x 1000 = $100,000

3. A borrower obtains a loan for $100,000 with a monthly payment of $632.07. What is the loan constant?

   Loan constant = ($632.07 ÷ $100,000) x 1,000 = 6.3207

Loan - to - Value Ratio (LTV)

Formulas:
LTV ratio = Loan ÷ Price (Value)

Loan = LTV ratio x Price (Value)

Price (Value) = Loan ÷ LTV ratio

Examples:
1. A borrower can get a $265,600 loan on a $332,000 home. What is her LTV ratio?

   LTV Ratio = $265,600 ÷ 332,000 = 80%

2. A borrower can get an 80% loan on a $332,000 home. What is the loan amount?

   Loan = $332,000 x .80 = $265,600

3. A borrower obtained an 80% loan for $265,600. What was the price of the home?

   Price (value) = $265,600 ÷ .80 = $332,000

Financial Qualification

Income ratio qualification

Formula:
Monthly Principal & Interest (PI) payment = Income ratio x Monthly gross

income

Example: A lender uses a 28% income ratio for the PI payment. A borrower grosses $30,000 per year. What monthly PI payment can the borrower afford?

Monthly PI payment = ($30,000 ÷ 12) x .28 = $700

How much can the borrower borrow if the loan constant is 6.3207? (See also-loan constants)

Loan amount = ($700 ÷ 6.3207) x 1,000 = $110,747.22

Debt ratio qualification

Formulas: *Debt ratio = (Housing expense + Other debt payments) ÷ Monthly gross income*

Housing expense = (Monthly gross income x Debt ratio) - Other debt payments

Example: A lender uses a 36% debt ratio. A borrower earns $30,000 / year and has monthly non-housing debt payments of $500. What housing payment can she afford?

Housing expense = ($30,000 ÷ 12 x .36) - 500 = ($900 - 500) = $400

Investment

Appreciation Calculations

Simple appreciation

Formulas: *Total appreciation = Current value - Original price*

Total appreciation rate = Total appreciation ÷ Original price

Average annual appreciation rate = Total appreciation rate ÷ number of years

One year appreciation rate = (Annual appreciation amount) ÷ (Value at beginning of year)

Examples:
1. A home purchased for $200,000 five years ago is now worth $300,000. What are the total appreciation amount, total appreciation rate, and average appreciation rate?

   Total appreciation = ($300,000 - 200,000), or $100,000

   Total appreciation rate = ($100,000 ÷ 200,000), or 50%

   Average annual appreciation rate = 50% ÷ 5 years = 10%

2. A home costing $250,000 is worth $268,000 one year later. What is the one-year appreciation rate?

   One-year appreciation rate = ($18,000 ÷ 250,000) = 7.2%

Compounded appreciation

Formula: *Appreciated value = Beginning value x (1+ annual rate) x (1+ annual rate) ......*
for the number of years in question

Example: A $100,000 property is expected to appreciate 5% each year for the next 3 years. What will be its appreciated value at the end of this period?

Appreciated value = $100,000 x 1.05 x 1.05 x 1.05 = $115,762.50

Rate of Return, Investment Value, Income

Formulas: Where Income = net operating income (NOI); Rate = rate of return, cap rate, or percent yield; and Value = value, price or investment amount:

Rate = Income ÷ Value

Value = Income ÷ Rate

Income = Value x Rate

Examples:
1. An office building has $200,000 net income and sold for $3,200,000. What was the rate of return?

   Rate = ($200,000 NOI ÷ 3,200,000 price) = 6.25%

2. An office building has $200,000 net income and a cap rate of 6.25%. What is its value?

   Value = ($200,000 ÷ 6.25%) = $3,200,000

3. An office building sells for $3,200,000 at a cap rate of 6.25%. What is its NOI?

   Income = $3,200,000 x 6.25% = $200,000

Basis, Adjusted Basis, and Capital Gain

Formulas: *Capital gain = Amount realized - Adjusted basis, where*

Amount realized = Sale price - Selling costs

Adjusted basis = Beginning basis + Capital improvements - Total depreciation

Total depreciation = (Beginning depreciable basis ÷ Depreciation term in years) x Years depreciated

Depreciable basis = Initial property value + Capital improvements - Land value

Example: Tip: work example backwards from last formula to first formula.

An apartment building was purchased for $500,000, with the land value estimated to be $100,000. The owner added a $100,000 parking lot. The

66

property was depreciated on a 40-year schedule (for present purposes!). Three years later the property sold for $700,000, and selling costs were $50,000. What was the capital gain?

1. depreciable basis = $500,000 purchase price + 100,000 parking lot - 100,000 land = $500,000

2. total depreciation = ($500,000 ÷ 40 years) x 3 years = $37,500

3. adjusted basis = $500,000 purchase price + 100,000 parking lot - 37,500 total depreciation = $562,500

4. amount realized = $700,000 sale price - 50,000 selling costs = $650,000

5. capital gain = $650,000 amount realized - 562,500 adjusted basis = $87,500

Depreciation

Formulas: *Annual depreciation = (Beginning depreciable basis) ÷ (Depreciation term in number of years)*

Depreciable basis = (Initial property value + Capital improvements - Land value)

Example: Property value = $500,000; land value = $110,000; depreciation term = 39 years

1. ($500,000 - 110,000) = $390,000 depreciable basis

2. ($390,000 ÷ 39 years) = $10,000 annual depreciation

Equity

Formula: *Equity = Current market value - Current loan balance(s)*

Example: A home that was purchased for $150,000 with a $100,000 loan is now worth $300,000. The current loan balance is $80,000. What is the homeowner's equity?

Equity = $300,000 value - $80,000 debt = $220,000

Net Income

Formula: *NOI = Potential rent - Vacancy loss + Other income - Operating expenses*

Note: NOI does not include debt payments!

Example: A building has 10 office suites generating annual potential rent of $10,000 each. Vacancy = 10% and annual expenses are $35,000. Vending machines yield

67

$5,000. What is the NOI?

$100,000 rent - 10,000 vacancy + 5,000 other income - 35,000 expenses = $60,000 NOI

Cash Flow

Formula: *Cash flow = (Net Operating Income - Debt service) where debt service is PI payment*

Example: A building generates $100,000 NOI after expenses and has a debt payment of $40,000. What is its cash flow?

Cash flow = $100,000 - 40,000 = $60,000

Investment Property Income Tax Liability

Formula: *Tax liability = (NOI + Reserves - Interest expense - Depreciation) x Tax bracket*

Example: An office building has NOI of $200,000, an annual reserve expense of $20,000, interest expense of $130,000 and annual depreciation of $50,000. Assuming a 28% tax bracket, what is its income tax liability?

Tax liability = ($200,000 + 20,000 - 130,000 - 50,000) x 28% = $11,200

Return on Investment

Formula: *ROI = NOI ÷ Price*

Example: An investment property generates a cash flow of $100,000 and appraises for $1,500,000. What is the owner's return on investment?

ROI = $100,000 ÷ 1,500,000 = 6.67%

Return on Equity

Formula: *ROE = Cash flow ÷ Equity*

Example: An investment property generates a cash flow of $100,000. The owner has $500,000 equity in the property. What is the owner's return on equity?

ROE= $100,000 ÷ 500,000 = 20%

Real Estate Taxation

Converting Mill Rates

Definition: 1 mill = $.001; a mill rate of 1 mill per $1,000 = .1%; a 1% tax rate = 10 mills

Formula:	$Tax = (Taxable\ value \div 1000) \times Mill\ rate$
Example:	A tax rate on a house with a $200,000 taxable value is 7 mills per thousand dollars of assessed valuation. What is the tax?

Tax = ($200,000 ÷ 1,000) x 7 mills = $1,400

Tax Base

Formula:	$Tax\ base = Assessed\ valuations - Exemptions$
Example:	A town has a total assessed valuation of $20,000,000 and exemptions of $4,000,000. What is the tax base?

$20,000,000 - 4,000,000 = $16,000,000

Tax Rate, Base, and Requirement

Formulas:	$Tax\ rate = Tax\ requirement \div Tax\ base$
	$Tax\ base = Tax\ requirement \div Tax\ rate$
	$Tax\ requirement = Tax\ base \times Rate$
Example:	A town has a tax base of $160,000,000 and a budget of $8,000,000. What is the tax rate?

Tax rate = ($8,000,000 ÷ 160,000,000) = .05, or 5%, or 50 mills

Special Assessments

Formula:	$Special\ assessment = Total\ special\ assessment\ cost \times Homeowner's\ share$
Example:	A homeowner owns 100' of an 800' seawall that must be repaired. The total assessment will be $80,000. What is the homeowner's assessment?

1. Homeowner's share = 100' ÷ 800' = .125, or 12.5%

2. Special assessment = $80,000 x 12.5% = $10,000

Commissions

Commission Splits

Formulas:	$Total\ commission = Sale\ price \times Commission\ rate$
	$Co\text{-}brokerage\ split = Total\ commission \times Co\text{-}brokerage\ percent$
	$Agent\ split = Co\text{-}brokerage\ split \times Agent\ percent$

Broker split = Co-brokerage split - Agent split

Example: A $300,000 property sells at a 7% commission with a 50-50 co-brokerage split and a 60% agent split with her broker. What are total, co-brokerage, agent's, and broker's commissions?

Total commission = $300,000 x .07 = $21,000

Co-brokerage splits = $300,000 x .07 x .50 = $10,500

Agent split = $10,500 x .60 = $6,300

Agent's broker's split = $10.500 - 6,300 = $4,200

Seller's Net

Formula: *Seller's net = Sale Price - (sale price x commission) - Other closing costs - Loan balance*

Example: A home sells for $260,000 and has a loan balance of $200,000 at closing. The commission is 7% and other closing costs are $2,000. What is the seller's net?

Seller's net = ($260,000 - (260,000 x .07) - 2,000 - 200,000) = $39,800

Price to Net an Amount

Formula: *Sale Price = (Desired net + Closing costs + Loan payoff)) (1 - Commission rate)*

Example: A homeseller wants to net $50,000. The commission is 7%, the loan payoff is $150,000, and closing costs are $4,000. What must the price be?

Sale price = ($50,000 + 4,000 + 150,000) ÷ .93 = $219,355

Closing Costs, Prorations

30-Day 12-Month Method

Formulas: *Monthly amount = Annual amount / 12*

Daily amount = Monthly amount / 30

Proration = (Monthly amount multiplied by the # months) + (Daily amount multiplied by the # days)

Example: An annual tax bill is $1,800. Closing is on April 10. What is the seller's share of the taxes?

1.   Monthly amount = ($1,800 ÷ 12) = $150; no. of mounts = 3

2.   Daily amount = ($150 ÷ 30) = $5.00; no. of days = 10

3.   Proration = ($150 x 3) + ($5 x 10) = ($450 + 50) = $500 seller's share

365-Day Method

Formula: *Daily amount = (Annual amount ÷ 365) or (Monthly amount ÷ Length of month)*

Proration = Daily amount multiplied by the # days

Example: An annual tax bill is $1,800. Closing is on April 10. What is the seller's share of the taxes?

1. Daily amount = ($1,800 ÷ 365) = $4.93

2. Jan 1 thru April 10 = (31 + 28 + 31 + 10) days, or 100 days

3. Proration = $4.93 x 100 days = $493 seller's share

Income Received in Advance (Rent)

Logic: *Credit buyer and debit seller for buyer's share*

Example: Seller receives $1,000 rent. The month is ¾ over.

1. Buyer's share is ($1,000 x 25%) = $250

2. Credit buyer / debit seller $250.

Expenses paid in Arrears (Tax)

Logic: *Credit buyer and debit seller for seller's share*

Example: Buyer will pay $1,000 taxes. The year is ¾ over.

1. Buyer's share is ($1,000 x 25%) = $250

2. Credit buyer / debit seller $750.

Insurance Coverage

Recovery with Co-Insurance Clauses

Formula: Recovery = (Damage claim) x (Percent replacement cost covered ÷ Minimum coverage requirement)

Example: An owner insures a home for $100,000. Replacement cost is $150,000. A co-insurance clause requires coverage of 80% of replacement cost to avoid penalty. Fire destroys the house. What can the owner recover from the insurer?

Claim recovery = $150,000 x (67% cost covered ÷ 80% required) = $125,625

Section III: Arizona Laws & Practices

Part I: Real Estate Law in Arizona

Sources of Real Estate Law

Article XXVI of the Arizona Constitution
- Adopted in 1962
- Authorizes Arizona licensees to engage in the limited practice of law
- Grants licensed salespeople and brokers the right to draft documents incidental to the transfer of real property
- Unique to Arizona; found in no other state
- Eliminates the slower work of attorneys
- Licensees
  - must represent one or both principals in the sale, exchange, trade, or leasing of real property
  - may not charge
  - may draft or fill out preliminary purchase agreements, earnest money receipts, deeds, mortgages, leases, assignments, releases, contracts of sale of realty, and bills of sale

Title 32, Chapter 20 -- Code of Real Estate

Basic law review
- Constitutional law
  - example: Article XXVI (26)
  - voted on by citizens
- Statutory law
  - example: Title 32, Chapter 20 of Arizona Revised Statutes
  - introduced in legislative committees
  - approved by one or both Arizona House of Representatives or Senate
  - signed into law, vetoed, or ignored by the governor
  - codified with a numerical label
  - becomes part of Arizona Revised Statutes (ARS)
- Administrative law
  - example: Arizona Department of Real Estate (ADRE)
  - state (or federal) agencies with the authority to make rules and the power to enforce them
- Case law
  - example: State Bar of Arizona v. Arizona Land Title & Trust Co. (1961)
  - laws made in courtrooms by judges and juries
  - may become legal precedent for adjudicating other cases
- Common law
  - example: which party pays for what title insurance at close of escrow
  - based on customs and traditions

Powers and duties of the Arizona Real Estate Commissioner
- Appointed by the Governor
- Candidates must have experience in a mix of
  - real estate
  - title insurance
  - banking or mortgage broker
  - plus 3 years of administrative experience

- Cannot have a financial interest in a brokerage or act as a real estate licensee at time of appointment
- Is authorized to administer the Arizona Department of Real Estate (ADRE)
  - ADRE regulates brokers and salespeople in real estate, cemetery, and membership camping
  - monitors prelicensing instruction, testing, and continuing education courses
  - oversees approved schools, competence of instructors, and quality and timeliness of teaching materials.
  - oversees activities of licensees, investigates complaints, participates in administrative hearings regarding licensee conduct
  - regulates the sale of subdivisions, unsubdivided lands, timeshares, condominiums, membership campgrounds, and cemeteries
- ADRE's critical functions are to:
  - establish and enforce minimum requirements for licensure
  - approve real estate schools and instructors
  - monitor and approve continuing education courses
  - issue public reports for residential developments
  - investigate complaints
  - enforce disciplinary actions
  - provide public information on licensees, companies, and developments
  - produce and distribute educational matter to licensees and the public
- The Commissioner may adopt rules deemed necessary to carry out ADRE's mission
- May adopt standardized forms needed to comply with state statutes
- Investigative authority:
  - may investigate any written and verified complaint against an entity or individual
  - may examine the books or records of any brokerage
  - may take testimony, examine and copy physical evidence, and subpoena witnesses
  - may establish an investigative and enforcement ADRE unit, as required by state law
- The Commissioner is required to execute and record in the County Recorder's Office, and make maps of them available upon public request
  - any territory near a military airport or ancillary military facility
  - military training route, restricted airspace, military electronic range
- The Department is required to make earth fissure maps prepared by the Arizona Geological Survey available electronically or in print to the public upon request

The Real Estate Advisory Board
- State law allows for a ten member advisory board
- Board consists of:
  - two members with Arizona brokerage experience
  - three with residential brokerage experience within five years of appointment
  - two developers/subdividers
  - three members who are not closely related to an Arizona licensee
- Members serve six year terms; no payment other than travel and subsistence reimbursement
- The board meets at least quarterly
- Board provides:
  - recommendations to the commissioner
  - input on specific questions and proposals from the Commissioner
  - annual evaluations of the Commissioner and ADRE to the Governor

AREC's Disciplinary Process and Procedures

Grounds for disciplinary action include
- procuring or attempting to procure a real estate license by fraud, misrepresentation, or false or misleading content on a license application
- substantial misrepresentation, false promises designed to influence, and dishonest, fraudulent dealings

- incompetence, defined as lack of basic knowledge or skill appropriate to one's license
- engaging in licensed real estate activities without holding a valid license
- conviction of a felony such as forgery, fraud, theft, extortion, or moral turpitude
- violation of criminal or administrative order, decree, or sentence; or federal, state law, regulation or rule
- failure to treat participants in a real estate transaction fairly
- failure to adequately respond to ADRE disciplinary procedures, such as failure to appear or provide required documents for a hearing

Violations of license law
- A license is in jeopardy if he or she
  - engages in financial improprieties as a licensee or party to a transaction
  - performs licensed activities without an active license
  - engages in real estate activities under a broker other than his or her own
  - violates advertising rules
  - fails to respond to a departmental investigation or to provide documents
  - participates in unacceptable record keeping, disclosure, or forgery
  - is dishonest on the original application for a license
  - is convicted of any crime
  - is successfully charged with incompetence, professional neglect, or was paid out from the real estate recovery fund
  - demonstrates dishonesty

Revocation and suspension procedures
- The Real Estate Commissioner may
  - suspend or revoke a license
  - deny issuance of a license
  - issue a letter of concern to a licensee
  - issue a provisional license
  - deny the renewal of a license within five years immediately preceding, demonstrated dishonesty
- A **suspended license** may be reinstated if certain conditions are met
- **Revocation** of a license generally means permanent loss of license
- A **letter of concern** requires modification or elimination of certain practices to avoid disciplinary actions
- A **provisional license** allows a licensee to practice under a consent order (a mutual agreement between ADRE and the licensee to stop or modify behavior)
- **Cease and desist orders** issued to a licensee by ADRE instruct a licensee to immediately stop inappropriate or illegal activities
- Most of these actions require **due process** including hearings, evidence, and witnesses
- A **summary suspension**, however, may demand a licensee to immediately stop activities
  - which **endanger public health, safety or welfare**
  - in cases of felony conviction
  - incarceration
  - on parole
- A licensee facing a disciplinary hearing may voluntarily surrender a license; if that happens, Arizona will never issue the person a real estate license again

Arizona's Real Estate Recovery Fund (ARERF)
- ARERF is a malpractice fund administered by ADRE
- Designed to compensate members of the general public injured by the actions of a real estate licensee where such members are unable to recover full damages through lawsuit and judgment
  - claims for payment from the fund are made to ADRE only after a verdict to determine settlement in a lawsuit is rendered
  - every licensee pays into the fund when initiating a license, $10 for salespeople; $20 for brokers
  - Arizona law requires the fund to have $600,000 in it as of June 30 each year

- o if the required balance isn't maintained, licensees levied a special assessment: an additional $10 per salesperson and $20 per broker at time of license renewal
- o for consumers, recovery fund payments are limited to $30,000 per claim and $90,000 for any number of claims
- o if the recovery fund pays out for a licensee, that licensee's license is revoked
- o a license revoked for recovery fund payout is reinstated if the licensee repays the fund with legal rate of interest, 16%, and retakes salesperson or broker prelicensing course.

Part II: Arizona Licensing Laws & Regulations

Arizona Licensing Requirements

Who must be licensed
- The purpose of licensing and regulation is to protect the public.
- Any person who aids another in selling, purchasing, exchanging, renting, leasing, or management of real property for compensation, including cemetery and membership camping sales and brokerage, requires a license
- A valid ADRE real estate license is required for anyone acting in the capacity of
  - o real estate broker or salesperson
  - o cemetery broker or salesperson
  - o membership camping broker or salesperson
- A valid license must be held by anyone who aids another or offers to aid another in
  - o the sale, purchase, exchange, rental or lease of real property
  - o business or commercial opportunities
  - o options
  - o cemetery plots
  - o membership camping contracts
  - o timeshare interests

License exemptions
- anyone or corporate entity selling, purchasing, exchanging, leasing, renting, or managing one's own property
- a person holding valid power of attorney for an isolated transaction
- an attorney in the performance of duties as an attorney
- a receiver, trustee in bankruptcy, or person acting under a court order
- a trustee selling under a deed of trust
- a residential leasing agent or on-site manager of one property for compensation
- Also exempt from licensing:
  - o real estate brokerage administrative personnel
  - o maintenance people
  - o clerical staff doing no work requiring a license

Unlicensed personnel
- Unlicensed personnel may not legally be part of a real estate team
  - o a legal real estate team is made up of active licensees working under the same employing broker
  - o an employing broker is the brokerage entity, not an individual

General licensing requirements
- Candidates for both Arizona salesperson and broker licenses must
  - o be at least 18 years of age
  - o be a resident of any state; no residency requirement
  - o complete 90 hours of approved real estate classroom education
  - o pass a school test

- o pass a state examination
- o if a salesperson candidate, must take an additional 6 hours of Introduction to Contract Writing class
- o if a broker candidate, must take an additional 9 hours of Broker Management Clinics
- o if a broker candidate, must demonstrate 3 years of full-time real estate experience in the past five years
- Salesperson and broker license candidates must submit an application which includes
    - o applicant identity information
    - o information on past license revocations or disciplinary action on any professional license in Arizona or other state
    - o criminal record, if any
    - o fingerprint clearance card or fingerprints
    - o required license fees
- Proofs of experience for broker candidates are affidavits from previous brokers and tax records
- New broker continuing education requirement:
    - o 9 hours of broker management clinics – 3 classes – for license renewal if responsible for contracts as well as statutory duties in the absence of the designated broker
    - o 9 hours of clinics also required for self-employed, sole proprietorship brokers

License Status & License Types

Activated and active licenses

- Successful candidates must first activate their licenses
    - o to activate means to "start up"
    - o an activated license means licensee now has a file at ADRE in Phoenix
    - o candidates have one year to activate a license after passing the state real estate examination
    - o inactive/activated licensees may not work at activities requiring an active license or earn commissions
- To work in the profession and earn commissions requires an active license
    - o an active license requires a licensee to be legally licensed through an employing broker
- Only a designated broker can, by law, earn a commission
    - o licensed salespeople cannot earn a commission directly or take money from the public for real estate activities
    - o all money from the public must go to and through a brokerage designated broker
    - o a broker takes commission income, subtracts any brokerage share, E&O insurance, and other costs and issues new payment to the salesperson for salesperson's commission earned.
- A brokerage designated broker also holds a licensee's physical license
    - o upon licensee hiring, ADRE sends licensee's license to the employing broker
    - o at severance, the employing broker sends the licensee's license back to ADRE
    - o licensees may get a copy of their license from the ADRE website
    - o brokerages are not required to display licensees' licenses; must show them on demand
- **Independent contractors v. employees**
    - o according to Internal Revenue Service Codes, most real estate licensees seldom meet IRS requirements to be employees
    - o real estate licensees do not adhere to specific hours of work; are not paid a salary or wages; are not issued a W-2 reporting employee income; and generally do not participate in employee benefits
    - o IRS income reporting for independent contractors is via a 1099 form
    - o many licensees sign an independent contractor agreement with their brokerages
    - o as independent contractors, licensees are not bound to brokerages by time; they may self-sever or be involuntarily severed for cause (violations of ethics or law, etc.) at any time
    - o brokers must provide reasonable supervision

- o employment contracts are between <u>principals and a brokerage</u>, not between principals and licensees
  - An original salesperson and broker license is for a period of 2 years up to and including the last day of the month of licensure
- **Continuing education**: to maintain an active or inactive Arizona real estate license, salesperson or broker must complete a minimum of 24 hours of continuing education every 2 years including:
  - o 3 hours of Agency Law
  - o 3 hours of Contract Law
  - o 3 hours of Disclosure
  - o 3 hours of Real Estate Legal Issues
  - o 3 hours of Fair Housing
  - o 3 hours of Commissioner's Standards
  - o 6 hours of any ADRE approved subject offered by an ADRE approved provider
  - o designated brokers, self-employed brokers, sole proprietorship brokers and licensees who may be assigned as temporary designated broker must take 21 hours of classes in required categories plus 9 hours of broker management clinics to retain their licenses
  - o associate brokers who do not fit into any of the above categories are not required to take the broker management clinics
  - o licenses are suspended for licensees who fail to renew licenses
  - o licensees with suspended licenses may not work in real estate or earn commissions

Temporary real estate licenses
- Temporary Broker's License
  - o issued if a broker dies, or is disabled by sickness, injury, or insanity
  - o may be issued to a licensed or unlicensed spouse, next of kin, administrator, personal representative, employee, legal guardian, or conservator of a licensed broker
  - o issued for the short-term purpose of winding up existing or pending business of the broker
- Temporary Cemetery Salesperson
  - o can be issued to person who applied for and otherwise qualifies for a cemetery salesperson license
  - o good for 90 days only after issuance

Temporary Designated Broker
- not a license change; not a temporary license
- must be appointed if a designated broker is out of direct control of a brokerage for at least 24 hours but less than 30 days
- requires a letter of appointment; no fees, no license change
- temporary designated broker cannot hire or fire or be sole signer on a trust account
- appointee can be any licensee with the brokerage or from outside the brokerage

Certificate of Convenience – membership camping
- one-time, 30 day; not a license change
- issued to a membership camping salesperson otherwise qualified for a license, who agrees to complete training

Holding multiple licenses; license change notifications
- In general, Arizona real estate licensees may hold only one license at a time
  - o exception: holders of cemetery sales licenses may also be employed by a general real estate brokerage at the same time
  - o exception: holders of membership camping licenses may also be employed by a general real estate brokerage at the same time
- A salesperson or broker shall notify ADRE in writing within 10 days of any change in the individual's personal information or qualifications

Appraiser license types
- Appraisers in Arizona must be licensed
- Licensed Residential Appraiser
  - may appraise non-complex one- to four-residential units with a transaction value of less than $1,000,000, and complex one-to four-residential units with a transaction value of less than $250,000
  - license requirements: 150 hours of classroom education, passage of an examination, 2,000 hours of appraisal experience (apprenticeship) in less than 18 months
- Certified Residential Appraiser
  - may appraise one- to four-residential units without regard to transaction value
  - license requirements: 200 hours of classroom education including 90 hours completed for the licensed residential appraiser program, passage of an examination, 2,500 hours of appraiser experience in less than 24 months, plus a bachelor's degree or higher
- Certified General Appraiser
  - may appraise all types of real property
  - license requirements: 300 classroom hours, exam passage, 3,000 hours of appraisal experience in less than 30 months - at least half of which must be in non-residential appraisals - plus a bachelor's degree or higher
- Trainee Appraiser: a new appraiser under the supervision of a licensed appraiser completing the required experiential hours
- Broker price opinions
  - provided by real estate licensees rather than licensed appraisers
  - gives an opinion of the price of real estate
  - may not be referred to as an "appraisal"

Part III: Easements, Encumbrances, Ownership & Conveyances

Easement Interests

Nature of easement interest
- Real property interest entitling one person's limited legal use of another's property for a specific designated use
- Non-possessory right which is written and recorded
- May be terminated with specific legal action but otherwise does not terminate with the sale of the land (i.e., is appurtenant)
- A license is a **personal privilege** to use the land of another for a limited purpose; it is not an interest in real property

Types of easement
- Appurtenant easement
  - "runs with the land"; attached to the land title; if the land is sold, the easement is transferred to the new owner
  - often created in Arizona to lawfully transfer landlocked land; land must have ingress (a way in) and egress (a way out)
  - **Arizona easements by necessity** run across servient tenements at the demand of dominant tenements
  - servient tenements are landowners who must respond to the demand for access to landlocked land by the dominant tenement

- o access roads and drives to landlocked property must be provided by the servient property by law
  - ▪ legal accessibility means the property is reachable by a two-wheel drive passenger vehicle or piece of fire apparatus (fire truck)
- o the **servient retains title**; **pays property taxes** on the land and easement
- o the **dominant tenement holds the recorded easement**; must pay road maintenance costs
- o roads which are subject to easements often cross U.S. Forest Service land in Arizona
  - ▪ the U.S. government must provide easements to private land
- • Easement in Gross
  - o **commercial easement in gross:** a utility or railway easement which can be assigned or transferred
  - o **personal easement in gross:** cannot be assigned or transferred; it terminates with the death of the grantor or upon conveyance of the property
- • Prescription easements
  - o resulting from the continuous, open, hostile, and notorious use of another's land for a period of 10 years in Arizona without the consent of the owner
- • Profit à prendre
  - o considered a type of easement
  - o the right to remove soil, minerals, fruit, timber or some other product of the land
  - o requires compensation to the owner
  - o is non-possessory
  - o limited to a specific purpose
  - o is in writing

Easement creation and termination
- • Created in four ways
  - o express grants, executed by separate deeds
  - o reservations in deeds
  - o easements by necessity to prevent landlocked land
  - o prescription easements – used for 10 years as previously described
- • Easements may be terminated in Arizona by
  - o agreement of the parties, using a recorded quit claim deed
  - o merger of the dominant and servient properties
  - o abandonment of the easement
  - o adverse possession

Encumbrances

Definitions
- • An encumbrance is a **claim, lien, charge, or liability** attached to or binding on real property
- • An encumbrance may lessen the value of a property or burden, obstruct, or impair its use
- • Encumbrances do not necessarily prevent transfer of title
- • An encumbrance is a right or interest in property held by someone other than the legal owner

Arizona monetary encumbrances
- • A charge or claim as security for payment of a debt or obligation
- • Affect title to the property involved

Non-monetary encumbrances
- • Non-monetary encumbrances affect the use and condition of property

Tax liens
- • Arizona property taxes and special assessments are liens on specific properties that take precedence over all other liens and encumbrances

Encumbrances: Mechanic's Lien

Who may file
- Arizona law allows mechanics (**repair and renovation contractors**) and materialmen (**suppliers of building and repair materials**) to file mechanic's liens
- Mechanic's liens in Arizona **favor subcontractors**, materialmen and laborers independent of the original contractor
- **Advance notice required**: For subcontractors and materialmen, a 20-day notice prior to the filing of a lien is required to alert the property owner, general contractor, or lender a lien will be filed; the 20 days begin with delivery of materials or completion of the labor
  - Both general and subcontractors in Arizona must record mechanic's liens within 120 days, which includes the 20 days of the 20-day notice
- Original contractors do not lose their right to lien or subrogate their lien position
- Mechanic's liens cover situations where the general contractor has been paid but the subcontractor has not

Who may not file
- Those who cannot file mechanic's liens:
  - unlicensed contractors and handypersons
  - those who have not given the required 20 day notice
  - those who cannot show proof of service
  - persons who do not hold a valid certification of registration
  - persons who do not have a written agreement with the owner of the property
- In Arizona, a subcontractor may not assert any claim against a property owner according to a subcontract

Lien priority
- Lien priority is first in time of recordation, first in priority for payment
- If notice of completion of project is recorded, the time for all parties to record their liens is reduced to 60 days
- If payment is not made after lien recordation, contractors must begin collection procedures via filing **a foreclosure action within 180 days** (6 months)

Lien release
- A lien release **must be recorded within 20 days** of the satisfaction of the lien

Non-Monetary Encumbrances

Deed restrictions
- Deed restrictions are generally placed on property when is it developed; they can restrict
  - square footage of structures
  - setbacks
  - styles of buildings
  - home businesses
  - fence heights

Covenants, conditions, and restrictions (CC&Rs)
- Similar to deed restrictions
- Placed on property by the original developer
- May be rewritten and revised by homeowner's associations
- If a person violates usage rules, homeowners must take legal action at their own expense
- A delay in taking actions causing loss of legal rights is called *laches*

Easements as encumbrances
- An easement is another type of non-monetary encumbrance found in Arizona

- appurtenant easements usually involve ingress and egress, resulting in a dominant tenement demanding an easement over a servient tenement
- an easement in gross may be a utility easement

Encroachments
- **Trespass** is an encroachment of unlawful entry by a person or structure
- **Nuisance** is also an encroachment which includes noise, smell and light

Homestead exemption
- Protects one's equity from a forced sale due to a judgment up to $150,000
- Is automatically assigned to the head of a household of a primary residence 18 years of age or older
- May be transferred to a new primary resident
- Can be lost in the case of abandonment or if the owner moves out of Arizona
- The only form of legal life estate in Arizona
  - Arizona is a community property state; dower and curtesy (forms of legal life estate) do not apply

---

Real Property Ownership

Cooperatives
- A **leasehold** in which tenants also own stock in the corporation which owns the building
- A corporation generally holds one title and one mortgage on the property
- Tenants receive stock in the corporation and a personal property interest in the form of a proprietary lease
- Board of directors of the corporation develops budgets; maintains the common areas
- Tenants generally form a stockholder association; have limited control over rents; and have limited approval of new tenants
- As a leasehold, tenants do not get income tax deductions for mortgage interest or property tax
- Cooperatives are rare in Arizona

Condominiums
- A condominium is a fractional fee simple ownership that includes a share of the common areas of the complex
- Individual units owned as tenancy in severalty, joint tenancy, community property with or without survivorship, or tenancy in common
- Owners receive a deed for the unit and often a second deed for the owner's share of the common areas
- Owners enjoy full tax benefits on loan interest payments
- In addition to residential units, business and commercial space condominiums are also available

Manufactured Homes
- A manufactured home **on a rental pad** is **personal property**
- A manufactured home **on land** is considered **real property**
- A manufactured homes considered personal property transfers with a bill of sale
- Requirements to sell manufactured homes
  - To represent a seller of a single- or doublewide on a rental pad, the state requires the agent to be a "dealer."
  - A dealer's license must be obtained from Arizona Department of Fire, Building, and Safety; this license is required to represent all factory-built structures including modular homes on rental pads
  - Agents representing manufactured homes for sale considered real property need a real estate license from ADRE

Community Property

- Most states in the U. S. Southwest are community property states
- Southwestern states model real property ownership laws after the Spanish and Spanish Land Grant Law
- 1800s Spanish property law held that husband and wife were equals in a marriage, not a combination of the husband and wife into the same entity

Community property key features

- husband or wife may devise (will) her or his property interest share to a third party. As a result, real property must be cleared through probate
- For married couples, Arizona has "**community property with right of survivorship**"
  - allows married couples to receive federal tax benefits for community property while avoiding probate
  - provides an automatic survivorship right
  - precludes any will excluding one partner in a marriage
  - married couples must specify community property with right of survivorship
  - the default method of holding interest in real property in Arizona for married couples is community property without the right of survivorship
- Real property acquired during a legally recognized marriage becomes community property in Arizona unless
  - the property was **owned prior** to marriage
  - the property was **willed or gifted** to only one party in the marriage
  - one party voluntarily **gives up his or her interest** in the property via a disclaimer deed
- Spouse of a married buyer or seller must sign listing contracts and contracts for sale
- Arizona real property owners can also hold as tenancy in severalty, joint tenancy, and tenancy in common

Timeshares

- **Timeshare**: a type of condominium ownership where the use of property is desired for a short period every year
- Considered **pre-paid vacations** in real estate by the IRS; **expenses** related to timeshare ownership **are not deductible** except mortgage interest
- Fractional vacation ownership is the major benefit of Arizona timeshares
- Timeshare includes a reservation system allowing owners to use at different times during a year
- Owners may also have allotments of time they can spend on other national and international locations

Types of timeshare ownership

- Arizona Revised Statutes define various types of timeshare ownership
  - a timeshare estate gives owners the right of ownership in a timeshare complex
  - timeshare use means a license, contractual, or membership **right of occupancy, not coupled with an estate in real property**; an estate is frequently deeded property and many Arizona timeshares are deeded
  - in **interval ownership**, an owner has a deed, title, and right to occupy for an agreed time each year
  - **vacation ownership** is based on a license to use a property while the developer retains fee simple ownership
  - newer concepts in timeshare include amenities such as luxury vehicles while occupying, or spending time allotments in luxury hotels or on ocean cruises

Homeowners' associations

- Many subdivisions and townhome and condominium developments require every owner to belong to a home owner's association (HOA)
  - developers complete building then turn management over to a property manager and/or HOA
- HOAs can select officers and boards of directors with the power to act on behalf of the association; responsible for activities from budgeting to selecting and paying vendors
- HOAs are required to operate within their bylaws and state laws

- Enforcement of HOA rules is often controversial
  - CC&Rs, enforced by HOAs, are encumbrances
  - enforcement of rules is considered by some as infringement of a property owner's right to quiet enjoyment
  - real estate professionals are charged with helping buyers determine if their planned use of a property is compatible with HOA rules
  - HOAs can place a lien against properties whose owners fail to pay assessments or penalties
  - since most HOAs are incorporated, complaints against them may be submitted to the Arizona Corporation Commission
  - HOAs can foreclose on properties for non-payment of assessments -- but not for failure to pay penalties
- Since HOA management does not require a real estate license, ADRE has little jurisdiction over HOAs

Conveyances by Deed

Alienation defined
- Alienation is the act of **transferring title** from one person to another
  - **voluntary alienation** is transferring with the consent of the owner such as sale, trade, or gift
  - **involuntary alienation** is transfer without owner consent, which may result from foreclosure, tax sale, judgment, escheat, eminent domain or adverse possession
  - **alienation by will** is transfer by a person's last will and testament
  - **alienation by descent** is transfer when a person dies intestate (no will)
  - when a person dies intestate, the deceased person's property is distributed according to Arizona's statute of **descent and distribution**

Deeds
- A deed is a written instrument in which a property owner conveys and transfers an ownership interest
  - the **grantor** is the original property **owner**
  - the grantee is the person receiving the property
- A deed is evidence of transfer of title
- Types of deeds differ according to the **covenants made** by the grantor
  - real property purchase contracts specify the type of deed the grantee will receive
  - the **most common deed** resulting from voluntary transfer in Arizona is the **warranty deed**

General warranty deed
- Provides the greatest protection for the grantee; greatest responsibilities for the grantor> It contains 5 warrantees for the grantor, called covenants or promises
  - the Covenant of **Seisin** promises the grantor owns the property and has the **right to convey** it
  - the Covenant of **Quiet Enjoyment** promises the **grantor will defend** the grantee against all claims made by third parties
  - the Covenant **Against Encumbrances** promises the property is **free from encumbrances** other than those identified in the deed
  - the Covenant of Warranty of Title promises the grantor will compensate the grantee for a loss if the title fails at any time
  - the Covenant of Further Assurance promises the grantor will obtain and deliver any instrument needed to make title good

Special warranty deed
- is used by new home builders, major corporations, trust departments
- offers the same covenants as the general warranty deed but limited to only when the grantor owned or was in possession of the property
- **limits responsibility** for claims to **only during ownership**

Bargain and sale deed
- Offers less protection for grantees
- Promises the **grantor has the right to convey** the property and **property is free from encumbrance**s except those identified in the deed
- Used often for involuntary alienation
- Includes treasurer's deed for a tax sale; sheriff's deed for mortgage foreclosure; trustee's deed for trust deed foreclosure

Quitclaim deed
- Quits or **gives up a person's interest** in real property
- Offers **no covenants**; just releases claims
- Often used for gifting, divorces, and to remove clouds on title

Disclaimer deed
- Executed so that one spouse in a marriage may hold title to real property separate from the other spouse
- If not executed, acquired real property is considered community property in Arizona

Deed validity
- In Arizona, a contract signed by a minor is automatically void
- A deed delivered to a minor or incompetent grantee is valid
- A deed to a **fictitious person** is **void**
- A deed to a person using a **fictitious name** is **valid**
- "Sound mind" in contract capacity means sane and free from the influence of alcohol or drugs
    - in Arizona, only a court of law can declare a person insane
- A grantor's name must be spelled consistently throughout a deed
- A misspelled name will not necessarily invalidate a deed if the grantor's identity is otherwise clear
- Most U.S. deeds cite nominal consideration in the transfer of real property
    - in Arizona, nominal consideration is $10
    - Arizona warranty deeds read: "For the amount of $10 or more & other valuable consideration, I _____ as Grantor here by convey to _____, as Grantee, all right, title & interest in that certain real property situated in _____ County in the State of Arizona and described as followed (legal description)
    - the words "...do hereby convey to..." are called "words of conveyance "
    - the required legal description must also be on all contracts which transfer real property
- In Arizona, a **habendum clause defines the interest** or estate being conveyed
- Deeds must be signed, sealed and delivered to be fully valid
    - deeds in Arizona are generally delivered by physically placing them in the hands of grantees or delivery by certified mail to a grantee from a title company
- Challenges to deeds are often settled with the help of title insurance companies enforcing guarantees found in deeds

Title & Recordation

Title search and abstract of title
- Title is the right of ownership of property and evidence of such rights
- A title search is required to determine marketable title
- In Arizona's title search procedure, title companies employ title examiners who search recorded documents for chain of title and other claims on the property
    - chain of title is linkage of one owner to the next throughout the history of the property
    - other claims could include forgery, fraud, or other encumbrances
- An abstract of title is a summary of all legal and conveyance actions affecting a property
- A clean or marketable title is one sufficiently free of defects to be transferable
- Most recorded documents appear in a title search before the transfer of property

Recordation
- Deeds are not required to be recorded in Arizona but approximately 95% are
  - recordation allows documents to be accessed publicly
  - an unrecorded deed can challenge legal ownership of the current property owner
  - unrecorded deeds have weaker claims because they were not processed properly
  - unrecorded deeds often have not been legally delivered

Leasehold Transfers

Assignment
- Title to leasehold property is transferred using an assignment of lease rather than a lease itself

Legal capacity
- To have the legal capacity to sign a lease and execute a lease in Arizona, a person must be at least 18 years of age or an emancipated minor
  - the age of majority in Arizona is 18
  - minors under the age of 18 may own real property but may not sell it because they do not have the legal capacity to convey real property via a contract
- An emancipated minor
  - is at least **16 years** of age
  - has been **emancipated** from his or her parents or guardians **via court action**
  - is **financially self-sufficient**, able to buy shelter, food, and healthcare without support
  - is an Arizona resident

Escheat

Escheat
- Property owned by a decedent **without a will or apparent heirs** will be taken by the state via escheat
  - the state will sell the property and will search for heirs for 7 years
  - a special appropriation from the legislature is used to repay heirs found within the 7 years
- The purpose of escheat is to **prevent real property from being abandoned**

Part IV: Land & Environmental Laws

Water Laws

Definitions
- **Potable water:** water which can be safely and agreeably consumed by humans
- **Water table:** the natural level at which water is located whether at or below the surface of the earth
- **Aquifer:** An underground layer of water-bearing gravel, rock, sand, or silt from where groundwater can be withdrawn with a water well
- **Erosion:** the gradual wearing away of land due to natural forces
- **Avulsion:** the rapid, sudden removal of land by natural forces
- **Alluvion:** the buildup of land by wind, water, and other natural causes
- **Alluvium:** multiple natural buildups of soil
- **Arizona wetlands:** consistently saturated land which supports a variety of plant life
  - often located on or near small rivers, tanks, marshes, and rainfall collection areas
  - comprise 1% of Arizona land

- o include the Colorado and Little Colorado in northern Arizona; Sonoran Desert and the San Pedro, Gila, Salt, and Little Colorado in southern Arizona; and special wetlands projects near Phoenix and Tucson

Surface Water
- Water at rest or flowing on the surface of the earth such as rivers, streams and lakes
  - o includes underground water from percolation or seepage which is not part of a defined underground waterway
- Arizona's interior watersheds - defined as non-Colorado River water - are governed by the **doctrine of prior appropriation**
  - o means "first in time, first in right" -- those with chronologically prior permits to use water have priority rights over new potential users
- Surface water use permits **are required**
  - o surface water use rights must be **maintained every 5 years** at minimum
  - o if use is not made in a 5-year period, the rights revert to the state

Waterways
- Arizona's only navigable waterway, the Colorado River, is governed by federal law and administered by the U.S. Department of the Interior through the Bureau of Reclamation
- The U.S. Army Corps of Engineers determines navigable and non-navigable waterways
- Army Corps of Engineers designations determine surface water ownership and use
- Whether a waterway is used for commerce is one factor in determining navigable waterways
- Property owners whose property includes surface waterways do not own the water in Arizona; they may be able to use and enjoy it
- The Colorado River provides approximately 30% of Arizona's water via a system of allocations
  - o Arizona's inability to use its full allocation has led to California and Nevada to attempt to increase their allocations at Arizona's expense
  - o historically Arizona did not have the ability to take, store, and deliver all Colorado River water allocated to the state
  - o the completion of the Central Arizona Project (CAP) and Waddell Dam expanded Lake Pleasant's reserve capacity to store water
- The right to use surface water in Arizona is limited as a function of the quantity of water available, the degree of natural recharge, and the priority of the user's rights (first in use, first in right) .
- Surface water use must be reasonable and beneficial
- The Arizona Department of Water Resources (ADWR) controls all water use in the state
- All surface water rights in the Gila River Basin are currently subject to adjudication before the Supreme Court of Arizona
  - o this is the result of claims for water rights by the Gila Indian Tribe
  - o the effects of the decision on this challenge is likely to have impact on both surface and ground water in Arizona

Ground Water
- **Ground water:** all water under the surface of the earth except water flowing in underground streams with definite banks and beds
- The **1980 Groundwater Management Code (GMC)** was enacted to control severe overdraft in Arizona
  - o Overdrafts occur when water is pumped out in greater quantities than replenished by natural recharge
- **GMC goal:** provide a means to allocate the state's limited groundwater to meet the changing needs of the state and augment Arizona's groundwater through water supply development
- The Code established **three levels of water management**:
  - o lowest level: general provisions that apply statewide
  - o next level: Irrigation Non-expansion Areas ((INAs)
  - o highest level: **Active Management Areas (AMAs);** most extensive provisions where groundwater overdrafts are most severe
- Originally four AMAs were created: Phoenix, Pinal, Prescott, and Tucson; Santa Cruz AMA, part of the Tucson AMA, was added

- o AMA boundaries are actually formed by water basins
- o the remainder of the state is made up of areas not yet designated for active management
- Groundwater use and rights are highly regulated in AMAs due to a long history of overdrafts and subsidence
  - o **subsidence occurs when surface ground water sinks** due to the loss of water pockets below the surface
- Within an AMA, a person must have groundwater right or permit to pump groundwater legally
  - o wells must be registered with ADWR; has fewer regulations than exempt wells in AMAs and INAs
- An irrigation grandfathered right confers the right to irrigate specific plots that have been irrigated with groundwater between 1975 and 1980
  - o land without an irrigation grandfathered right may not be irrigated with groundwater
  - o under GMC, irrigate means to apply water to two or more acres of land to produce plants for sale or human consumption or as feed for livestock
  - o an irrigation grandfathered right specifies how much groundwater can be used; the amount will vary over time according to a formula established in management plans
  - o an irrigation grandfathered right may not be sold apart from its associated land
- A type 1 right is associated with land permanently retired from farming and converted to non-irrigation use such as building a new industrial plant or subdivision
  - o a type 1 right is conveyed with the land like an irrigation grandfathered right
  - o the maximum that can be pumped annually using a type 1 right is three acre feet per acre
- Groundwater withdrawn under a type 2 right can only be used for non-irrigation purposes, including industry, livestock watering, and golf courses
- Type 2 rights may be sold separately from the land or well; it may be possible to lease a portion of a type 2 right but if sold, the right may not be divided
- The owner of a type 2 right may, with ADWR approval, withdraw groundwater from a new location within the AMA
- **Most Arizonans receive domestic water through service area rights**; service area rights authorize cities, towns, private water companies, and irrigation companies to withdraw groundwater to serve their customers
- Withdrawal permits allow new withdrawals for non-irrigation use within AMAs.
- There are 8 types of withdrawal permits with use ranging from poor-quality groundwater permits to general industrial permits
- Permits are subject to the quality and purpose of groundwater use
- **There is no new irrigation permitted in AMAs**; no new land may be put into production in an AMA; only grandfathered irrigation is permitted
- In an AMA, **anyone offering subdivided or unsubdivided land for sale or lease must demonstrate an assured supply of water** to the ADWR before the land can be publically marketed
- To receive an assured water supply certificate from ADWR, a developer must demonstrate that
  - o the water supply is of sufficient quantity and quality to **sustain the development for 100 years**
  - o the proposed use is consistent with the management plan
  - o the water provider has the financial capacity to construct development water delivery and treatment systems
- A developer in a service area (city, town, private water company) can obtain a designation of assured water supply from ADWR
  - o if the subdivision will be served by a designated provider, a written commitment for service is all that's required for the designation
- To support groundwater management goals, ADWR adopted new assured water supply rules in the 1990s
  - o these rules require **new developments to be sustained by predominantly renewable supplies** such as surface water including effluent and Colorado River water delivered by the Central Arizona Project
- ADRE's website advises prospective home buyers **to investigate water availability before purchasing**; information on the site includes
  - o definitions of adequate water supply and inadequate water supply
  - o property served by a water provider designated as having an adequate water supply
  - o no water supply determinations outside AMAs

- o   a current map of areas in Arizona outside AMAs
- Arizona allows collection of water in dry wells
    - o   dry wells ae bored holes in which the depth is larger than the width, and in which storm water may be collected
    - o   gray water and effluent may not be collected in dry wells

---

Environmental Regulation

The Arizona Department of Environmental Quality (ADEQ)

- Established by the Arizona Legislature as state's environmental agency under the Environmental Quality Act of 1986
- **Mission**: to protect and enhance public health and the environment
- Administers the state's environmental laws and designated federal laws to prevent the pollution of air, water, and land use, and ensure clear up of pollution when it occurs
- **Core functions:** environmental planning, permitting, compliance and enforcement, monitoring and data analysis, cleanups, and educational outreach
- ADEQ focuses on air quality, water quality, and waste

Air Quality Division

- Responsibilities include:
    - o   ambient air monitoring
    - o   pollution forecasts
    - o   locating and evaluating pollution sources
    - o   issuing permits to industry and other facilities
    - o   vehicle inspection programs

Water Quality Division

- Ensures Arizona's public water system delivers safe drinking water
- Identifies water pollution problems and establishes standards to deal with them
- Investigates complaints and violations of Arizona water quality laws, rules and permits
- Issues permits
- Manages the quality of watersheds
- Monitors the quality of surface and groundwater
- Regulates the discharge and treatment of wastewater

Waste Programs Division

- Responsibilities include:
    - o   assuring property handling, storage, and treatment of wastes
    - o   correction of operation and maintenance of underground storage tanks (USTs)
    - o   investigating complaints and violations of Arizona solid waste laws and regulations
    - o   investigating, managing, and remediating soil and groundwater pollution
    - o   promoting prevention and recycling
- **Hazardous wastes:** listed by the federal government; contain mix of **ignitable, corrosive, reactive, unstable, or toxic** characteristics
- Arizona homeowners are not liable for cleanup of state or federal superfund sites
- Homeowners who release of hazardous materials may be held liable for cleanup; this liability extends to non-residential use of property
- Primary residential hazards:
    - o   radon which can be trapped in large quantities in a structures
    - o   asbestos originally used for insulation and in construction
    - o   mold

Common Arizona real estate environmental issues

- Carbon monoxide
- Electromagnetic fields (EMFs)
- Groundwater contamination

- Lead
- Pesticides
- Polychlorinated biphenyls (PCBs)
- Underground storage tanks
- Clandestine drug labs, typically meth labs, use extremely hazardous chemicals in the illegal manufacture of methamphetamine, ecstasy, or LSD
  - these labs create a dangerous environment and cause structural damage
  - upon discovery of a drug lab or arrest of its operator, the **discovery becomes an emergency in Arizona**
  - Arizona law requires remediation of the lab site **within 12 months** of lab removal
  - a registered drug lab remediation firm must do the remediation
  - once remediation is complete, every buyer who signs a contract to buy the property must receive **within 5 days of signing the contract**, notice of the past presence of the lab and owner's arrest
  - the buyer must acknowledge receipt of the notice and **has 5 days to elect to cancel** the contract
  - a prospective rental tenant must also receive such notice prior to signing a rental agreement; if notice is not provided, a tenant may void the rental agreement
  - failure to provide required notice carries a $1,000 fine and liability for any harm resulting from failure to disclose
- Marijuana cultivation
  - With the allowance of medical marijuana in Arizona, damage from unlawful growing has become a disclosure issue
  - Illegal growers often rent homes and dangerously reroute plumbing for water and electricity for grow lamps
  - Areas near growing areas are subject to mold due to increased moisture
  - Venting humid air through dark interior spaces such as attics also stimulates the growing of mold

Land Descriptions

Methods of legal description
- Three forms of land description are recognized in Arizona as legal land description, i.e., recognized in a court of law:
  - government rectangular survey
  - metes and bounds survey
  - lot, block, and tract
- More than one description method can be used for one parcel of land

The government rectangular survey
- The 1785 Continental Congress passed a land ordinance dividing public land into "small, affordable" parcels known as townships
- All public land west of the Appalachians and north of the Ohio River, and all western lands – including Arizona – and except Texas were surveyed using the government rectangular survey
- The government rectangular survey resulted in the creation of **35 principal meridians** and **baselines** throughout the U.S.
- Arizona's primary baseline and meridian intersect approximately 20 miles south of Phoenix
- Original surveyors tried to choose a lasting natural monument for the initial points and chose the confluence of the Gila and Salt rivers in Arizona
- All non-Indian reservation land in Arizona is located in the **Gila and Salt River Base Line and Meridian (G&SRBM)**
- Today, the G&SRBM meridian runs approximately along 115th Avenue in Phoenix, and the base line is Base Line Road
- Arizona has two principal meridians and base lines
  - in addition to the G&SRBM, a small portion of the northeast corner of Arizona on the Navajo Nation was made the Navajo Meridian and Base Line in 1869
- Arizona uses correction lines and fractional sections to account for the curvature of the earth

- Less-than-full sections within townships which are interrupted by state borders and rivers are called government lots
- Arizona's rectangular survey land descriptions **begin with the smallest unit and end with the largest**, G&SRBM, which is the entire state
  - an example begins with halves and quarters of sections, section number(s), township designation, and then principle baseline and meridian

Metes and bounds

- Land descriptions too small to be fully identified by governmental rectangular survey may also include a metes and bounds survey
- Arizona has brass markers or "**brass caps**" embedded throughout the state; these are artificial **monuments** used as a starting point of metes and bounds surveys
- Where markers are not available, surveyors often use local points of **height and depth references** called **datums**
- Local datum points include the Arizona Divide west of Flagstaff on Interstate 40, where the elevation is officially determined and surface water drains north and south
- Datum points are also used to reference **air lots** for legal description
  Air lots are air-specific elevation boundaries over a parcel of land such as building built over properties such as railway yards using caissons for support.

Units of measure

- Common legal description conversions are:
  - 16.5 feet, and 25 links = 1 rod
  - 4 rods, and 66 feet = 1 chain
  - 80 chains, 320 rods, and 2,760 yards = 5,280 feet
  - 10 square (sq.) chains, 160 sq. rods, 4,840 sq. yards, and 43,560 sq. feet = 1 acre

Subdivision Law

Subdivision or subdivided land

- A subdivision or subdivided land is defined as improved or unimproved land which is divided for purposes of sale or lease into 6 or more parcels, **any of which is 36 acres or less**

Unsubdivided land

- Unsubdivided land is land divided for the purpose of sale or lease, whether immediate or future, into 6 or more lots, parcels, or fractional interests **36 acres or more but less than 160 acres each**
- Parcels **more than 160 acres are not regulated** under Arizona subdivision law
- Rules for developing unsubdivided lands are nearly the same as for subdivided land
  - the application and questionnaire for developing unsubdivided land is smaller in scope and requires less information

Subdivision disclosure: the Commissioner's Public Report (CPR

- The Arizona Subdivision Law is a disclosure law
- For the protection of buyers, subdividers and developers must obtain a Commissioner's Public Report (CPR) before any properties can be sold
- The CPR provides complete and accurate material facts related to the subdivision
- **CPR contents**: To obtain a CPR, developers must file a notice to subdivide and complete the ADRE's subdivided land questionnaire, containing
  - information on the owner, investors, and developer
  - true condition of title
  - a description of topographical characteristics of the land
  - location of services such as sewage treatment
  - a map of the subdivision called a plat, filed with the office of county recorder
  - the legal description of the parcel or parcels
  - information on proposed utilities and utility providers,
  - state of access for the subdivision
  - approved waste disposal collection

- o assurance of adequate water supply as required by Arizona water law
  - o location of the nearest public schools
  - o proposed gas, electricity, and telephone facilities
  - o information on subdivision financing
  - o indebtedness
  - o common area maintenance fees and improvements
  - o estimates of annual taxes and special assessments
  - o a copy of restrictive covenants
  - o business history of the developer
  - o information on the real estate brokerage representing the developer
  - o disclosures, such as proximity to a military airport
- The ADRE evaluates the questionnaire and inspects to verify the application
- Developer must pay an application fee
- Developers and brokerages may advertise lot availability **but may not close sales until the application is approved and CPR issued**
- **Lot reservations** for unimproved lots and conditional sales contracts for lots with improvements **may be accepted prior to CPR**
  - o a maximum of $5,000 per reservation or contract may be accepted
  - o deposit monies must be held in escrow
  - o developers may not use deposit monies for building activities
  - o lot reservations and conditional sales contracts may be rescinded any time prior to CPR and all deposit monies returned as per Arizona state law
- A developer may advertise the subdivision prior to CPR but **all advertising must be approved** by ADRE prior to issuance of CPR
- After CPR is issued, ADRE prior approval of development is not required but a number of legal restrictions for subdivision will be applied
- A commissioner's public report may be prepared by a title insurance company employed by a developer
  - o a developer may also prepare the CPR; both the developer or title company then sends it to ADRE for approval; this speeds up the CPR process
- All buyers of lots and homes in subdivisions **must receive a copy of CPR within 2 to 10 days** of signing a purchase contract
- CPR copies are generally sent certified mail to record receipt
- The buyer must attest to receipt of CPR, and that the buyer has read and understands it

Contract rescission
- A subdivision purchaser has contract rescission rights for
  - o **7 days after signing** a purchase contract
  - o **Up to 6 months** if the buyer(s) have not personally **inspected** the property
  - o Up to 3 years if promised access isn't delivered
- Purchase contracts for unsubdivided land may be voided for up to 3 years

Advertising Requirements
- ADRE subdivision advertising requirements include
  - o accurate descriptions of the subdivision
  - o promises made to consumers
  - o escrowed funds for improvements
  - o average surface area of standing water
  - o timing of completion of amenities
  - o use of contests, lotteries, and prizes in subdivision promotion

Part V: Disclosure & Consumer Protection

Arizona Agency Disclosure

Disclosure purpose and requirements
- Principals in an Arizona real estate transaction **have the right to know how they are represented** by a brokerage
  - in the sale and purchase of real property, **broker representation** can consist of representing the buyer as **buyer broker**; seller **as seller's broker**; or **both** buyer and seller
- Arizona licensees have specific agency disclosure requirements that are part of their fiduciary duty under agency law
  - agency law calls for disclosure of an **agent's relationship to a buyer**
  - disclosure is required if licensee/principal relationship includes relatives, close friends, business partners, investors, or whether a business relationship will result from the transaction
  - a listing broker must also **disclose and present all offers** to a seller until closing
  - agents must **disclose a buyer's potential to pay a higher price** but never suggest a seller may accept a lower price
  - licensees must make certain clients understand nature and amounts of earnest money
  - disclosure of a buyer's financial situation should be sufficient for the seller to be confident in the buyer's ability to complete the transaction prior to accepting a purchase offer
  - an agent should disclose her or his **informed opinion of the property value**, and it should be based on fact
  - **commissions paid** by the seller and shared with cooperating brokers must be disclosed in writing
  - by agency law, salespeople and brokers have the responsibility to **explain the content of contracts** before signing
  - agents must disclose any and all extra money they might earn from referring clients to other industry entities
  - dual agency requires informed consent on the part of both buyer and seller; if the same licensee or brokerage represents the buyer and seller in a transaction, both principals must approve of this relationship; **disclosure of dual agency** is mandatory in Arizona
- Licensees must never discourage a client from seeking legal advice
- Agency disclosure and election should be discussed by the principal(s) and brokerage before discussions of the real estate transaction

Disclosure forms
- Various Arizona forms deal with agency disclosure
  - the Arizona Agency Disclosure and Election form allows real estate clients to select buyer or seller representation or both; the Arizona purchase contract confirms agency representation
  - while many actions create agency and several forms confirm it, only two forms employ brokerages to work for clients: the **Buyer-Broker Exclusive Employment Agreement** and a **listing agreement**.

Property Disclosure

Disclosure requirements
- A principal's agent in Arizona has the duty to discover and disclose any known facts about a property
  - facts may materially affect the value and desirability of a property
  - facts may or may not be known to other parties in a transaction, or may or may not be easily observable
  - agents should use due diligence to search for property defects

- Defects which may not be disclosed, or are not required to be disclosed are:
  - the site of a natural death, suicide, homicide, or any felony crime
  - occupancy or ownership of a person exposed to HIV or diagnosed with AIDS or other disease not transmitted through common occupancy of real property (disclosing this is a federal fair housing violation)
  - stigmatized property, such as property reputed to be haunted
- Sellers have the duty to
  - disclose any known property defects in writing
  - answer buyer questions regarding property condition
  - disclose any information that would prevent a previous statement from becoming inaccurate or misleading
  - correct any incorrect assumption the other party is relying on to make decisions
- Buyers are responsible for
  - actual notice, i.e., the buyer must make a physical inspection of the property
  - constructive notice, such as checking public records for liens, lis pendens, judgments, or attachments on the property

Seller's property disclosure form
- Seller disclosure statements are available in Arizona to help in property disclosure; these detailed forms help sellers attest to:
  - ownership and property information
  - building and safety concerns
  - utilities
  - environmental information
  - sewer and water treatment
  - past and present property conditions
  - past and present wood destroying organism infestation
  - repairs made by licensed or unlicensed contractors
  - previous fire or flood damage
  - location of property near designated polluted areas

Consumer Protections

Federal protections
- Federal laws and acts with impact on Arizona real estate include the following:
  - Consumer Protection Act of 1968
  - Truth in Lending Act (TILA)
  - Equal Credit Opportunity Act (ECOA)
  - Interstate Land Sales Full Disclosure Act
  - Fair Housing Act
  - Real Estate Settlement Procedures Act (RESPA)
  - Financial Institutions Reform Recovery and Enforcement Act (FIRREA)
- Federal agencies whose rules and regulations affect Arizona real estate include the
  - Internal Revenue Service (IRS)
  - Environmental Protection Agency (EPA)
  - Housing and Urban Development (HUD)

State protections
- State statutes that provide consumer protection
  - the **Arizona Landlord and Tenant Act**(s) provide guidelines for landlord/tenant relationships and rights
  - general laws such as Arizona's **anti-spam law** apply to real estate and other businesses in the state
  - **subdivision law** is designed to help Arizona residents make educated and informed decisions regarding development purchases
  - Arizona also has its own fair housing, water, and environmental laws
- Statewide, several agencies accept and take action on consumer complaints regarding real estate practices and have enforcement power, including the:

- o Arizona Department of Real Estate (ADRE)
- o Arizona Corporation Commission
- o State Attorney General's Office

Arizona consumer fraud protection statutes

- **Fraud**: any deception, unfair act or practice, false statement, false pretense, false promises, or misrepresentation made by a seller or advertiser of merchandise
  - o concealment, suppression or failure to disclose any material fact may be consumer fraud
  - o "merchandise", according to the state attorney general's office, specifically includes real estate
- **Office of Arizona Attorney General:** charged with protecting the public from consumer fraud, antitrust, and anti-competitive practices
- Arizona Attorney General can seek remedies against violations of the **Consumer Fraud Act** within one year of the date of a claim
- Puffing, exaggerated or superlative comments, which are not intended as fact, are not considered misrepresentations or fraudulent
- Arizona's **Telephone Solicitations Act** requires telemarketers to make certain disclosures and prohibit misrepresentations

Codes of ethics

- Voluntary codes of ethics and behavior are also important in Arizona
  - o the Arizona Association of Realtors® and local associations all subscribe to the National Association of Realtors® code of ethics and professional behavior
  - o AAR takes and resolves complaints involving member behavior
  - o AAR mediates conflicts between parties or holds hearings
  - o salespeople and brokers can lose MLS rights and/or be fined, or directed to take continuing education at this level
- By law and professional standards with regard to public welfare, Arizona real estate licensees are expected to be honest, truthful, of good character, and competent
- Competency includes a minimum understanding of the following:
  - o general purpose and legal effect of real estate principles and practices
  - o purpose and legal effect of related forms, including agency contracts, real estate contracts, deposit receipts, deeds, mortgages, deeds of trust, security agreements, bills of sale and property management
  - o relationships between a principal and agent, principles of real estate and business opportunity practice, applicable canons of business ethics, provisions or Arizona real estate law and commissioner's standards
- Designated brokers are charged with maintaining compliance and professional standards of licensees employed at their brokerage

Violations and penalties

- Violations of statutory law are generally subject to civil and criminal remedies
- While many real estate disputes are resolved in civil actions, some violations are subject to criminal law
  - o an unlicensed person who accepts a finder's fee is potentially committing a class 6 felony, for example
- Consumer complaints can endanger licensee licenses, corporate standing, or legal standing

Part VI: Regulated Activities & Relationships

Advertising

Definition

- Per ADRE, virtually everything a licensee does to circulate his or her name – other than "keep in touch" or "thank you" items such as birthday cards – falls under the definition of advertising

Rules and regulations
- **"Blind ads"** -- advertisements which suggest no salesperson or broker is taking part in the sale -- are prohibited
- Designated brokers must supervise all advertising
- Non-managing licensees are also responsible for ad compliance
- **Broker's identification**. The employing broker's name must be clear and prominent in ads
    - the name may be the employing broker's legal or dba name; "prominent" means conspicuous or in a position of importance
    - the employing broker's name must be included in classified ads, real estate advertising guides, magazine ads and on the top of flyers
    - the employing broker's name must be spelled out in its entirety; using just a franchise name – without the full name of the local affiliate – is not in compliance
    - on websites, name of the employing broker must be visible on the first page of the site without scrolling down
    - web pages must also identify the employing broker on each page or link
    - employing broker identity also applies to e-mails
- Real estate team advertisements may only include identities of licensed salespeople or associate brokers who are employed **at the same brokerage**
- No statute or rule requires inclusion of telephone numbers or address of the employing broker or licensee in an advertisement
- All advertising must contain accurate claims and representations, and fully stated factual material
- A licensee's name must be set forth in a way that would allow a consumer to find the licensee in ADRE records or on the department website
- Licensees advertising their own property for sale must include the words "owner/agent" on all property signs and in all advertisements
- Licensees who advertise property subject to another's listing must display the name of the original listing broker in a clear and prominent manner
- The term "acre", either alone or modified, may only be used when referring to an area of land representing 43,560 square feet

Commissions

Commissions
- Commission rates are **negotiable**
- Brokerage-designated brokers may determine internal policy for commission ranges
- Designated brokers should supervise commission rates

Commission sharing
- Seller and buyer agents often work together and share commission income in Arizona
    - gross commissions are often split between buyer's and seller's salespeople who cooperate in a transaction

Commission regulations
- Only a designated broker can accept money from the public; **salespeople and associate brokers cannot take money from the public** for real estate services
    - Arizona forbids payment of commissions to unlicensed people or licensees with inactive licenses
    - designated brokers are responsible for:
        - collecting and paying **errors and omission insurance**
        - implementing independent contractor and employee employment agreements
        - salesperson and broker expectations and performance standards
        - office and brokerage operational policies
- Finder's fees payable to members of the general public are not allowed
    - exception: in property management, a tenant can refer new tenants and receive a credit reward on their rent.

- Referral fees paid to licensees who refer new business to other licensees are allowed --these are licensee to licensee, broker to broker payments

Commission disputes
- Conflicts often resolved in Arizona civil courts
- Proof a plaintiff was a qualified licensed broker or salesperson at the time of the dispute is required
- **ADRE does not address commission disputes** regarding earning, splitting, or non-payment of compensation
- The Arizona Association of Realtors® will mediate or otherwise attempt to resolve commission disputes; AAR only has jurisdiction over its members in these disputes

Referral Fees and Finders Fees

- Referral fees are legal in Arizona because the referring salesperson and receiving salesperson both hold active licenses
  - in a referral transaction, the referring salesperson's broker sends payment to the receiving salesperson's broker
  - broker-to-broker payment is fully lawful
- Finder's fees are prohibited by Arizona law
  - a finder's fee is an unlicensed person payment for potential leads for new business
  - broker payments to the general public for leads is prohibited
  - in general, only licensees may share in commissions
  - attorneys are exempt from licensing laws but cannot take a commission; they must charge flat fees
  - ADRE feels only those who have earned a license should be able to earn commissions
  - commissions are performance based; paid only when a transaction is completed
  - exemption exists in property management and leasing: a current tenant can get rent reductions on a limited basis for recruiting new tenants

Recordkeeping & Documentation

Responsibilities
- Designated brokers responsible for the supervision of sales contract preparation and procedures

Recordkeeping requirements
- All official transaction files must be held in main brokerage office
  - may be kept offsite with ADRE approval
  - official transaction files and employment records must be open for ADRE review at reasonable times
- Required copies to be in transaction files include
  - earnest money receipts confirming proper handling
  - closing statements showing all receipts, disbursements and adjustments
  - sales contracts
  - if applicable, copies of employment agreements

Agency Relationships

Governing principles
- Arizona law, professional standards, and agency principles govern relationships between brokerages and their clients, including the following:
  - licensee owes a fiduciary duty to a client and must **promote a client's interest**, and **deal fairly** with all other parties in a transaction

- licensees must **disclose information** that materially or adversely affects consideration paid by any party to a transaction, including principal's ability to perform, property defects, and any encumbrances
- licensees must perform actions without delay
- licensees are prohibited from **allowing controversy** with another licensee to interfere with a client's transaction
- required **written disclosures**: real estate license status, whether a principal is related to the agent, any ownership entanglements, any financial conflicts of interest
- licensee may not accept compensation or **represent more than one party** in a transaction without written permission from all parties
- licensee may not accept any compensation for goods and services from a transaction without written permission of principals
- all client and customer service must conform to professional standards of practice
- salespersons and brokers are prohibited from **operating outside of their expertise** without disclosure to clients
- licensees must provide **reasonable care** regarding information gathering and communication with clients
- licensees are not required to have additional expertise other than that required by their license
- a salesperson may not permit or facilitate occupancy of a person's real property by a third party without written authorization or allow possession prior to close of escrow unless instructed by the owner
- a licensee must recommend a client seek legal or other professional advice regarding the risks of pre- and post-possession of a property
- Real estate professionals are bound by agency law in Arizona

Fiduciary duties
- Arizona agency rules and laws include the following statutory requirements for fiduciary duty
  - loyalty
  - obedience
  - disclosure
  - confidentiality
  - reasonable care and diligence
  - accountability
- Of these six, the requirement for confidentiality extends forever and beyond close of escrow

Dual agency
- Dual or limited agency is allowed in Arizona
  - in dual or limited agency, a brokerage may represent both parties in a transaction
  - dual agency occurs when one licensee represents both buyer and seller, or two licensees in the same brokerage represent buyer and seller
- Dual agency is common in smaller Arizona communities where there is a limited number of local brokerages
- Arizona requires **informed consent** of all principals in a dual or limited agency situation
  - informed consent means principals must be fully informed of the potential problems with limited or dual agency, and agree to the relationship **in writing**
- Difficulties to avoid
  - conflicts of interest when licensees within the same brokerage are charged with getting the highest price for the seller and lowest price for the buyer
  - maintaining confidentially with two clients within one brokerage

Transactional brokerage
- Transactional brokerage is not allowed in Arizona
  - a licensee must represent a principal to use the powers granted in Article 26; therefore, Arizona licensees cannot function as transactional brokers
- Transactional brokers, also called facilitators or intermediaries, are not agents
  - in transactional brokerage, salespersons and brokers are not agents because they represent neither the buyer or seller

- transactional brokers have no responsibility for advocacy or fiduciary duties but must be fair and honest in their dealings with both principals
- transactional brokers provide paperwork preparation and contract management service rather than represent clients in negotiations and other activities of an agent

---

Employment Contracts (Listings)

Employment contract requirements

- Employment contracts must
  - be written in clear, unambiguous language
  - fully set forth all material terms including broker compensation
  - have a definite duration showing dates of inception and expiration
  - be signed by all parties to the agreement
- Not assignable to another brokerage unless all parties agree
- Not required for a licensee to represent a party
- Licensees may not attempt to procure a real estate employment agreement from a party already subject to an exclusive agreement under another broker

---

Handling of Funds

Deposits

- Brokers must immediately deposit all entrusted funds in a neutral escrow depository or broker trust account federally insured or guaranteed account in a depository located in this state
  - each deposit must be made via deposit slips
  - receipts and documentation must identify each transaction, date and amount of deposit, and the parties to the transaction

Application of funds

- Trust monies must be used only for the purpose for which they were deposited
- Trust account monies may not be commingled with brokerage or personal funds
- No more than $3,000 of brokerage money may be kept in a broker trust account for account maintenance

Records

- A broker must maintain complete records of all monies received in connection with a real estate transaction
- Records must be kept in the main brokerage office or offsite with ADRE permission
- Records should conform to acceptable accounting practices

Part VII: AZ Finance & Taxation Practices

Financing Documents

Trust deeds

- Arizona is primarily a deed of trust, or trust deed state, although mortgages are still offered and exist in Arizona
- A **deed of trust** is a security instrument that **pledges the property as collateral for loan**
  - three parties to the instrument: the trustor, beneficiary, and trustee
  - the **trustor** is the **borrower**, who holds equitable interest in the property
  - the beneficiary is the lender
  - the **trustee** holds "bare legal title" (legal title without the right of possession) and is **neutral third party** to whom the trustor gives power of sale

- The security instrument is combined with a **promissory note**, which is the financing instrument consisting of
  - evidence of debt
  - promise to repay
  - terms and conditions of repayment
- Under Arizona law, six entities can serve as trustees
  - banking institutions
  - real estate brokers
  - title or escrow companies
  - insurance agents
  - attorneys
  - public fiduciaries

Lien theory state

- Because Arizona is a lien theory state
  - title transfers at close of escrow
  - a deed is evidence of transfer of title
  - a voluntary, specific lien is placed on the property
  - the beneficiary becomes the lienor
  - the trustor becomes the lienee

Foreclosure in Arizona

Foreclosure characteristics

- Deeds of trust provide quick and inexpensive foreclosure as a non-judicial procedure
  - mortgages require court action to foreclose
  - deed of trust foreclosure avoids lengthy mortgage redemption periods
  - statutes of limitations do not apply since trustors give up legal title and there is no redemption period
  - after a trustee's sale, a deed conveys to the auction winner and there is no post-sale redemption period
  - deeds of trust have a 90-day reinstatement period in which loans can be made good by repaying back payments and any fees and penalties
  - unlike mortgage foreclosure, there is no acceleration of debt, which greatly enhances the possibility of reinstating the original loan program
- Deficiency judgments may not be allowed
  - lenders may not sue to get back balances if a property sells in foreclosure for less than the loan amount
- In Arizona, anti-deficiency statutes apply only to residential properties (not commercial) that are single family or duplexes and property less than 2.5 acres
  - state anti-deficiency statutes can be over-ridden on federal government-backed loans

Deed of trust foreclosure process

- Steps in the foreclosure process:
  1. default on the terms and conditions of the loan
  2. recordation of notice of default and notice of trustee's sale
  3. beneficiary notifies the trustor of default, instructs trustee to conduct a sale
  4. an election to sell is recorded (called **constructive notice**); trustor is notified via certified mail (**actual notice**); minimum time prior to trustee's sale is 90 days
  5. notice of the sale published in a general circulation newspaper approved by ADRE for three weeks
  6. auction held on courthouse steps or property site
  7. on the day of the auction, auction rules are established and the beneficiary enters a reserve bid
  8. an auction winner and back of winner are determined
  9. the deed goes to the highest bidder with payment
- Excess money after the loan and fees are paid, goes to the trustor

- o before the trustor is paid, all recorded interests are settled including the loan amount to the lender
- The trustee is paid from proceeds of the sale; does not receive payment unless a property goes into foreclosure

Land Contract Financing

Land contract basics
- Allowed in Arizona; less common than deeds of trust and mortgages
- Allows for **quick property repossession** in cases of buyer default
- **Title does not transfer in a land contract;** upon default, payments made to sellers are forfeited during a statutory reinstatement period
- Reinstatement periods based on amount of buyer's equity in the property:
  - o less than 20% -- 30 days
  - o at least 20% but less than 30% -- 60 days
  - o at least 30% but less than 50% -- 120 days
  - o at least 50% -- 270 days (9 months)

Arizona Property Tax Concepts

Right to tax
- States, counties, and municipalities are granted the right to tax real property

Tax lien
- Placed against real property on January 1 of each year to secure payment of taxes
  - o Arizona taxpayers who owe more than $100 are allowed to pay annual taxes in two installments
  - o the first payment is due October 1 of the current year, the second is March 1 of the following year
  - o property tax payers who owe less than $100 must pay in full on October 1
- Failure to pay property taxes and special assessments can lead to a **tax lien** and foreclosure

Tax collection
- On mortgaged properties, tax payments and homeowner's insurance premiums are held in escrow and paid when due by the lender
- Burdened taxpayers can make installment payments
  - o must pay interest on installment payments
  - o interest rate is called the legal rate in Arizona
  - o the legal rate is the highest interest rate allowed for borrowers who do not agree to a negotiated rate
  - o the legal rate in Arizona is currently 16%
- The schedule for tax payments, activities, and penalties in Arizona is:
  - o January 1.......................... Property taxes become a lien on property
  - o Month of January.................. County assessor mails a notice of evaluation
  - o late August/early September.... Property owners receive a bill
  - o October 1.......................... First half of the current year's tax bill due
  - o November 15..................... First half current year's taxes delinquent
  - o March 1 .... Second half of the current year's taxes due
  - o May 1............................. Second half current year's taxes delinquent
  - o September .... Delinquent notices are sent to unpaid owners
  - o February.......................... Tax lien sold for eventual payment of taxes

Tax rates
- Arizona's highest property tax rate is
  - 19% for commercial real estate
  - 16% for agricultural
  - 10% for residential

Part XIII: Leasing & Property Management

Arizona Residential Landlord & Tenant Act

Purpose and applicability
- Purpose of Arizona Residential Landlord and Tenant Act (ARLTA): to **protect the rights** and **identify the responsibilities** of landlords and tenants
  - landlord/tenant relationship is regulated by Arizona statutory law
- ARLTA applies to residential rental units
- **Does not apply to:** mobile homes, commercial and vacant land rentals, and membership camping

Exemptions
- Exempted from the ARLTA are:
  - residential institutions
  - purchasers under a contract for sale
  - fraternal and social organization housing
  - hotel/motel/recreational lodging
  - employees of landlords living in a rental unit as a perk
  - condos and proprietary leases (cooperatives)
  - public housing under the federal government

Landlord responsibilities
- A landlord in Arizona must
  - provide tenants with the name and address of the property owner or manager
  - provide a free **copy of the ARLTA** or information on how it can be obtained
  - provide tenants with a signed copy of the lease form documenting existing damage to the property, and written notification the tenant may be present at the move-out inspection
  - provide possession of the residence
  - comply with applicable **building codes**
  - make necessary **repairs**
  - keep common areas clean
  - **maintain** all electrical, plumbing, heating, and air-conditioning equipment, and provide for trash removal
  - **supply running water** and reasonable amounts of hot water
  - **respond within 14 days** if the tenant asks for the security deposit to be returned
    - the landlord's response will also include return of deposit and an itemized list of deductions taken for damage repair
  - follow strict procedures to dispose of personal property left in a dwelling
  - give a tenant a minimum of **48 hours written notice to enter** unless an emergency
- A landlord in Arizona **may not**
  - require tenants to sign a lease which **waives tenant rights**
  - allow someone to live rent free in exchange for the landlord not maintaining the residence
  - **refuse** to rent a residence on the basis that the potential tenant has **children**
  - **lock out tenants** for residential lease default

Landlord rights
- A landlord may
  - issue a **five-day pay or quit notice**, or otherwise **initiate eviction action** for violation of rent agreements

- enter without consent in emergencies
  - with consent, a landlord my only enter at reasonable times
- collect security deposits to cover non-payment of rents and potential damages to the property
  - security deposits may not exceed more than one and one-half of one month's rent amount
  - other deposits for pets, cleaning, redecorating, etc. may also be required

Tenant responsibilities

- A tenant must
  - pay agreed upon rent on time
  - keep the residence **clean and safe**
  - remove and dispose of trash
  - keep plumbing fixtures clean
  - use electrical appliances, heating and air conditioning and plumbing in a reasonable manner
  - ask when the move out inspection will be
- A tenant may not
  - deliberately or negligently **damage the property**
  - use the property for anything other than a residence unless agreed upon otherwise
  - **withhold rent** because a landlord breaks oral promises
  - withhold payment of rent, with few exceptions
  - **unreasonably withhold consent for a landlord to enter** the property for inspections, to perform agreed upon repairs and services, or to show the property to prospective or actual buyers, mortgagees, tenants, workmen, or contractors

Tenant rights

- A tenant may
  - **recover twice any amounts** wrongfully withheld in a court action
  - notify the landlord of her or his intent to fix a problem at landlord expense if a landlord fails to fix a maintenance or repair problem which can be fixed for less than $300 or equal to one-half monthly periodic rent payment
    - if the landlord does not fix the problem within 10 days of tenant notice, the tenant may hire a licensed contractor to make the repair, submit a bill to the landlord, and deduct the cost of the repair from rent
  - **give notice of breach of lease** if landlord fails to provide essential services
    - after notice, tenant may arrange for utilities and deduct the cost from rent
    - tenant may find substitute housing during the period of non-compliance and be excused from paying rent during that period
  - **deliver notice of landlord's failure** and tenant's intent to terminate the lease within 10 days for a landlord's material failure to comply with terms of the lease
    - a landlord's non-compliance impacting health and safety has a 5-day deadline
  - terminate a rental agreement if a victim of domestic violence and if
    - notice of the circumstances is submitted to the landlord within 30 days of the event
    - a copy of a protective order is provided to serve the perpetrator or a written departmental report from a law enforcement agency reporting the violence is provided
  - break a lease under the **Service Member's Civil Relief Act** if an active member of the armed forces upon receiving permanent change of station orders of deployment for at least 90 days

Property Management

Manager's functions and services

- Property managers and property management brokerages
  - secure suitable tenants
  - collect and record rental deposits and rents
  - assist in maintenance and security of property for client owners

Management agreements
- Principal parties are property owners and a licensed broker; purpose is to establish respective responsibilities and manager's compensation
- Agreements must
    - be written in clear and unambiguous language
    - specify a start and end date for contract term and length of services
    - contain a cancellation policy suitable to all
    - specify type and frequency of reports
    - be signed by all parties
- Agreements may
    - include automatic renewal provisions
    - provide for liquidated damages for early cancellation or termination
    - allow management firm to transfer funds, handle owners' monies
- Agreements may not
    - be assigned to a different broker without written consent of the property owner

Lease Agreements

Features
- A written or verbal agreement transferring exclusive right of possession and use of rental real estate for a specific period of time
- Lease is a combination of a conveyance document and contract to pay rent and other obligations
- Landlords retain a reversionary right in a lease; it requires the property to be transferred back to the owner upon termination of the lease
- Lessee's interest in rental property is called a leasehold estate

Lease validity
- The validity of a lease is determined by contract law: requirements include:
    - **capacity to contract** in Arizona: must be at least 18 years of age and of sound mind
    - mutual agreement of the terms
    - must be for **legal use**
    - be **in writing in order to be enforceable** in a court of law for terms of **more than one year** (one year plus one day)
        - Statute of Frauds in Arizona allows for the enforcement of oral leases of less than one year
    - **signatures** of the lessor(s) and lessee(s)
    - description of the premises
        - a complete address and unit number; a legal description is not required
    - uses restricted in the lease
        - may be any lawful manner or as described in the ARLTA
    - **term of lease**; by definition a lease is an estate which ends
        - most have beginning and end dates; even open-ended leases will eventually end **possession**
        - in Arizona, landlord must give tenant actual occupancy of the leased premises
    - **consideration, or rent**

Lease terms
- Most leases in Arizona require rent to be paid in advance
- Lease specifies when rent is due and past due
- Unless prohibited by the lease, lessee may assign or sublet all or part of leased premises; assignment with novation makes a new tenant fully responsible for the lease
    - lease may prohibit assignment without written consent of the landlord
    - in a sublease, the original tenant remains fully responsible for the terms of the lease
        - the tenant becomes sublessor when he or she subleases to a sublessee
        - sublessee makes rental payments to the sublessor, who then pays rent to the original landlord

- o often called a sandwich lease
- Leases may include a sales clause, allowing the property owner to market and transfer the property
- A lease option allows tenants the option to purchase the property at the conclusion of the lease
- A lease may set forth rules regarding:
  - o parking
  - o occupancy limits
  - o policies on return deposits
  - o leasehold improvements
  - o renter's insurance
  - o pets
  - o guests
  - o noise
- Rules in a lease may not violate the ARLTA or state and federal fair housing laws

Termination
- Lease terminations are triggered:
  - o by expiration
  - o via agreement of the parties, called surrender
  - o by forfeiture due to default
  - o by a merger of leasehold and freehold estate when tenant buys rental unit
  - o through abandonment, destruction, or condemnation of the rental premises

Part IX: Other Related AZ Practices & Laws

Business Brokerage Transactions

Commercial opportunity transactions
- A commercial opportunity transaction is where a business and all real property associated with it are jointly conveyed
- Building space owned by the owner is transferred in the sale
  - o real property transfers with a deed
  - o parking areas, green space, and other real property also transfer
- As real property is conveyed, **salesperson employed by the seller must hold an active Arizona real estate license**; no special license or certification is required

Business opportunity transactions
- Business opportunity transactions concern conveyances of businesses located in leased facilities; all business assets are personal property and no real property conveys
- **Do not require salesperson to have an active Arizona real estate license**
  - o business assets to be sold include fixtures, equipment, supplies, inventory, "blue sky" or customer loyalty and goodwill, trade name, non-compete agreement, and training
  - o personal property transfers via a bill of sale
- licensed salespersons or brokers often used for their marketing and transaction management skills
  - o a licensed generalist can pursue business sale transactions: no special license or certification is required

Transfer of a business
- Commercial sales begin with letter of intent and preliminary agreement
- Title company with business and commercial experience typically used to close
- Transfer documents are based on escrow instructions
- Instruments and agreements include: promissory note, chattel securing agreement, Uniform Commercial Code (UCC) filing statements, bill of sale, non-compete agreement, and compliance documents for bulk sales laws
- The UCC and bulk sales law ensure certain financed inventory is protected via rules concerning vendors, and collateral

Realtor® Boards & Associations

Local and regional organizations
- Arizona is divided into local and regional professional real estate boards and associations to encourage cooperation between brokerages via multiple listing services
- Local associations and boards belong to the Arizona Association of Realtors® (AAR), which is a part of the National Association of Realtors® (NAR)

National Association of Realtors® ethics
- The NAR mandates a code of ethics which is binding on both members and non-members
  - ethics guide the professional behavior of real estate licensees
  - NAR code violations may be pursued by both licensees and members of the general public
  - a grievance committee reviews all complaints to determine if enough evidence exists to refer the compliant to the professional standards committee
  - grievance committee procedures allow for evidence, testimony and due process
  - penalties range from letters of warning to fines or suspension from AAR or MLS privileges
- Only members of a local or regional board or association are Realtors®, and may call themselves Realtors®

Multiple Listing Services

Functions and features
- Primary function of boards is to operate a multiple listing service (MLS) for their members
- MLS members have access to vital details about a property and sellers' offerings
  - MLS provides detailed accounting of properties for sale or rent; represents inventory for sale in a particular area
  - MLS-listed properties categorized by residential homes for sale, vacant land, commercial and industrial, business opportunities, and a variety of leases
  - MLS helps seller and buyer agents cooperate to find and acquire property for clients
  - Restricted public MLS access available, but with limited information

Arizona-specific Math

Calculating acreage of single parcels
- There are **640 acres in a section**
- Each comma in a rectangular survey description is read "of the…"
- To calculate acreage, **multiply the halves and quarters** in the description and **divide the total into 640**
  - the SE2, (of the) NW4, (of the) NE4 equals 2 x 4 x 4 = 32 divided into 640 equals 20 acres.

Calculating acreage of multiple parcels
- The word "and" in an Arizona land description separates parcels in **different** sections
- Calculate the acreages for each parcel and add them
  - (Parcel A) the size of E2 of the NE4 of Sec. 11 <u>and</u> (Parcel B) the SE4 of the NW4 of Sec. 4:
    - Parcel A: 2 x 4 = 8 divided into 640 = 80 acres
    - Parcel B: 4 x 4 = 16 divided into 640 = 40 acres
    - 80 + 40 = 120 acres for the full amount of land
- A semi-colon in Arizona land description separates parcels within the <u>same</u> section

- To calculate the acreage of parcels in the same section, also calculate the acreages for each parcel and add them
  - the size of SW4, NE4; N2, S2, SW4; NE4, Sec 31 is 4 x 4 = 16 divided into 640 = 40 acres; the second parcel in the same section is 2 x 2 = 4 x 4 = 16 divided into 640 acres = 40 acres; the third parcel is 4 divided into 640 = 160 acres for a total land size of 40 + 40 + 160 = 240 acres

Calculating property taxes
- **"Full cash value"** -- determined by annual appraisal
- **"Assessment ratio"** -- a percentage of full cash value determined by property classification
- **"Assessed value"** -- the assessment ratio times the full cash value
- Tax rates stated as a specific amount **for every $100 of assessed value**
- Tax bill is the result of applying the tax rate to the assessed value
- Calculation method
  - Full cash value X assessment ratio = assessed value
  - Divide assessed value by 100 to get the number of 100's
  - Multiply the tax rate by the number of 100's to get the tax bill amount
- Tax calculation example
  - The tax rate in a given jurisdiction is $9.00 for every $100 of value and the assessment ratio for owner-occupied residential properties is 10%; the full cash value of a residential property is determined to be $160,000
  - assessed value = $160,000 x 10% = $16,000
  - number of 100's = $16,000 divided by 100 = 160
  - tax bill = 160 x $9.00 (tax rate) = $1,440.00

Closing Cost Prorations

Calculating closing cost prorations
- In Arizona, number of days in a year is normally based on a calendar year: 365 days, and 366 in a leap year
- A bank year may be specified instead, which is 360 days of 12 equal 30-day months
- The day of close of escrow "belongs" to the buyer
- Calculation method

  - Identify the method to be used (365 v 360) and which party owns the day of closing
  - Compute the cost per day
  - Calculate the actual number of days to be prorated
  - Multiply the number of days to be prorated by cost per day
  - Determine whether the amount should be a debit or credit to the buyer or seller

- Calculation example
  - An annual homeowner's association assessment is $720 per year, prepaid by the seller; closing is September 17; day of closing belongs to the buyer
  - cost per day = $720 / 365 days (not a leap year) = $1.9726 rounded to $1.973
  - paid days "used" by seller at closing = 31 (Jan) + 28 (Feb) + 31 (Mar) + 30 (Apr) + 31 (May) + 30 (Jun) + 31 (Jul) + 31 (Aug) + 16 (Sep) = 259 days
  - paid days "unused" by seller at closing = 365-259 = 106
  - amount to be prorated = 106 x $1.973 = $209.14
  - since the seller is owed money for his prepayment, credit the seller and debit the buyer

Section IV: National Practice Tests

Test 1: Rights; Interests and Estates; Ownership

1.1   Which of the following would be defined as real estate as opposed to real property?

   a. Wells, driveways, and signs on a parcel of land.
   b. Mobile homes temporarily parked on a parcel of land.
   c. Timber that has been cut and is lying on a parcel of land.
   d. Business equipment an owner or tenant has placed on a parcel of land.

1.2   Which of the following would be considered a property improvement?

   a. An alteration to land to make it more useful.
   b. An increase in the value of a property.
   c. A chicken coop permanently attached to land.
   d. A parcel of land that has passed a percolation test.

1.3   Which of the following best describes the physical boundaries of land?

   a. The surface of the earth and infinite space above the surface.
   b. The center of the earth and infinite space above the earth.
   c. The surface of the earth and all water and minerals on or below the surface to the center of the earth.
   d. The surface of the earth and the air rights above the surface to the point defined by local zoning.

1.4   The "bundle of rights" refers to a set of rights

   a. enjoyed by the owner of a property.
   b. that is synonymous with the Bill of Rights.
   c. guaranteed to citizens by the Statute of Rights.
   d. specified in a deed or land contract.

1.5   Which of the following best describes the legal concept of personal property?

   a. Any item which is acquired in a fee simple sale transaction.
   b. Any item of property that is not definable as real property.
   c. Any movable property owned by an individual, partnership, or corporation.
   d. Any item that is not a natural item affixed to the earth.

1.6   The right to encumber a property means that the owner can

   a. sell the property to an encumbered party.
   b. pledge the property as collateral for debt.
   c. lease the property.
   d. assign the bundle of rights to another.

1.7   A property owner leases 60 acres of agricultural land for a renewable period of 5 years. In the context of real estate rights, this lease represents a(n)

   a. transfer of a portion of the bundle of rights.
   b. encroachment on the bundle of rights.
   c. conveyance of the complete bundle of rights.
   d. encumbrance of the tenant's rights.

1.8   A homeowner is very upset over a drone that a neighbor flies over his house. He takes his case to court to end this possible violation of rights. Does he have a case, and on what basis?

a. No. The neighbor is not physically on his property.
b. No. The drone is in the air, so he cannot exercise any surface rights.
c. Yes. The owner has the right to stop encroachments.
d. Yes. The drones infringe on his air rights.

1.9   Littoral rights apply to which of the following?

a. Boatable ponds entirely contained within the boundaries of an owner's property.
b. Streams and rivers.
c. Navigable lakes, seas, and oceans.
d. Navigable streams and rivers.

1.10   A retired couple has just bought a retirement home with a pier on a large lake. In this case the retirees' water rights extend to

a. the high water mark of the body of water at the shoreline.
b. the low water mark of the body of water at the shoreline.
c. the center of the lake.
d. the end of the pier.

1.11   A waterfront homeowner has just died. What will become of the water rights the owner enjoyed while living in the home?

a. They revert to the state when the property is sold.
b. They are extinguished.
c. They are a personal right belonging to an individual owner, not attaching to the real property.
d. They transfer with the property when the property is sold.

1.12   Riparian rights concern which of the following bodies of water?

a. Lakes.
b. Seas and oceans.
c. Streams and rivers.
d. Navigable lakes.

1.13   Which of the following best describes a "fixture?"

a. Any item of personal property positioned within the boundaries of a parcel of real estate.
b. An item of personal property that has been converted to real property.
c. An item of real property temporarily placed on land for the purpose of conducting a business.
d. An item of personal property that has been left in one location for a period of six months.

1.14   An item may be considered personal property as opposed to real property provided that

a. the owner intended to remove it after a period of time.
b. it can be removed without altering the appearance of the structure.
c. it is unnecessary to the physical integrity of the structure.
d. the owner installed it at some time after acquiring the real property.

1.15   Two people own a house, each having an undivided equal interest. Which of the following best describes what each party owns?

a. Fifty percent of the physical house and the land it rests on.
b One hundred percent of the home and the land.
c. Fifty percent of the estate consisting of the indivisible whole of the real property.
d. Each owns one hundred percent of the estate represented by the real property and fifty percent of the physical house and the land it rests on.

1.16 A real property interest that includes the right to possess is considered

    a. an estate in land.
    b. a leasehold estate.
    c. a fee simple estate.
    d. the bundle of rights.

1.17 The right to control land usage by zoning and eminent domain is an example of

    a. a public interest.
    b. a police interest.
    c. an encumbrance.
    d. an estate in law.

1.18 If the duration of an owner's rights in an estate is not determinable, the owner has

    a. a tenancy at sufferance.
    b. a leased fee simple estate.
    c. a freehold estate.
    d. a leasehold estate.

1.19 The distinguishing feature of a leasehold estate is

    a. ownership of an interest by a tenant.
    b. temporary ownership of the full bundle of rights in a property.
    c. unlimited ownership of one right in the bundle of rights in a property.
    d. that the estate is limited by a lease term.

1.20 A landowner conveys a parcel of property with the provision that the land cannot be developed for retail purposes. The new owner immediately begins to develop a retail shopping outlet, the grantor finds out and takes the property back. What kind of estate did this landowner convey?

    a. Fee simple absolute.
    b. Life estate with reversion.
    c. Life estate with condition subsequent.
    d. Fee simple defeasible.

1.21 Ned grants his sister Alice an estate for as long as she lives. Her descendants, however, cannot inherit the estate. What kind of estate is it?

    a. An estate pur autre vie.
    b. An estate for years.
    c. An ordinary life estate.
    d. A legal life estate.

1.22 Homestead estates are examples of

    a. a conventional life estate.
    b. a legal life estate.
    c. an estate created by an owner's agreement.
    d. a fee simple absolute.

1.23 Louis owned a boat and a house before marrying Barbara. While she was single, Barbara owned a new car. The two got married and bought a second home. As a wedding present, Barbara's father bought Louis a motorcycle. Under the law of community property, what property can Louis sell without his wife's consent or signature?

a. The boat and house.
b. The boat, house, and motorcycle.
c. The second home and the motorcycle.
d. The boat and motorcycle.

1.24 Katelyn rents an apartment for one year. What rights has she acquired under the leasehold?

a. The right to exclude everyone from the premises.
b. The right to encumber the fee interest.
c. The right to sell the premises.
d. The right to possess and use the premises.

1.25 An estate from period-to-period will continue as long as

a. the tenant makes, and landlord accepts, regular rent payments.
b. the term specified in the lease.
c. the period is less than a year.
d. the landlord has not sold the property.

1.26 An estate at will

a. cannot be terminated.
b. is terminated only if so stated in the lessee's last will and testament.
c. terminates on the death of lessor or lessee.
d. terminates on the date specified in the lease agreement.

1.27 A tenant continues to occupy an apartment after lease expiration without the consent of the landlord. This type of estate is called

a. an estate at sufferance.
b. a holdover estate.
c. a canceled leasehold.
d. a hostile leasehold.

1.28 A tenant without a lease has been sending the landlord monthly rent checks, and the landlord continues to accept the payments. What kind of leasehold estate exists?

a. Estate for years.
b. Estate from period to period.
c. Estate at will.
d. Estate at sufferance.

1.29 A fee or life estate is held by an individual. This form of estate is referred to as a(an)

a. tenancy in severalty.
b. tenancy by the entireties.
c. absolute fee simple.
d. legal fee simple.

1.30 Six people have identical rights in a property and enjoy an indivisible interest. However any of the owners may sell or transfer his/her interest without consent of the others. This form of ownership is a

a. joint tenancy.
b. homestead ownership.

c. tenancy in common.

d. estate in severalty.

1.31 The "four unities" required to create a joint tenancy include which of the following conditions?

a. Parties must acquire respective interests at the same time.

b. Parties must be residents of the same state at the time of acquiring the interest.

c. Parties must be family members.

d. Parties must have joint financial responsibility.

1.32 Unlike tenants in common, joint tenants

a. own distinct portions of the physical property.

b. cannot will their interest to a party outside the tenancy.

c. may own unequal shares of the property.

d. cannot encumber their interest to outside parties.

1.33 Which of the following life estates is created by operation of law rather than by the owner?

a. Conventional life estate.

b. Ordinary life estate.

c. Legal life estate.

d. Community property life estate.

1.34 Which of the following is true of a homestead?

a. A homestead interest cannot be conveyed by one spouse.

b. A homestead interest cannot be passed to the children of the head of household.

c. A homestead interest is a form of conventional life estate.

d. A homestead is a primary or secondary residence occupied by a family.

1.35 A tenant in common can

a. sell or transfer his interest without the consent of the other tenants in common.

b. use his or her interest in the estate to encumber the entire estate.

c. sell, encumber or transfer his or her interest only to the other tenants in common.

d. sell, encumber or transfer his or her interest only with the consent of all the other tenants in common.

1.36 Which of the following would be considered community property?

a. Property acquired before marriage

b. A motorcycle bought after the marriage with separate property funds

c. Income derived from community property

d. A mother's heirloom wedding ring gifted to the wife after her wedding

1.37 When real property is held in a land trust, who controls the property?

a. The trustor

b. The trustee

c. The beneficiary

d. The mortgagee

1.38 In a community property state, John marries Patricia. Prior to the marriage John owned an SUV. During the marriage, John bought a Buick, John and Patricia bought a second property with money earned from Patricia's job, and each individual received a motorcycle from Patricia's uncle as a gift. What property is community property in this marriage?

a. The SUV, the Buick, and the second property.

b. The SUV, the Buick, the second property, and the motorcycles.

111

c. The Buick and the second property.

d. The Buick, the second property, and the motorcycles.

1.39 Which of the following is true of a cooperative?

a. A cooperative may hold an owner liable for the unpaid operating expenses of other tenants.

b. The owners have a fee simple interest in the airspace of their respective apartments.

c. Owners may sublease their apartments even if they sell their stock in the cooperative.

d. The proprietary lease is guaranteed to have a fixed rate of rent over the life of the lease term.

1.40 Which of the following is true of a tenancy in common?

a. The co-owners must be related.

b. The owners enjoy an indivisible interest.

c. The tenants must acquire their interests at the same time.

d. The tenants must pay equal amounts for their interest in the estate.

1.41 Carissa and Robert acquire a condominium as tenants in common. In this circumstance, Carissa can

a. sell her interest to a third party without the consent of Robert.

b. use her interest in the estate to mortgage the entire estate.

c. sell her interest only to Robert.

d. sell encumber or transfer her interest only with the consent of Robert.

1.42 When a tenant in common dies, what happens to the tenant's interest in the estate?

a. It is divided equally among the surviving tenants in common.

b. The surviving tenants must buy the interest from the deceased tenant's heirs or sell their interests to the heirs.

c. It becomes a joint tenancy.

d. It passes by probate to the deceased tenant's heirs.

1.43 Which of the following is true of a joint tenancy?

a. The tenants can determine the size of the share owned by each tenant.

b. The size of the tenant's shares is determined by the amount of equity each has invested in the property.

c. The tenants have an equal and indivisible ownership interest.

d. There can be no more than two co-owners, and each has a fifty percent interest.

1.44 In contrast to a tenancy in common, in a joint tenancy

a. there is a single title to the property.

b. there are as many titles to the property as there are co-owners.

c. title is held by a trustee.

d. co-owners who are married hold separate titles.

1.45 If a joint tenant sells his or her interest to an outside party,

a. the new owner becomes a tenant in common with the other owners, who continue to hold a joint tenancy with each other and a tenancy in common with the new owner.

b. the joint tenancy continues with the new owner as the third joint tenant.

c. the joint tenancy terminates and all owners become tenants in common.

d. the joint tenancy terminates and the owners must create a new joint tenancy to include the new owner.

1.46 When a joint tenant dies, what happens to the tenant's interest in the estate?

a. It passes to the decedent's heirs, who become joint tenants.

b. It passes as a tenancy in common to the decedent's heirs.

    c. The joint tenancy terminates and becomes a tenancy in common with the decedent's heirs and the surviving tenants as co-owners.

    d. It passes to the surviving joint tenants.

1.47   Under what conditions can two individuals own a property as tenants by the entireties?

    a. If they so elect at the time of acquiring title.

    b. If they are blood relatives.

    c. If they are married.

    d. If they incorporate.

1.48   When an estate is held in a trust, which party holds legal title?

    a. The beneficiary.

    b. The trustor.

    c. The trustee.

    d. The grantor.

1.49   Tanya buys a 4-bedroom condominium. As the new owner, she has the right to

    a. sell or mortgage the unit without impediment from individual owners of neighboring units.

    b. sell the interest in the physical unit separately from the interest in the common elements.

    c. prevent non-owners from using the unit owner's portion of the common elements.

    d. exclusively possess and use those portions of the common areas structurally or functionally necessary for the operation of the unit.

1.50   A condominium owner's share of maintenance and operations expenses are based on

    a. the unit's pro rata share of floor space.

    b. the unit's pro rata share of the property value as defined in the declaration.

    c. the number of shares the owner purchased in the condominium association.

    d. the assessed value of the condominium unit.

1.51   By contrast to a condominium, the owner of a cooperative owns

    a. shares in a corporation or association and a proprietary lease in a physical unit.

    b. a fee simple interest in a physical unit plus a tenancy in common in common elements.

    c. a tenancy in common in a physical unit and the common areas.

    d. a ground lease in the physical unit's pro rata share of land and a proprietary lease in the unit.

1.52   In a cooperative, real property is owned only by

    a. the individual unit owners.

    b. the individual unit owners and the cooperative association.

    c. the cooperative developer.

    d. the corporate entity of the cooperative association.

1.53   In a time-share freehold, owners acquire

    a. undivided interests in the property as tenants in common.

    b. a renewable periodic tenancy from for a portion of a year.

    c. a pro rata share of a leased fee.

    d. a tenancy in severalty for a portion of a year.

Test 2: Encumbrances; Liens; Title Transfer and Recording; Leases

2.1   Which of the following describes an encumbrance?

   a. A third party's right encroach upon a property without the permission of the property owner.
   b. A third party's right to claim the sale proceeds of a property that has been mortgaged as collateral for a loan.
   c. A third party's interest in a real property that limits the interests of the freehold property owner.
   d. Another's right to acquire a freehold interest in a property against the property owner's wishes.

2.2   Which of the following is true of easements in general?

   a. They involve the property that contains the easement and a non-owning party.
   b. They apply to a whole property, not to any specific portion of the property.
   c. They only involve the legal owner of the property.
   d. They may require a specific use, but cannot prohibit one.

2.3   Mr. King wants to offer 100 acres of his property for sale. Since the property is landlocked, he will have to put in a driveway to the road that will run across his remaining property. What kind of easement will he have to grant?

   a. An easement in gross.
   b. A commercial easement.
   c. A personal easement.
   d. An easement appurtenant.

2.4   If property Alpha has a court-ordered easement across property Beta in order for Alpha to have access to a public road, the easement is a(n)

   a. easement by prescription.
   b. personal easement.
   c. easement by necessity.
   d. easement in gross.

2.5   An encroachment is

   a. an easement that has not been recorded on the title of the burdened property.
   b. an unauthorized physical intrusion of one property into another.
   c. a right granted by a property owner to the owner of an adjoining property to build a structure that protrudes across the property boundary.
   d. a structure that does not comply with a zoning ordinance.

2.6   A court might grant an easement by prescription if

   a. a town needs to dig a trench across an owner's property to install a sewer line to a neighboring property, and the owner refuses permission.
   b. a property owner sells the front half of a lot and wants to continue using the driveway to access the rear of the lot.
   c. a trespasser has been using an owner's property for a certain period with the owner's knowledge but without permission.
   d. a property owner wants to prevent the owner of an adjoining property from building a an improvement that blocks her view.

2.7 The purpose of a deed restriction is to enable an owner to specify

    a. the form of ownership in which a property may be held.
    b. how long a property must be owned before it can be legally transferred.
    c. what groups of people are legally excluded from future ownership of a property.
    d. how a property may be used and what improvements may be built on it.

2.8 Melinda purchases a house and finances it. The lender in turn places a lien on Melinda's title. The lien in this mortgage transaction is

    a. evidence of debt incurred by a property owner.
    b. a promissory note granted by a property owner as security for a debt.
    c. the creditor's claim against the property as collateral security for the loan.
    d. the document required to clear clouded title.

2.9 In a lien-theory state, what kind of interest does a mortgage lender have in the liened property?

    a. A possessory interest.
    b. A tenancy-by-mortgagee interest.
    c. A legal interest in a pro rata share of the property.
    d. An equitable interest.

2.10 How is a lien terminated?

    a. Payment of the debt that is the subject of the lien and recording of the satisfaction.
    b. Transfer of the property that has the lien.
    c. Recording of another lien that is superior.
    d. Death of the lienor or lienee.

2.11 A judge rules in favor of the creditor in a court proceeding and places a judgment lien against all the debtor's assets, including his real property. This is an example of a(n)

    a. voluntary junior lien.
    b. involuntary superior lien.
    c. involuntary specific lien.
    d. involuntary general lien.

2.12 A real estate tax lien, a federal income tax lien, a judgment lien, and a mortgage lien are recorded against a property. Which lien will be paid first when the property is sold?

    a. Real estate tax lien.
    b. Federal income tax lien.
    c. Judgment lien.
    d. Mortgage lien.

2.13 A lien holder can change the lien priority of a junior lien by agreeing to

    a. change the date of recording.
    b. lower the amount of the claim.
    c. cancel the lien.
    d. subordinate the lien.

2.14 Which of the following accurately describes the act of foreclosure?

    a. A court-ordered acceleration of loan payments.
    b. The final step in a bankruptcy filing.
    c. A proceeding to enforce a lien by forcing the sale or transfer of a secured property.
    d. A proceeding to take equitable title to a property that was liened as security for a mortgage loan.

2.15 A property is secured by a mortgage that does not contain a "power of sale" clause. To foreclose, the lien holder will have to

a. file a deficiency suit.
b. file a foreclosure suit.
c. file a suit to quiet title.
d. obtain a quit claim deed.

2.16 A homeowner defaults on his mortgage loan. In the subsequent foreclosure action, the lender takes title to the liened property directly instead of initiating a court-ordered public sale. This is an example of

a. strict foreclosure.
b. judicial foreclosure.
c. non-judicial foreclosure.
d. deed in lieu of foreclosure.

2.17 A property owner gives Deanna permission to cross his property as a shortcut to her kindergarten school bus. One day the property owner dies. What right was Deanna granted originally, and will it survive the owner's death?

a. A personal easement in gross, which continues after the owner's death.
b. An easement by prescription, which continues after the owner's death.
c. A license, which continues after the owner's death.
d. A license, which terminates upon the owner's death.

2.18 On two adjacent properties, there is an easement that allows property A to use the driveway that belongs to property B. Here, property A is said to be which of the following in relation to property B?

a. Subservient estate.
b. Servient tenement.
c. Senior tenant.
d. Dominant tenement.

2.19 A property owner who is selling her land wants to control how it is used in the future. She might accomplish her aim by means of

a. an injunction.
b. a deed restriction.
c. an easement.
d. a land trust.

2.20 What distinguishes a lien from other types of encumbrance?

a. It involves a monetary claim against the value of a property.
b. It lowers the value of a property.
c. It is created voluntarily by the property owner.
d. It attaches to the property rather than to the owner of the property.

2.21 Which of the following defines actual notice?

a. It is notice published in a newspaper.
b. It is knowledge one could have or should have obtained.
c. It is notice explicitly stated in a legal document.
d. It is knowledge received or imparted through direct experience.

2.22 Which of the following defines constructive notice?

    a. It is notice published in a newspaper.
    b. It is knowledge one could have or should have obtained.
    c. It is notice explicitly stated in a legal document.
    d. It is knowledge received or imparted through direct experience.

2.23 Ownership of real estate can be transferred voluntarily or involuntarily. The three ways title can be transferred voluntarily are by

    a. grant, deed, and will.
    b. escheat, deed, and covenant.
    c. title certificate, will, and deed.
    d. sale contract, deed, and warrant of seizin.

2.24 What is the function of recording a deed?

    a. It makes the deed valid.
    b. It causes title to pass.
    c. It gives constructive notice of ownership.
    d. It removes all prior recorded encumbrances.

2.25 The only clause that is actually required in a deed is the

    a. habendum clause.
    b. granting clause.
    c. reserving clause.
    d. tenendum clause.

2.26 The type of deed that offers the grantee the fullest protection against claims to the title is the

    a. general warranty deed.
    b. special warranty deed.
    c. quitclaim deed.
    d. bargain and defend deed.

2.27 What is one of the purposes of a lawsuit to "quiet title"?

    a. To force the grantor to defend the title against a third party claim.
    b. To terminate a co-ownership estate when one co-owner is unwilling.
    c. To keep the owner's name out of the title records.
    d. To have an encumbrance removed if the lienholder cannot prove its validity.

2.28 Which of the following best describes the documentary stamp tax?

    a. A transfer tax based on the price of the property being conveyed.
    b. A tax a title company must pay in order to examine title records in the recorder's office.
    c. A tax collected by attorneys and paid to the state when transfer documents are prepared.
    d. A tax on stamps used to certify the authenticity of a conveyance.

2.29 The court proceeding that generally settles a decedent's estate is called

    a. testate.
    b. probate.
    c. escheat.
    d. distribution.

2.30   If an owner of real property dies intestate and has no legal heirs, what will happen to the property?

    a. It will escheat to the state or county.
    b. It will transfer to the decedent's executor.
    c. It will be divided equally among adjoining property owners.
    d. It will become a public easement.

2.31   A municipality wants to build a sewage treatment facility which will require the acquisition of several parcels of privately owned land. What legal power enables the municipality to buy the necessary properties, even against the owners' wishes?

    a. Estoppel.
    b. Escheat.
    c. Alienation.
    d. Eminent domain.

2.32   An adverse possessor must be able to successfully demonstrate that he or she has been

    a. openly possessing and claiming the property without the owner's consent.
    b. occupying the property without an occupancy permit.
    c. using the property intermittently and without permission over a period of years.
    d. building a permanent structure on the property.

2.33   A buyer has signed a contract to purchase a property, but is uncertain of the condition of the title. Which of the following parties is legally responsible for knowing the condition of the title?

    a. The County Recorder.
    b. The seller's agent.
    c. The buyer.
    d. The mortgage lender.

2.34   A break in the chain of title to a property results in

    a. a clouded title.
    b. a title plant.
    c. a lien of indeterminate ownership.
    d. a duplicate title.

2.35   Wayne and Leota obtain an insurance policy that protects them from liabilities and losses resulting from title defects. The kind of policy they bought is a

    a. a homeowner's insurance policy.
    b. standard owner's title insurance policy.
    c. lender's title insurance policy.
    d. private mortgage insurance policy.

2.36   An owner transfers title to a property to a buyer in exchange for a motorcycle. This is an example of

    a. voluntary alienation.
    b. involuntary liquidation.
    c. hypothecation.
    d. 1031 exchange.

2.37   A person wishes to convey any and all interests in a property to another without assurance of the property's marketability. This party would most likely use which of the following types of deed?

    a. A sheriff's deed.
    b. A special warranty deed.
    c. A partition deed.
    d. A quitclaim deed.

2.38 Jennifer owns a one-half interest in a condominium as a tenant in common with her business partner. If Jennifer has several heirs and dies without a will, the property will

    a. pass to the heirs by the laws of descent and distribution.
    b. escheat to the state.
    c. pass to the surviving spouse based on homestead law.
    d. pass to the surviving heirs according to the provisions of the will.

2.39 A drifter secretly lives in an abandoned shack on a large ranch property. After twenty years, the person makes a claim of ownership to the shack and the land immediately surrounding it that he had cleared. This claim will likely be

    a. upheld through adverse possession.
    b. upheld because of the length of possession.
    c. declined through the doctrine of prior appropriation.
    d. declined because possession was secretive.

2.40 To be marketable, title must be

    a. insured.
    b. free of undisclosed defects and encumbrances.
    c. abstracted by an attorney.
    d. guaranteed by a title certificate.

2.41 Which of the following types of leasehold estate lacks a specific term?

    a. Estate for years.
    b. Estate from period-to-period.
    c. Estate at will.
    d. Estate by the entireties.

2.42 A landlord generally has the right to enter the leased premises

    a. at any time without notice.
    b. for specified reasonable purposes.
    c. provided the tenant gives prior permission.
    d. only thirty days prior to lease expiration.

2.43 When a tenant rents an apartment, he or she is usually responsible for

    a. compliance with the rules and regulations of the building.
    b. payment for any alterations to the leased space.
    c. recording the lease in title records.
    d. occupying the premises throughout the lease term.

2.44 Under landlord-tenant laws, landlords must treat tenants fairly and honestly. In a residential leasehold, this requirement would include

    a. insuring the tenant against loss of personal property.
    b. providing required building support and services.
    c. guaranteeing that a fair rent is being charged.
    d. insuring the property for the value of the leasehold.

2.45 While a one-year lease is in effect, the tenant dies of a sudden illness. In this situation,

    a. the lease automatically terminates.
    b. the tenant's estate has the option of canceling the contract.
    c. the landlord can record a lien against the leased fee interest.
    d. the tenant's estate is still obligated under the lease.

2.46   Three students rent a house together, and all three sign a one-year lease. Six months later, two students move out. Which of the following is true of the remaining rent obligation?

a. The remaining tenant is responsible for the full rent obligation.
b. The remaining tenant is responsible for one third of the rent obligation.
c. The lease is cancelled due to abandonment. Therefore, the rent obligation is extinguished.
d. The departing tenants have no further rent obligation.

2.47   A tenant transfers a portion of the leasehold interest to another party. The instrument that accomplishes this transfer is a(n)

a. deed.
b. novation.
c. sublease.
d. reconveyance

2.48   Vijay enters into a lease for his new store. The provisions of the lease require Vijay to pay the operating expenses of the premises such as janitorial and repair expenses. This is an example of a

a. gross lease.
b. percentage lease.
c. land lease.
d. net lease.

2.49   A tenant obtains a full-service lease where the landlord agrees to pay all operating expenses in exchange for an additional $5.00 rent per square foot. Another term for this lease is a(n)

a. gross lease.
b. proprietary lease.
c. exchange lease.
d. full service net lease.

2.50   Which of the following circumstances is the most likely scenario for a ground lease?

a. A developer wants to acquire a necessary parcel that separates two parcels she already owns.
b. An owner-developer wants to retain ownership of the land portion of the improved real property.
c. A fast food company wants to place a restaurant in an existing building without buying either land or improvement.
d. A farmer wants to sell his property to a mining company.

2.51   A tenancy at will can usually be terminated by

a. either party giving proper notice.
b. either party without notice.
c. a sublease, with the lessor's approval.
d. an assignment by the lessor.

2.52   Under the Uniform Residential Landlord and Tenant Act, if a lease does not state a clear expiration date, the lease is regarded as

a. invalid.
b. a tenancy from period-to-period.
c. a tenancy at will.
d. a tenancy for years.

2.53 The Uniform Residential Landlord and Tenant Act generally does not apply to

a. a hotel.
b. a single-family residence.
c. a unit in an apartment building that has fewer than ten units.
d. a duplex in which the owner occupies one of the units.

2.54 In executing a condominium lease, a tenant has acquired

a. a temporary transfer of legal title.
b. a limited freehold interest in the air space of her unit.
c. a temporary possessory interest.
d. a title conveyance in exchange for rent.

2.55 When a tenant acquires a leasehold estate through a lease, what does the property owner acquire?

a. A freehold estate for years.
b. A reduced leasehold estate.
c. A defeasible estate.
d. A leased fee estate.

2.56 When an owner leases her property, she temporarily relinquishes the right to

a. transfer the property.
b. encumber the property.
c. occupy the property.
d. maintain the property.

2.57 Which of the following happens when a leased property is sold?

a. The buyer acquires title subject to the lease, which remains in effect.
b. The lease is cancelled.
c. The lease expires within thirty days unless renewed.
d. A new lease is automatically executed.

2.58 If a lease does not state a specific ending date, when does it terminate?

a. Immediately, since it is an invalid lease.
b. After one year.
c. When either party gives proper notice.
d. Whenever the property is sold.

2.59 In accordance with the statute of frauds,

a. leases in excess of one year must be recorded to be enforceable.
b. oral leases are not enforceable.
c. a five-year lease must be in writing to be enforceable.
d. an unwritten lease is fraudulent.

2.60 Which of the following is true of a sublease?

a. The subtenant takes over sole responsibility for performance of the original lease contract.
b. The original tenant retains primary responsibility for performance of the original lease contract.
c. It does not convey any of the leasehold interest.
d. It conveys the entire leasehold interest.

Test 3: Land Use; Legal Descriptions; Contract Law

3.1 Which of the following is true regarding master planning and zoning?

    a. The aggregate of zoning ordinances is the master plan.
    b. A master plan eliminates the need for zoning ordinances.
    c. Master planning is a county-level function; zoning is limited to the city level.
    d. Zoning ordinances are a primary means of keeping land use in harmony with the master plan.

3.2 The basic intent of zoning ordinances is to

    a. establish the basis for public ownership of land for the common good.
    b. establish subdivision rules and regulations.
    c. specify usage for every parcel within the zoning authority's jurisdiction.
    d. restrict development in unincorporated areas.

3.3 Why do zoning authorities create different types of zones?

    a. To ensure that a variety of building structures are available in the community.
    b. To separate land uses so that they do not interfere with each other.
    c. To preserve high density land uses.
    d. To discourage industrial and commercial users from relocating.

3.4 The key consideration in granting a zoning exception known as a special exception is which of the following?

    a. Hardship
    b. Change of zones
    c. The public interest
    d. The use was legal prior to the new zone creation

3.5 The intensity of land usage generally refers to what?

    a. The number of residential building lots per acre.
    b. The number of people per square mile.
    c. The number of building permits issued per year within a zoning jurisdiction.
    d. The area of a commercial or industrial facility in relation to the size of the site.

3.6 How does Planned Unit Development zoning vary from ordinary zoning?

    a. It applies only to office parks.
    b. It incorporates a number of different zones within a single property boundary.
    c. It requires that multiple tracts of land be developed according to a single design.
    d. It requires developers to obtain a separate building permit for every structure.

3.7 Which of the following situations is most likely to represent an illegal nonconforming use?

    a. A homeowner in a residential zone converts her residence to a private school.
    b. A homeowner builds a toolshed in a neighborhood where there are no toolsheds.
    c. A storeowner remodels a storefront in accordance with regulations, and then the zoning is changed to residential.
    d. A new zoning ordinance outlaws two-story additions after a homeowner completes an addition.

3.8 What is the difference between a variance and a nonconforming use?

    a. A variance, once granted, is unconditional and permanent.
    b. A variance is granted by the zoning board if the owner has a justifiable reason.
    c. A nonconforming use is allowed if the owner requests it in advance of building.
    d. A nonconforming use violates current zoning, but a variance does not.

3.9 A document certifying that a structure complies with building codes and is ready for use is referred to as a(n)

    a. inspection report.
    b. satisfaction bond.
    c. certificate of occupancy.
    d. user permit.

3.10 Which of the following is true of an eminent domain proceeding?

    a. It cancels the property owner's mortgage loan balance.
    b. It leaves the property owner with equitable title in place of legal title.
    c. It conveys legal title to the acquiring entity.
    d. It clouds the chain of title by canceling the original grant.

3.11 Among other provisions, the Superfund Act (CERCLA) and Superfund Amendment and Reauthorization Act of 1986 provided that

    a. large development projects undergo an environmental impact survey immediately after completion of construction.
    b. industrial users of real estate comply with air quality standards.
    c. the EPA would give financial help to homeowners to remedy any hazardous situation resulting from radon, asbestos, or lead-based paint.
    d. parties responsible for improper disposal of hazardous waste could be charged for the cleanup costs.

3.12 Public land use planning strives to balance which of the following potentially conflicting interests?

    a. Individual property rights and the public's interest.
    b. Public policy makers and community business leaders.
    c. Tenant occupancy specifications and construction contractors.
    d. Individual property owners and municipal planning agencies.

3.13 Zoning, building codes, and environmental restrictions are forms of local land use control known as

    a. master planning.
    b. preemption.
    c. police power.
    d. concurrency.

3.14 If a municipality exerts its power of eminent domain against a certain property owner, what happens?

    a. The owner must pay higher property taxes or give up the property.
    b. The owner must cede an easement without receiving any compensation.
    c. The municipality annexes the property.
    d. The owner must sell the property in exchange for market-value compensation.

3.15   To be valid, a local zoning ordinance must

   a. reasonably promote community health, safety and welfare.
   b. comply with federal zoning laws.
   c. apply only to unique properties.
   d. published periodically in the local newspaper.

3.16   Why do communities require building permits?

   a. To promote development.
   b. To establish the basis for an inspection.
   c. To promote certificates of occupancy.
   d. To ensure that improvements comply with codes.

3.17   What is the purpose of residential zoning?

   a. To increase home values in a neighborhood.
   b. To regulate the density of dwellings in the residential zone.
   c. To prevent families from residing in commercial and industrial sites.
   d. To maximize intensity of usage.

3.18   A non-profit organization wants to erect an urgent care facility in a residential zone. Given other
       favorable circumstances, the local authorities may grant permission by allowing

   a. a special exception.
   b. an illegal nonconforming use.
   c. an easement.
   d. a license.

3.19   A property that conformed with zoning ordinances when it was developed but does not conform to
       new ordinances is said to be

   a. an illegal special exception.
   b. a variance.
   c. a legal nonconforming use.
   d. unmarketable.

3.20   The approval process for development of multiple properties in an area includes submission of

   a. a covenant of restriction.
   b. a plat of subdivision.
   c. a court order.
   d. a developer's pro forma.

3.21   A legal description of a property is one which

   a. accurately identifies the boundaries of the property as distinct from all other properties.
   b. accurately describes the location and dimensions the lot and improvements on the property.
   c. is accepted by a licensed surveyor as suitable for inclusion in a survey of the property.
   d. is written by an attorney licensed to practice real estate law in the state in which the property is
      located.

3.22   The essential elements of the metes and bounds system are

   a. parallels, base lines, and meridians.
   b. boundaries, distances, and a base line.
   c. reference points, angles, and distances.
   d. lot numbers, sections, and ranges.

3.23   In the Rectangular Survey System, a range is the area in between

  a. any row of sections in a township.
  b. two consecutive meridians.
  c. a principal meridian and a base line.
  d. a parallel and a meridian.

3.24   In the Rectangular Survey System, a tier is defined by

  a. six consecutive sections of a township.
  b. two consecutive meridians.
  c. two consecutive parallels.
  d. a parallel and a meridian.

3.25   In the Rectangular Survey System, what are the dimensions of a township?

  a. One mile square.
  b. Six miles by six miles, or 6 miles square.
  c. Thirty-six miles square.
  d. The north and south boundaries are one mile apart; the east and west boundaries are
      indeterminate.

3.26   What portion of a section is ten acres?

  a. 1/8.
  b. 1/16.
  c. 1/32.
  d. 1/64.

3.27   The lot and block system of legally describing property is used for

  a. farm properties.
  b. any property in an unincorporated area.
  c. properties where metes and bounds is not acceptable.
  d. properties in a subdivision.

3.28   A certain legal description contains the phrase, "...northwesterly along Erie Road to the POB...".
       What kind of description is this?

  a. Plat survey.
  b. Government grid.
  c. Metes and bounds.
  d. Rectangular survey.

3.29   How many sections are there in a township?

  a. One.
  b. Six.
  c. Twelve.
  d. Thirty-six.

3.30   In the Rectangular Survey System, a section contains how many acres?

  a. 640.
  b. 320.
  c. 160.
  d. 40.

3.31 The valuable consideration necessary to make a contract valid must be

a. money.
b. something tangible.
c. something of value traded in exchange for something of value.
d. something of equal value with whatever is received in exchange.

3.32 A real estate sales contract, to be enforceable, must

a. contain a legal description of the property.
b. be written on a form approved by the state bar association.
c. be acknowledged by three witnesses.
d. be recorded within three days to be enforceable.

3.33 How much time does a seller have to accept a buyer's offer?

a. Forty-eight hours from the time of the offeror's signing of the offer.
b. Twenty-four hours from the time of the offer's delivery to the seller.
c. Within 24 hours following the stated expiration.
d. A reasonable time, or until the expiration date on the offer.

3.34 A buyer submits an offer to a seller and then dies in a car accident. Before learning of the buyer's death, the seller accepts the offer. Which of the following is true?

a. The seller can force the buyer's estate to go through with the purchase.
b. The buyer's death terminated the offer.
c. The seller must make a new offer with the same terms to the buyer's heirs.
d. The buyer's heirs have the option of enforcing the contract.

3.35 Which of the following contracts can be assigned to another party?

a. An exclusive listing agreement.
b. A personal services agreement.
c. A contract for the sale of undeveloped land.
d. An employment contract between a broker and a salesperson.

3.36 An implied agency relationship may be deemed to exist if

a. the parties do not disavow an express contract that has expired.
b. the parties act is if there is a contract.
c. an offering party does not receive written notice that the offer has been rejected.
d. the parties promise to perform their part of the agreement if the other party performs.

3.37 Which of the following is an executory contract?

a. An expired lease.
b. A sale contract before closing.
c. A recorded sale contract.
d. An option to buy after it is exercised.

3.38 A bilateral contract is one in which

a. both parties promise to do something in exchange for the other party's performance.
b. both parties receive equal consideration.
c. two parties agree to perform a service together.
d. both parties promise to do something if the other party performs first.

126

3.39   A homeseller signs a listing agreement with a broker then subsequently revokes the listing. Which of the following is true?

a. The seller continues to have contractual obligations to the broker.
b. The contract remains in full force until the expiration date.
c. The broker may have a claim for marketing expenses expended during the listing term.
d. The seller cannot sign a listing agreement with another broker.

3.40   A breach of contract is

a. a termination of the contract by the mutual consent of the parties.
b. financial damage suffered by a party because another party has nullified a contract provision.
c. a lawsuit to force a party to discharge the contract.
d. the failure of a party to perform according to the terms of the contract.

3.41   What is rescission?

a. The act of withdrawing an offer before it has been accepted.
b. The act of declaring that a contract is no longer in effect for a given party.
c. The act of declaring a contract unenforceable.
d. The act of modifying the terms of an offer.

3.42   To be valid, a valid contract must

a. reflect a mutual understanding or agreement.
b. use precise wording in a document.
c. not be executable.
d. be created only by an attorney.

3.43   Two parties enter into a contract. The agreement fulfills all the requirements for a valid contract, with no disqualifying circumstances. Given this situation, it is still possible that the contract may be

a. void.
b. illegal.
c. unenforceable.
d. voidable.

3.44   The guardian for a mentally incompetent party enters into an oral contract with another party to buy a trade fixture on behalf of the incompetent party. This contract

a. does not meet validity requirements.
b. is possibly valid and enforceable.
c. must be in writing to be valid.
d. is valid but unenforceable.

3.45   A prospective homebuyer submits a signed offer with the condition that the seller pay for the inspection at closing. The seller disagrees, crosses out the provision, then signs and returns the document to the buyer. At this point, assuming all other contract validity items are in order, the original offer is now

a. an accepted offer, therefore a valid contract.
b. an executable option.
c. a counteroffer.
d. an invalid offer.

3.46 A construction contractor executes a contract with a buyer. In the agreement, the contractor promises to complete construction by November 20. This promise can be construed as

a. an option.
b. mutual consent.
c. a meeting of the minds.
d. valuable consideration.

3.47 A seller contracts to sell a property that she does not own. The sale contract for this transaction

a. is executable.
b. must be in writing.
c. is void.
d. is illegal yet potentially enforceable.

3.48 The statute of limitations requires that parties to a contract who have been damaged or who question the contract's provisions

a. must act within a statutory period.
b. must select a specific, limited course of action for recouping their losses.
c. must arbitrate prior to taking court action.
d. must wait a statutory period before they may take legal action.

3.49 The purpose of the statute of frauds is to

a. invalidate certain oral contracts.
b. require certain conveyance-related contracts to be in writing.
c. nullify oral leases and listing agreements.
d. eliminate fraud in real estate contracts.

3.50 A seller immediately accepts a buyer's offer but waits ten days before returning the accepted document to the buyer. Meanwhile, the offer has expired. Which of the following is true?

a. The buyer is bound to the contract since it was accepted immediately.
b. The buyer has no obligations to the seller whatsoever.
c. The buyer may not rescind the expired offer.
d. The seller may sue for specific performance.

4.1   The agency relationship is defined by

a. the Realtor Code of Ethics.
b. the laws of agency, or in some states, by statute.
c. the law of real estate contracts.
d. the agreement between a principal and an agent.

4.2   Which of the following is true of the connection between compensation and the agency relationship?

a. An agreement to give and receive compensation creates an agency relationship.
b. If an agency relationship exists, the principal must provide valuable consideration to the agent.
c. The relationship is independent of any compensation arrangement.
d. If an agency relationship exists, the agent is entitled to compensation.

4.3   One of the parties to an agency relationship defaults, and the agreement terminates. Which of the following is true?

a. All obligations are extinguished.
b. Both parties must continue to perform all other obligations of the agreement.
c. The defaulting party may have a financial consequence.
d. The damaged party has no claim against the defaulting party.

4.4   Among the fiduciary duties imposed on a real estate agent is the requirement to

a. refuse offers the agent knows will be unacceptable to the principal.
b. present all offers to the principal regardless of their amount.
c. advise the principal against accepting an offer that is below full price.
d. advise a prospect that the principal will not accept the prospect's offer in order to elicit a better offer.

4.5   One of the agent's fiduciary duties that continues even after a listing agreement expires is

a. obedience.
b. diligence.
c. confidentiality.
d. disclosure.

4.6   The standard of care and competence that a principal can expect from an agent is generally that which is

a. specified in the agency agreement.
b. necessary to earn the promised compensation.
c. necessary to procure a customer.
d. comparable to that of other practitioners in the area.

4.7   Agent Michael is showing his new listing to a buyer who informs him that he has just inherited five million dollars. Michael is now bound by fiduciary duty to

a. keep the information in confidence.
b. disclose the information to the buyer's agent.
c. disclose the information to the seller.
d. verify the buyer's statements before disclosing them to the client.

4.8 Agent Gerry has executed an exclusive buyer broker agreement with the Andersons. The agent subsequently places an offer with Melinda, the exclusive selling agent for the Lincolns, to buy their lakefront property. The offer contains provisions for the Lincolns to pay the brokerage commission, which the Lincolns agree to. Given this set of circumstances, Gerry owes the full set of fiduciary duties to

a. the Andersons.
b. the Lincolns.
c. Gerry's broker.
d. Melinda's broker.

4.9 A subagent is the agent of

a. the seller.
b. the buyer.
c. a broker who has an agency relationship with a client.
d. the client's and the customer's agents.

4.10 Which of the following is a dual agency situation?

a. Two agents share the exclusive right to represent the same client on all transactions.
b. One agent represents both sides in a transaction.
c. A selling agent from one brokerage works with a listing agent from another brokerage to complete a transaction.
d. One agent represents two sellers at the same time.

4.11 The duties of a transaction broker or facilitator include

a. preserving the confidentiality of information received from either party.
b. helping the two parties achieve their respective objectives.
c. disclosing material facts that affect the value of the property to both parties.
d. choosing to obey the instructions of one party and informing the other party of the decision.

4.12 In which of the following contact situations would a seller's agent be expected to disclose his agency relationships?

a. The agent is showing the client's property to a prospective buyer.
b. The agent tells an acquaintance at a party about the client's property.
c. The agent answers questions about the client's property for a telephone caller responding to a newspaper ad.
d. The agent is showing a potential buyer houses in a certain price range in the multiple listing book.

4.13 The essential foundation of the agency relationship consists of

a. mutual respect, compensation, and confidentiality.
b. diligence, results, and compensation.
c. service, marketing, and respect.
d. good faith, trust and confidence.

4.14 Audrey wants to take a vacation. To do so, she authorizes an agent to conduct the operations of one of her business enterprises. The kind of agency she has established is

a. limited.
b. general.
c. universal.
d. special.

4.15 A property seller empowers an agent to market and sell a property on his behalf. The kind of agency represented is

    a. general.
    b. special.
    c. universal.
    d. no agency.

4.16 Implied agency arises when

    a. an agent accepts an oral listing.
    b. a principal accepts an oral listing.
    c. a party creates an agency relationship outside of an express agreement.
    d. a principal agrees to all terms of a written listing agreement, whether express or implied.

4.17 An agency relationship may be involuntarily terminated for which of the following reasons?

    a. Condemnation of the property.
    b. Mutual consent.
    c. Full performance.
    d. Renewal of the agent's license.

4.18 A principal discloses that she would sell a property for $500,000. During the listing period, the house is listed and marketed for $530,000. No offers come in, and the listing expires. Three weeks later, the agent confides to a customer that the seller would have sold for less than the listed price. Which of the following is true?

    a. The agent has violated the duty of confidentiality.
    b. The agent has fulfilled all fiduciary duties, since the listing has expired.
    c. The agent is violating the duties owed this customer.
    d. The agent has created a dual agency situation with the customer.

4.19 A principal instructs an agent to market a property only to families on the west side of the university campus. The agent refuses to comply. In this case,

    a. the agent has violated fiduciary duty.
    b. the agent has not violated fiduciary duty.
    c. the agent is liable for breaching the listing terms.
    d. the agent should obey the instruction to salvage the listing.

4.20 An owner's agent is showing a buyer a residential property for sale. The buyer notices water stains on the foundation walls and floor, and informs the agent. The appropriate course of action for the agent is to

    a. immediately contract to paint the ceiling.
    b. immediately contract to repair the roof.
    c. suggest the buyer make a lower-price offer.
    d. inform the seller.

4.21 The meaning and salient characteristics of the agency relationship should be disclosed to the client

    a. prior to completing a listing agreement.
    b. prior to or upon completion of an offer.
    c. upon the initial contact with the person.
    d. prior to showing properties.

4.22 When must a listing agent disclose his or her agency relationship to prospective tenants or buyers?

    a. Immediately prior to the initial contact.
    b. Upon initial contact.
    c. Whenever substantive communication is made beyond casual conversation.
    d. Immediately following any offer executed by the customer.

4.23 A buyer agent or tenant representative should disclose his or her agency relationship to the owner's agent

    a. immediately prior to the initial contact.
    b. upon initial contact.
    c. immediately prior to substantive contact.
    d. immediately following any offer executed by the landlord.

4.24 An agent is operating as a disclosed dual agent on a transaction. In this case, the agent

    a. may not represent one party's interests to the detriment of the other.
    b. must operate without a listing agreement.
    c. must be obedient and loyal to both parties.
    d. must require that the principals refrain from disclosing any material facts to him.

4.25 An agent informs a buyer that a provision in a contract is very commonplace. After explaining the clause, the agent assures the buyer that the clause does not mean anything significant. If something goes wrong with the transaction, the agent could be liable for

    a. violating duties owed a customer.
    b. misinterpreting the clause.
    c. intentional misrepresentation.
    d. practicing law without a license.

4.26 When a broker enters into a listing agreement, the broker has agreed to accept which of the following?

    a. Fiduciary and contractual obligations with the client.
    b. Fiduciary relationships with client and customer.
    c. Contractual obligations with cooperating brokers.
    d. Fiduciary obligations with the customer.

4.27 The degree of authority granted by a residential brokerage listing agreement generally allows the agent to

    a. create contractual obligations for the client.
    b. negotiate the selling price between client and customer.
    c. hire inspectors, and other individuals to prepare the property for marketing.
    d. market, sell and show the property.

4.28 A salesperson, without an oral or written listing agreement, brings potential buyers to the seller. The seller says, "You can bring me buyers if you want, but I'm not paying you a commission." The salesperson then continues to direct buyers to the property. Which of the following is true about this situation?

    a. There is no agency relationship, and therefore the seller will owe no commission if one of the salesperson's buyers buys the property.
    b. An implied agency may have been created, with obligations to perform for both seller and agent.
    c. The seller and agent have an illegal, undisclosed agency relationship.
    d. The agent has an open exclusive agency listing with no commission agreement, and therefore owes no fiduciary duties to the seller.

4.29 An agent enters into a listing agreement with a homeseller, but then becomes too busy to professionally fulfill the terms of the agreement. To solve the dilemma, the agent assigns the agreement to another licensee in the office. Which of the following is true about this situation?

a. The agent cannot assign the listing agreement.
b. The new listing agent acquires the full set of fiduciary duties owed to the client.
c. The new broker has to split any commission that results with the assigning broker.
d. The original broker has to disclose the assignment to the seller.

4.30 From an agent's point of view, the most desirable form of listing agreement is a(n)

a. exclusive agency.
b. exclusive right to sell.
c. open listing.
d. net listing.

4.31 What is a multiple listing?

a. A listing shared by a listing agent and a selling agent.
b. A listing that a listing agent delegates to a subagent.
c. A listing that is entered in a multiple listing service to enable cooperation with member brokers.
d. A listing that authorizes a listing agent to market more than one property for a seller.

4.32 Which of the following conditions is necessary for a customer to qualify as "ready, willing, and able" in the context of a commissionable transaction?

a. The customer's offer must be accepted.
b. The customer must be legally competent to undertake the transaction.
c. The customer must have a commitment from a lender.
d. The customer must have no business relationship with the agent.

4.33 Although a listing broker may delegate listing tasks to an employed licensee, the broker may not delegate the authority to

a. obtain and distribute compensation.
b. provide cooperating brokers with information about the property.
c. advertise the property.
d. inspect the property for hazardous substances.

4.34 Agent Peter has an open listing with Frank. Paul is Peter's broker. Agent Perry's customer buys Frank's house. Patrick has a commission agreement with Frank. Who is most likely to be compensated in this scenario?

a. Peter, since he has a written listing agreement.
b. Paul, since he is Peter's broker
c. Perry, since he found the customer.
d. Patrick, since he has a commission agreement.

4.35 If an agent has an exclusive listing to sell a property, and the property is then taken by eminent domain, what is the status of the listing?

a. The seller's obligations under the listing are assigned to the agency that takes the property.
b. It becomes a voidable contract.
c. The commission clause of the agreement is canceled.
d. It may be terminated against the agent's will.

4.36 A broker obtains an exclusive listing to sell a house, but after two months, he abandons the listing because the seller is too demanding and hot-tempered. What can the seller do in this situation?

a. Have the licensee's license revoked for negligence.
b. Sue the broker for money damages.
c. Sign a listing agreement with another broker and force the first broker to pay the commission.
d. Force the broker to perform the contract without compensation.

4.37 An owner agrees to pay a broker for procuring a tenant unless it is the owner who finds the tenant. This is an example of a(n)

a. exclusive right-to sell agreement.
b. exclusive agency agreement.
c. open listing.
d. net listing.

4.38 A landlord promises to compensate a broker for procuring a tenant, provided the broker is the procuring cause. This is an example of a(n)

a. exclusive right-to rent agreement.
b. exclusive agency agreement.
c. open rental listing.
d. net lease listing.

4.39 A property owner agrees to pay a broker an open-ended commission as the difference between the sale price and a net amount, provided the owner receives a minimum amount of proceeds from the sale at closing. This is an example of a(n)

a. exclusive right-to sell agreement.
b. exclusive agency agreement.
c. open listing.
d. net listing.

4.40 In the context of agency law, the legal difference between an owner representation agreement and a buyer representation agreement is

a. the client.
b. the commission amount.
c. fiduciary duties.
d. regulatory approvals.

4.41 A multiple listing authorization gives a broker what authority?

a. To list the owner's property in a multiple listing service.
b. To sell several properties for the owner at once.
c. To represent both seller and buyer, if necessary, in selling the property.
d. To delegate the listing responsibilities to other agents.

Test 5: Brokerage Business; Sale Contracts

5.1   Which of the following business entities is generally prohibited from brokering real estate?

   a. Sole proprietorship.
   b. Partnership.
   c. Corporation for profit.
   d. Non-profit corporation.

5.2   A joint venture may generally broker real estate if the co-venturers

   a. form a business trust.
   b. form a co-operative association.
   c. are properly licensed.
   d. are limited partners.

5.3   A licensed salesperson may work only for

   a. a client who has signed a listing agreement with a licensed broker.
   b. a single employing broker who has an active broker's license.
   c. a client who has signed an authorization agreement with a licensed salesperson.
   d. an employer who has an active or inactive broker's license.

5.4   Which of the following activities is a licensed salesperson allowed to engage in?

   a. Accept a listing that is in an associate's name.
   b. Accept a commission directly from the MLS.
   c. Offer a property for lease on behalf of the employing broker.
   d. Sign a contract with a management company on behalf of a client.

5.5   If a salesperson has worked on a completed transaction that involved a listing agent, a selling agent, and several subagents for each of these, from whom will the salesperson receive any compensation that is due?

   a. The listing agent.
   b. The selling agent.
   c. The seller.
   d. The employing broker.

5.6   A property has sold for $380,000. The listing agreement calls for a commission of 6.5%. The listing broker and selling broker agree to share the commission equally. What will the listing agent receive if the agent is scheduled to get a 40% share?

   a. $4,445.
   b. $3,556.
   c. $2,667.
   d. $4,940.

5.7   A real estate salesperson finds a buyer to a For Sale By Owner property. The home sells for $245,000, and the seller agrees to pay a commission of 3%. The salesperson is on a 65% commission schedule with her broker, who pays her 65% minus office expenses of $500. How much will the salesperson receive from this transaction?

   a. $4,778.
   b. $4,452.
   c. $4,278.
   d. $3,175.

5.8 A salesperson makes a listing presentation to a homeseller and obtains a signed listing agreement. The first thing the salesperson must now do is

a. make a final pricing determination for the property.
b. negotiate the commission with the client.
c. complete the signing of the listing.
d. explain the agency relationship to the client.

5.9 Juan shows a customer a property that is listed by another brokerage firm. He obtains an offer that is $5,000 less than the listing price. How should Juan deal with this offer?

a. Advise the buyer that the offer will be rejected.
b. Present the offer to the seller at the earliest possible moment.
c. Ask the listing broker to lower the listing price.
d. Counter the offer.

5.10 A broker receives an earnest money deposit from a buyer and signs the check over to the listing agent as a partial commission advance. What is wrong with this procedure?

a. Nothing, provided the deposit clears the bank and doesn't bounce.
b. The broker and the agent are guilty of price fixing.
c. The broker has illegally converted security funds for business use.
d. The agent may not be able to return the advance if the transaction falls through.

5.11 Under what circumstance may a property listed for sale with a brokerage be advertised without identifying the broker?

a. When the salesperson is an out-of-state licensee.
b. When the ad is restricted to the brokerage's website.
c. When the advertisement is a silent ad.
d. Never.

5.12 Competing brokers in a county seat agree on a standard commission rate for principals within the county. This is a possible violation of

a. fair trade and anti-trust laws.
b. the Statute of Frauds.
c. contract law.
d. the Uniform Commercial Code.

5.13 What is co-brokerage?

a. An owner agent and a buyer agent combine efforts to complete a sale.
b. Outside brokers assist a listing agent in procuring a buyer.
c. An owner or buyer lists with several brokers to complete a transaction.
d. Agents from a single agency cooperate to generate listings for the broker.

5.14 Which of the following may associate his or her name or title with the term "Realtor®"?

a. Any active or inactive broker in the country.
b. Any duly licensed, active agent or broker.
c. Any member in good standing in a properly chartered real estate trade organization.
d. Only members of the National Association of Realtors®.

5.15 Real estate sales agents are legally authorized to

a. represent their employing broker in procuring clients and customers.
b. act directly on a client's behalf to discharge the broker's listing responsibilities.
c. negotiate and execute contracts for sale on behalf of the client.
d. take on the listing responsibilities for other listings in MLS.

5.16 How does the position of an independent contractor licensee (IC) differ from that of an employee licensee?

    a. The IC is responsible for his or her own taxes; the broker does not withhold.
    b. The IC must obtain his or her own training; it is not provided by the broker.
    c. The employee is not entitled to company benefits.
    d. The IC must abide by all office meeting schedules.

5.17 A salesperson's commission rate and structure is established by

    a. state regulation.
    b. competitive conditions.
    c. agreement with other brokers in the market.
    d. negotiations with the client.

5.18 In obtaining offers from a buyer, an agent must be careful to

    a. pursue only those offers which are at or near the listing price.
    b. balance the owner's price expectations with the buyer's opinion of value.
    c. avoid disclosing what price the owner will accept.
    d. avoid completing offers that are beneath market value.

5.19 Commingling is the practice of

    a. blending escrow funds on a number of properties in one escrow account.
    b. mixing socially with prospects at open houses or other marketing functions.
    c. allocating commission funds from a transaction for use in the agency's business.
    d. mixing escrow funds with the broker's operating funds.

5.20 Three leading agencies charge identical commission rates for brokering office properties in Phoenix. Based on this information alone, which of the following is true?

    a. There is insufficient evidence of anything other than a normal business practice.
    b. The brokers have engaged in legal collusion.
    c. The brokers have allocated the Phoenix market.
    d. The brokers have illegally fixed prices.

5.21 A real estate sale contract is an executory contract until

    a. the completed sale transaction is recorded.
    b. the buyer and seller have agreed to all provisions and have signed the contract.
    c. all the obligations and promises are performed and the transaction is closed.
    d. the loan has been approved, the title insurance has been obtained, and the closing date is set.

5.22 In assisting a buyer or seller to complete an offer to purchase, what should an agent do to reduce the risk of committing an unauthorized practice of law?

    a. Use a standard contract promulgated by a state agency or a real estate board.
    b. Observe ethical standards promulgated by real estate trade organizations.
    c. Offer legal advice only on points of the contract that the agent is absolutely certain about.
    d. Write contract terms that are fair to both buyer and seller.

5.23 To be enforceable, a contract for the conveyance of real estate must

    a. be acknowledged by witnesses.
    b. be written.
    c. be recorded.
    d. have an expiration date.

5.24 A buyer makes an offer to purchase a house, and the seller accepts the offer. However, before the salesperson can inform the buyer of the seller's decision, the buyer delivers a written notice that she is opting out and cancelling the agreement. At this point, which of the following is true?

   a. The contract has been legitimately cancelled and is null and void.
   b. The seller must give the buyer an opportunity to make a new offer.
   c. The buyer must perform under the terms of the contract
   d. The seller must notify the buyer in writing that the buyer is in default.

5.25 Which of the following is an essential element of a valid contract for the sale of real estate?

   a. A valid blank form that the contract is written on.
   b. A habitable property.
   c. An offer and acceptance.
   d. A marketable title.

5.26 What kind of interest does the buyer acquire once a real estate sale contract is signed by the principal parties?

   a. Legal title.
   b. Lienholder interest.
   c. Reversionary interest.
   d. Equitable title.

5.27 A contingency in a sale contract is

   a. a promise by buyer or seller to perform a specific action.
   b. a condition that, if unmet, renders the contract unenforceable.
   c. one of several alternative actions that buyer or seller may take to satisfy contract requirements.
   d. an optional, unilateral action that either party may take at the request of the other party.

5.28 A clause in a sale contract stipulates that the seller must provide evidence that the property is free of active termite infestation. On the day of closing, the buyer learns that inspection service did not provide the required written documentation. The buyer then proceeds to declare that the sale is off. Which of the following is true of this situation?

   a. The seller can sue for specific performance.
   b. The buyer will be in default, and liable for damages, if he does not complete the transaction.
   c. The buyer may be able to have the contract canceled.
   d. The contract is automatically void.

5.29 A buyer signs an earnest money agreement and gives it to the broker who showed her the property she is buying. After leaving the broker's office, she reconsiders and decides she prefers a different property. How long does she have to take back her offer?

   a. Until the seller communicates acceptance of the offer.
   b. Until the earnest money deposit check is cashed.
   c. She can take it back at any time, but must forfeit the earnest money.
   d. She cannot take it back until after the expiration date of the offer.

5.30 On Wednesday, Fred offers to sell his property to Jack for $275,000, with the offer to remain open until 5 p.m. the next day. On Thursday morning, Sally offers Fred $280,000 for the property and Fred accepts. At 1 p.m. on Thursday afternoon, Jack accepts. Which of the following is true of this situation?

a. The acceptance by Sally creates a contract and terminates Fred's offer to Jack.
b. Fred has entered into contracts with both Jack and Sally to sell the same property.
c. Fred's acceptance of Sally's offer is invalidated by Jack's acceptance, because Fred's offer to Jack was made prior to Sally's offer to Fred.
d. No contract has been created because it is impossible to have two valid sale contracts for the same property.

5.31 Among the items that normally must be disclosed in a sale contract or its addenda is/are the

a. buyer's financial capability.
b. buyer's source of funds for the down payment.
c. seller's acceptable price range.
d. agency relationships and property condition.

5.32 To create an enforceable option-to-buy contract, there must be an exchange of

a. a promise to sell and a promise to buy.
b. valuable consideration and a right to buy.
c. valuable consideration and a promise to buy.
d. a down payment and a post-dated contract for sale.

5.33 Mary Carboy buys a house from Jim Schmidt and at the same time obtains an option to purchase the adjoining vacant lot for $10,000 within one year. A few months later, Carboy informs Schmidt that she is ready to exercise her option, but finds that Schmidt has received an offer of $12,000 from another party. Schmidt states that he will accept the offer unless Carboy is willing to match the $12,000 offer. Which of the following is true of this situation?

a. Schmidt must sell to Carboy for $10,000.
b. Carboy must pay $12,000 or lose the property.
c. Schmidt may sell to Carboy or the other party, but the price cannot exceed $10,000.
d. If the other party delivers payment before Carboy does, the option is canceled.

5.34 Which of the following is true regarding the assignability of an option?

a. It is assignable only if the contract specifically allows assignment.
b. It is never assignable.
c. It is assignable only if the option is exercised.
d. It is always assignable unless the contract prohibits assignment.

5.35 Which of the following is true of a contract for deed transaction?

a. At the end of the contract period, the vendee receives equitable title, provided all required periodic payments have been made.
b. The vendee has no right to possess or occupy the property during the contract period.
c. At the end of the contract period, the vendor conveys legal title, provided the vendee has fulfilled all obligations.
d. The vendor may cancel the contract at any time before the final payment has been received.

5.36 Several buyers are competing for the last available home in a desirable new subdivision. One buyer calls the owner-developer directly on the phone and offers $20,000 over and above the listed price. The developer accepts the offer. At this point,

a. the parties have a valid, enforceable sale contract on the home.
b. the parties have completed a verbal, executory contract.
c. the parties may not cancel their contract.
d. the developer could not entertain other offers on the property.

5.37 An owner completes a sales contract on her property with a buyer. Before closing, the seller runs into financial trouble and assigns the contract to her principal creditor. The buyer cries foul, fearing the property will be lost. Which of the following is true?

a. The buyer can sue the assignee to disallow the illegal assignment.
b. The buyer can take legal action against the assignor.
c. The assignor has completed a legal action.
d. The sale contract is nullified.

5.38. A due-on-sale clause in a sale contract puts parties on notice that

a. the full price of the property is due the seller at closing.
b. any loans surviving closing become immediately payable.
c. all of the seller's debts must be retired before or upon closing.
d. any conveyance may trigger an acceleration of any loans secured by the property.

5.39 A tenant has an option-to-purchase agreement with the landlord that expires on June 30. On July 1, the tenant frantically calls the landlord to exercise the option, offering the apology that she was busy with a death in the family. Which of the following is true?

a. Since options contain grace periods, the landlord must sell.
b. The tenant loses the right to buy, but can claim the money paid for the option from the landlord.
c. The landlord does not have to sell, but must renew the option.
d. The option is expired, and the tenant has no rightful claim to money paid for the option.

5.40 Two parties enter into a contract for deed agreement. In this form of agreement,

a. title is conveyed to the buyer, but the seller retains possession for a stipulated time period.
b. the buyer contracts to pay all cash at closing in exchange for the deed.
c. the seller retains legal title while the buyer makes partial payments until the contract is fully executed.
d. the buyer immediately acquires legal title and takes possession.

6.1   If the price of an item is increasing, one can usually assume that

a. demand for the item is decreasing in relation to supply of the item.
b. demand for the item is increasing in relation to supply of the item.
c. supply of the item is increasing.
d. demand for the item and supply of the item are increasing.

6.2   When the market for an item has achieved market equilibrium, which of the following statements is true?

a. New suppliers will enter the market and drive the price down.
b. Demand will slowly taper off, driving the price down.
c. Unmet demand for the item is directed toward demand for some other item.
d. Supply and demand are equal, and price and value are equal.

6.3   As an economic product, real estate is distinguished by

a. its homogeneity.
b. its variety.
c. the uniqueness of every parcel.
d. its ability to appreciate in value.

6.4   The city of Stevensville has declared a moratorium on new construction. If demand is increasing, what will be the likely effect on real estate prices in the area?

a. Prices level off.
b. Prices continue to follow the trend that preceded the moratorium.
c. Prices fall.
d. Prices rise.

6.5   If Okapi, Inc., a company that markets its sports clothing worldwide, moves into Stevensville and hires 100 employees, it is reasonable to expect that the town will experience

a. an immediate rise in the demand for industrial real estate, but no other changes in the real estate market.
b. an increase in demand for all types of real estate.
c. a housing boom, but no other changes in the real estate market.
d. an immediate increase in the prices for industrial and office real estate, but no impact on the residential market.

6.6   What is "absorption?"

a. The amount of new space that is added to available space over a period of time.
b. The number of houses that are built over a period of time.
c. The amount of space that is occupied at any given time.
d. The number of available units that become occupied over a period of time.

6.7   When vacancies are declining in a real estate market, it is common for the market to experience

a. rising prices.
b. falling prices.
c. falling construction activity.
d. falling absorption.

6.8   The price for any product is a function of four fundamental determinants of value. These are

     a. durability, feasibility, mobility, and location.
     b. desire, utility, scarcity, and purchasing power.
     c. popularity, recognizability, promotion, and rebate.
     d. fungibility, costs, convenience, and uniqueness.

6.9   A town is rapidly growing, but all the buildable vacant lots in the most desirable area have already been occupied. In this case, it is likely that the price of existing homes in that area

     a. will stabilize, since the population must stabilize.
     b. will increase.
     c. will decline, since no further building can take place.
     d. will not show any predictable movement.

6.10   If there is a significant undersupply of homes in a market, construction will tend to increase. This is an example of

     a. supply outstripping demand.
     b. demand outstripping value.
     c. consumer optimism.
     d. the market tending toward equilibrium.

6.11   If commercial real estate rental prices are falling in a market, it is likely that

     a. demand has outstripped supply of space.
     b. the market is in equilibrium.
     c. the market is over-supplied.
     d. employment is increasing.

6.12   A construction boom in a market is an indication that prices

     a. have been increasing.
     b. have been declining.
     c. have been in equilibrium.
     d. have exceeded supply.

6.13   Why is real estate traditionally considered a relatively illiquid economic product?

     a. Its physical form is fixed.
     b. Real estate is defined as land, not water.
     c. It is often difficult to convert to cash.
     d. It cannot be moved.

6.14   What does "base employment" refer to in the context of real estate demand?

     a. The lowest category of employment in terms of wages and desirability
     b. The number of persons employed in base industries in an area
     c. The number of persons employed on military bases in an area
     d. The labor pool available for employment in all industries in an area

6.15   What is "vacancy" in real estate market economics?

     a. A property that has no owner-occupant
     b. The total number of properties of a certain type that are on the market at a given time
     c. The absence of certain types of users in a given market area
     d. The total existing space of a certain type that is unoccupied at a given time

6.16 A moratorium on new construction is an example of

a. local government influencing the real estate market, regardless of demand.
b. the natural result of demand exceeding supply in a local market.
c. government promotion of the free market concept in the local real estate market.
d. a government policy that aims to restrain a trend of rising prices in the local real estate market.

6.17 Of the following potential influences on a local real estate market, which one would be considered local, rather than regional, national, or global?

a. Changes in money supply
b. Federal Reserve interest rates
c. In- and out-migrations of major employers
d. Trade imbalances with foreign trading partners

6.18 There is a lot of new construction going on in the town of Florence. Which of the following would most likely be the immediate effect on the real estate market?

a. Demand increases and prices rise.
b. Vacancy rises and prices fall.
c. Absorption and vacancy decrease.
d. Supply decreases relative to demand.

6.19 What kind of real estate users are most concerned with neighborhood quality, access to services, property amenities, and quality of life in their demand for real estate?

a. Retail
b. Office
c. Industrial
d. Residential

6.20 One distinguishing feature of real estate as an economic product is

a. its easy convertibility to cash.
b. its quick response to changes in supply-demand balance.
c. its susceptibility to swings in the local economy.
d. the easy substitutability of one item for another.

6.21 Bill Parsons paid $150,000 for a house to operate as a rental property, figuring that he could rent it out at a rate of $900 a month. In paying a price based on the property's ability to generate a desired future income, Parsons was motivated by the economic principle known as

a. substitution.
b. anticipation.
c. supply and demand.
d. utility.

6.22 Which of the following situations illustrates the principle of contribution?

a. A homebuyer makes a down payment of 20% instead of the 10% the lender requires.
b. A homeowner adds a third bathroom to a house and thereby increases the appraised value by $10,000.
c. The appraised value of a house goes up by $20,000 over a two-year period because of the prices recently paid for other houses in the neighborhood.
d. Because of a decline in mortgage interest rates, a homeowner in a certain market is able to list her house at a higher price.

6.23 When a property owner combines two adjacent properties to create a single property with a higher value than the sum of the values of the two separate properties, the applicable principle of value is called

a. assemblage.
b. accretion.
c. progression.
d. subdivision.

6.24 What is the difference between market value and market price, if any?

a. There is no difference.
b. Market value is a broker's estimate; market price is a precise number derived by a licensed appraiser.
c. Market value is an average price derived from comparable sales; market price is a price based on the cost of creating the property.
d. Market value is an estimate; market price is the price at which a property sold.

6.25 The first step in the appraisal process, regardless of the appraisal method, is to

a. identify the highest and best use of the property to be appraised.
b. collect and analyze property data.
c. estimate the value of the land as if it were vacant.
d. define the appraisal problem and the purpose of the appraisal.

6.26 In the final step of an appraisal, the appraiser reconciles the value estimates derived by the various appraisal approaches by

a. disregarding the high and low extreme results.
b. averaging the results of all three approaches.
c. weighing the applicability of the approaches and considering the quality of data supporting each approach.
d. choosing the result that is closest to the average for properties in the immediate neighborhood.

6.27 Which of the following statements properly describes the central concept of the sales comparison approach?

a. Find the median price of recently sold comparable properties and add or subtract dollar amounts in the subject property to account for competitive differences.
b. Make dollar adjustments to the sale prices of comparable properties to account for competitive differences with the subject.
c. Find at least three comparable properties that are currently for sale and make dollar adjustments to the listing prices to account for competitive differences with the subject.
d. Apply an appreciation factor to the price at which the subject property most recently sold and make dollar adjustments to account for competitive differences with comparable properties currently for sale.

6.28 One of the strengths of the sales comparison approach is that it

a. takes into account the subject property's investment value.
b. reveals the profit margin of the builder or developer of the subject property.
c. discovers the underlying value of the subject property apart from the influence of competing properties.
d. takes into account the competitive value of specific amenities of the subject property.

6.29 In making dollar adjustments in the sales comparison approach, the appraiser

    a. adds value to a comparable that is inferior to the subject property.
    b. adds value to the subject property if it is inferior to a comparable.
    c. subtracts value from a comparable that is inferior to the subject property.
    d. subtracts value from the subject property if it is inferior to a comparable.

6.30 The best comparable property for use in the sales comparison approach is the one that

    a. requires the most and largest adjustments.
    b. requires the fewest and smallest adjustments.
    c. sold most recently at the highest price.
    d. is located closest to the subject property.

6.31 A house is being appraised using the sales comparison approach. The house has three bedrooms, two bathrooms, and a patio. The appraiser selects a comparable house that has three bedrooms, 3 bathrooms, and no patio. The comparable house just sold for $200,000. A bath is valued at $7,000, and a patio at $2,000. Assuming all else is equal, what is the adjusted value of the comparable?

    a. $202,000.
    b. $207,000.
    c. $195,000.
    d. $205,000.

6.32 Which of the following statements properly describes the central methodology of the cost approach to appraisal?

    a. Apply a depreciation factor to the reported actual cost of acquiring and improving the subject property.
    b. Estimate the cost of building the improvements on the subject property.
    c. Estimate the land value and add to this the actual cost of the improvements adjusted for competitive differences with similar properties.
    d. Add the estimated land value and cost of improvements and subtract the accrued depreciation of the improvements.

6.33 One of the strengths of the cost approach is that it

    a. takes into account the amount of money required to develop a similar property.
    b. is very accurate for a property with new improvements that represent the highest and best use.
    c. results in an actual price in dollars instead of an estimated value.
    d. reveals the owner's return on money invested in the cost of development.

6.34 The principle underlying depreciation from physical deterioration is that

    a. eventually, a property loses all of its value.
    b. a property loses a portion of its value each year because of economic obsolescence.
    c. a property loses the same increment of value each year over the economic life of the property.
    d. the value lost to depreciation is incurable.

6.35 A property is being appraised by the cost approach. The appraiser estimates that the land is worth $30,000 and the replacement cost of the improvements is $95,000. Total depreciation from all causes is $10,000. What is the indicated value of the property?

    a. $135,000.
    b. $130,000.
    c. $125,000.
    d. $115,000.

6.36 Which of the following statements properly describes how to apply the income capitalization approach to appraisal?

a. Apply a rate of return to the price paid for an income property.
b. Divide the income a property generates by a rate of return.
c. Estimate the amount of income a property must generate to return the capital amount invested in it.
d. Estimate the rate of return a property owner receives from income generated by the property.

6.37 A strength of the income capitalization approach is that it

a. uses a rate of return that is required for all potential purchasers in a market.
b. yields an accurate projection of investment income.
c. uses a method that is also used by investors to determine how much they should pay for an investment property.
d. can be used with any type of property in any market.

6.38 A property is being appraised using the income capitalization approach. Annually, it has an estimated gross income of $60,000, vacancy and credit losses of $3,000, and operating expenses of $20,000. Using a capitalization rate of ten percent, what is the indicated value (to the nearest $1,000)?

a. $370,000.
b. $400,000.
c. $570,000.
d. $600,000.

6.39 An apartment building that sold for $450,000 had monthly gross rent receipts of $3,000. What is its monthly gross rent multiplier?

a. 12.5
b. .01.
c. .08.
d. 150.

6.40 A rental house has monthly gross income of $1,200. A suitable gross income multiplier derived from market data is 14.1. What estimated sale price (to the nearest $1,000) is indicated?

a. $169,000.
b. $102,000.
c. $203,000.
d. $173,000.

6.41 A certified appraiser is one who has received certification by

a. a licensed real estate school.
b. the Appraisal Institute.
c. the state in which the appraiser operates.
d. the Appraisal Review Board.

6.42 The act that required federally-related appraisals to be conducted by a certified appraiser is known as

a. The Financial Institutions Reform, Recovery and Enforcement Act (FIRREA).
b. The Uniform Standards of Professional Appraisal Practice Act (USPAPA).
c. The Appraisal Foundation Authorization and Reform Act (AFAR).
d. The Federal Institution for Regulation and Enforcement of Appraisal Act (FIREAA).

6.43 As a component of real estate value, the principle of substitution states that

a. if two similar properties are for sale, a buyer will purchase the cheaper of the two.
b. if one of two adjacent homes is more valuable, the price of the other home will tend to rise.
c. if too many properties are built in a market, the prices will tend to go down.
d. people will readily move to another home if it is of equal value.

6.44 Highest and best use of a property is that use which

a. is physically and financially feasible, legal, and the most productive.
b. is legal, feasible, and deemed the most appropriate by zoning authorities.
c. entails the largest building that zoning ordinances will allow developers to erect.
d. conforms to other properties in the area.

6.45 Lynne just bought a house. She paid $187,500, for it, even though it had been listed at $195,000. An adjoining property owner, Ken, had tried to buy the property for $185,000, but had been refused. He now offers Lynne $190,000 for the house. Lynne is interested, so she hires an appraiser. The appraiser returns an estimate of value of $200,000. Which of these numbers can be called the market value?

a. $187,500.
b. $190,000.
c. $195,000.
d. $200,000.

6.46 A notable weakness of the sales comparison approach to value is that

a. there may be no recent sale price data in the market.
b. the approach is not based on the principle of substitution.
c. the approach is only accurate with unique, special purpose properties.
d. sale prices cannot be compared, since all real estate is different.

6.47 In the market data approach, an appraiser

a. chooses nearby comparables, adjusts the subject for differences, and estimates the value.
b. gathers relevant price data, applies the data to the subject, and estimates the value.
c. selects comparable properties, adjusts the comparables, and estimates the value.
d. identifies the price previously paid, applies an appreciation rate, and estimates the value.

6.48 In the sales comparison approach, an adjustment is warranted if

a. the buyer obtains conventional financing for the property.
b. the seller offers below-market seller financing.
c. a comparable is located in another, albeit similar neighborhood.
d. one property has a hip roof and the other has a gabled roof.

6.49 To complete the sales comparison approach, the appraiser

a. averages the comparable values.
b. weights the comparables.
c. identifies the subject's value as that of the middle value of the comparables.
d. identifies the subject's value as that of the nearest comparable.

6.50 One weakness of the cost approach for appraising market value is that

a. builders may not pay market value for materials or labor.
b. market value is not always the same as what the property cost.
c. comparables used may not have similar quality of construction.
d. new properties have inestimable costs and rates of depreciation.

6.51　The cost of constructing a functional equivalent of a subject property is known as

a. reproduction cost.
b. replacement cost.
c. restitution cost.
d. reconstruction cost.

6.52　An office building lacks fiber optic cabling to accommodate the latest communications equipment. This is an example of

a. physical deterioration.
b. economic obsolescence.
c. incurable depreciation.
d. functional obsolescence.

6.53　A home is located in a neighborhood where homeowners on the block have failed to maintain their properties. This is an example of

a. curable external obsolescence.
b. incurable economic obsolescence.
c. functional obsolescence.
d. physical deterioration.

6.54　In appraisal, loss of value in a property from any cause is referred to as

a. deterioration.
b. obsolescence.
c. depreciation.
d. deflation.

6.55　In the cost approach, after estimating the value of the land and the cost of the improvements, the appraiser

a. estimates depreciation, subtracts depreciation from cost, and adds back the land value.
b. subtracts deterioration from cost, estimates land depreciation, and totals the two values.
c. estimates depreciation of land and improvements and subtracts the total from original cost.
d. estimates obsolescence and subtracts from the cost of land and improvements.

7.1   What is a lien-theory state?

    a. A state in which a mortgagee holds legal title to a secured property.
    b. A state in which a mortgagee has equitable title to a secured property.
    c. A state that allows a real estate owner's creditors to record liens against the owner's property.
    d. A state in which a lien is considered as a conveyance.

7.2   What is the function of a note in a mortgage or trust deed financing arrangement?

    a. It is the lender's security instrument in the collateral property.
    b. It is evidence of ownership of the mortgage or trust deed.
    c. It contains the borrower's promise to maintain the value of the property given as collateral for a loan.
    d. It is evidence of the borrower's debt to the lender.

7.3   When homebuyer Henry pledges his newly purchased home as collateral for a mortgage loan, the evidence of the pledge is the

    a. trust deed or mortgage.
    b. promissory note.
    c. loan commitment.
    d. loan receipt.

7.4   The borrower in a mortgage loan transaction is known as the

    a. mortgagee.
    b. mortgagor.
    c. lienor.
    d. trustee.

7.5   If a borrower obtains an interest-only loan of $200,000 at an annual interest rate of 6%, what is the monthly interest payment?

    a. $1,200.
    b. $600.
    c. $500.
    d. $1,000.

7.6   If a borrower's monthly interest payment on an interest-only loan at an annual interest rate of 6% is $500, how much was the loan amount?

    a. $72,000.
    b. $100,000.
    c. $120,000.
    d. $50,000.

7.7   A borrower of a $50,000 interest-only loan makes annual interest payments of $3750. What interest rate is the borrower paying?

    a. 7.5%.
    b. .75%.
    c. 3.75%.
    d. 8.5%.

7.8 Maria borrows $100,000 and pays two points for the loan. How much does she pay in points?

a. $200.
b. $2,000.
c. $1,200.
d. It depends on the interest rate.

7.9 Which of the following is true of an amortizing loan?

a. The amount of annual interest paid is the same for every year of the loan term.
b. Part of each periodic payment is applied to repayment of the loan balance in advance and part is applied to payment of interest in arrears.
c. Except for any points that may be paid, the interest on the loan balance is usually paid in advance.
d. The interest rate is reduced each year to maintain equal payments even though the outstanding loan balance is smaller.

7.10 For a loan that is not backed by the Federal Housing Administration or Veterans Administration, and for which the borrower is making a down payment of less than 20%, the lender is likely to require the borrower to obtain

a. a subrogation agreement.
b. private mortgage insurance.
c. a letter of credit.
d. a co-signer on the note.

7.11 What is a loan-to-value ratio?

a. The percentage of a lender's portfolio that is composed of mortgage loans.
b. The ratio of borrowed principal plus total interest to the appraised value of the collateral property.
c. The ratio of a lender's return on a mortgage loan to the value of the collateral property.
d. The fraction of the appraised value of the property offered as collateral which the lender is willing to lend.

7.12 The difference between what a borrower has to pay to purchase a property and the amount a lender will lend on the property is the

a. mortgage insurance coverage amount.
b. lender's profit margin.
c. buyer's down payment.
d. origination fee.

7.13 The Equal Credit Opportunity Act prohibits a lender from

a. refusing a loan because the borrower does not match the lender's target market.
b. including income from self-employment in the borrower's qualifying income.
c. requiring both spouses to sign the loan application form.
d. refusing a loan because a borrower has a defective credit report.

7.14 A loan applicant has an annual gross income of $72,000. How much will a lender allow the applicant to pay for monthly housing expense to qualify for a loan if the lender uses an income ratio of 28%?

a. $2,160.
b. $1,680.
c. $1,068.
d. $840.

7.15 AMC Bank discovers, in considering buyer Bob's application for a mortgage loan, that Bob has borrowed the down payment from an uncle and has to repay that loan. Bob should expect that AMC Bank will

a. refuse the application.
b. adjust the applicant's debt ratio calculation and lower the loan amount.
c. increase the loan amount to enable the borrower to pay off the loan to the relative.
d. require the borrower to make payments to an escrow account for repayment of the relative's loan.

7.16 The Federal Reserve's Regulation Z applies to which loans?

a. All loans.
b. All loans secured by real estate.
c. All loans secured by a residence.
d. All loans over $25,000.

7.17 If a particular loan falls under Regulation Z's right of rescission provision,

a. the lender has the right to change the terms of the loan within a certain period.
b. the lender has the right to accelerate repayment of the loan because of a change in the borrower's credit status.
c. the borrower has the right to pay off the loan ahead of schedule with no penalty.
d. the borrower has a limited right to cancel the transaction within a certain period.

7.18 Under the Equal Credit Opportunity Act, a lender, or a real estate agent who assists a seller in qualifying a potential buyer, may not

a. tell a rejected loan applicant the reasons for the rejection.
b. ask the buyer/borrower about his/her religion or national origin.
c. ask the buyer/borrower to explain unconventional sources of income.
d. use a credit report that has not been provided to the borrower.

7.19 A conventional mortgage loan is one that is

a. backed by the Federal National Mortgage Association.
b. insured under Section 203(b) of the Federal Housing Administration loan program.
c. guaranteed by the Government National Mortgage Association.
d. not FHA-insured or VA-guaranteed.

7.20 The assumability of an FHA-insured loan is

a. unrestricted.
b. limited by when the loan was originated.
c. limited to owner-occupied properties.
d. prohibited on all existing loans under current regulations.

7.21 A VA certificate of eligibility determines

a. how long an individual served in the military.
b. the maximum loan amount an approved lender can give to veterans.
c. how much of a loan the VA will guarantee.
d. whether a lender is approved to issue VA-guaranteed loans.

7.22 A borrower obtains a 30-year, fully amortizing mortgage loan of $50,000 at 8%. What is the principal balance at the end of the loan term?

a. $2,000.
b. $50,000.
c. $220.
d. Zero.

151

7.23   Which of the following describes a purchase money mortgage financing arrangement?

a. A bank gives a buyer a senior mortgage loan that fully covers the cost of purchasing the property.
b. The buyer gives the seller a mortgage and note as part of the purchase price of the property.
c. A land trust holds title to the property while the buyer makes periodic installment payments to the seller.
d. The seller uses the purchase money obtained from the buyer's mortgage loan to repay the seller's outstanding loan balance.

7.24   A homeowner borrows money from a lender and gives the lender a mortgage on the property as collateral for the loan. The homeowner retains title to the property. This is an example of

a. intermediation.
b. forfeiture.
c. hypothecation.
d. subordination.

7.25   Which of the following correctly describes the flow of money and documents in a mortgage loan transaction?

a. The borrower gives the lender a note and a mortgage in exchange for loan funds.
b. The lender gives the borrower a mortgage and receives a note in exchange for loan funds.
c. The borrower receives a note in exchange for a mortgage from the lender.
d. The lender gives the borrower a note, loan funds and a mortgage.

7.26   In a deed of trust transaction, which of the following occurs?

a. The beneficiary conveys title to a trustee in exchange for loan funds.
b. The trustee conveys title to a beneficiary in exchange for loan funds.
c. The trustor conveys title to a trustee in exchange for loan funds from the beneficiary.
d. The trustee conveys title to a trustor in exchange for loan funds from the beneficiary.

7.27   A lender lends money to a homeowner and takes legal title to the property as collateral during the payoff period. They are in a

a. title-theory state.
b. lien-theory state.
c. state allowing land trusts.
d. state where hypothecation is illegal.

7.28   A lender who charges a rate of interest in excess of legal limits is guilty of

a. redlining.
b. usury.
c. profit-taking.
d. nothing; there are no legal limits to interest rates.

7.29   A lender is charging 2 points on a $60,000 loan. The borrower must therefore pay the lender an advance amount of

a. $120.
b. $300.
c. $1,200.
d. $3,000.

7.30 The difference between a balloon loan and an amortized loan is

    a. an amortized loan is paid off over the loan period.
    b. a balloon loan always has a shorter loan term.
    c. an amortized loan requires interest-payments.
    d. a balloon loan must be retired in five years.

7.31 A distinctive feature of a promissory note is that

    a. it is not assignable.
    b. it must be accompanied by a mortgage.
    c. it is a negotiable instrument.
    d. it may not be prepaid.

7.32 When the terms of the mortgage loan are satisfied, the mortgagee

    a. may retain any overage in the escrow account.
    b. may inspect the property before returning legal title.
    c. may be entitled to charge the borrower a small fee to close the loan.
    d. may be required to execute a release of mortgage document.

7.33 In addition to income, credit, and employment data, a mortgage lender requires additional documentation, usually including

    a. an appraisal report.
    b. a criminal record report.
    c. a subordination agreement.
    d. a default recourse waiver.

7.34 The three overriding considerations of a lender's mortgage loan decision are

    a. points, interest rate, and loan term.
    b. the location of the mortgaged property, the borrower's cash, and the amount of the borrower's equity.
    c. the ability to re-pay, the value of the collateral, and the profitability of the loan.
    d. the amount of the loan, the borrower's income, and the down payment.

7.35 The reason lenders consider the loan-to-value ratio important in underwriting is that

    a. they don't want to lend borrowers any more money than necessary.
    b. they want to ensure there is more than enough collateral to cover the loan amount.
    c. borrowers can only afford to borrow a portion of the entire purchase price.
    d. the higher the loan-to-value ratio, the more profitable the loan.

7.36 The Equal Credit Opportunity Act (ECOA) requires lenders to

    a. extend equal credit to all prospective borrowers.
    b. consider the income of a spouse in evaluating a family's creditworthiness.
    c. discount the income of a person involved in child-rearing or child-bearing.
    d. specialize lending activity by geographical area for improved customer service.

7.37 Lenders use an income ratio in qualifying to

    a. insure a borrower has the earning power to make the loan payments.
    b. compare a borrower's earnings to the borrower's short-term debt.
    c. identify the highest possible interest rate that the borrower can afford.
    d. quantify the borrower's assets to the fullest extent.

7.38   The debt ratio formula used to qualify borrowers is

       a. total debt divided by debt payments.
       b. gross income divided by assets.
       c. gross income divided by debts.
       d. debt payments divided by gross income.

7.39   At the closing of a mortgage loan

       a. the borrower pays off the note and receives clear title.
       b. the lender issues a firm loan commitment.
       c. the parties complete all loan origination documents and the loan is funded.
       d. the borrower's loan application is complete and the file closed.

7.40   Which laws or regulations require mortgage lenders to disclose financing costs and annual
       percentage rate to a borrower before funding a loan?

       a. The Equal Credit Opportunity Act.
       b. Truth-in-Lending laws and Regulation Z.
       c. The Real Estate Settlement and Procedures Act.
       d. Federal Fair Housing Laws.

7.41   Which laws or regulations prevent mortgage lenders from discriminating in extending credit to
       potential borrowers?

       a. The Equal Credit Opportunity Act.
       b. Truth-in-Lending laws.
       c. The Real Estate Settlement and Procedures Act.
       d. Federal Fair Housing Laws.

7.42   Which laws or regulations require mortgage lenders to provide an estimate of closing costs to a
       borrower and forbid them to pay kickbacks for referrals?

       a. The Equal Credit Opportunity Act.
       b. Truth-in-Lending laws.
       c. the Real Estate Settlement and Procedures Act.
       d. Federal Fair Housing Laws.

7.43   Which of the following are methods used by the Federal Reserve System to regulate the money
       supply?

       a. Selling securities, printing money, and controlling lending underwriting requirements.
       b. Buying securities, changing the discount rate, and controlling banking reserves.
       c. Printing money, changing interest rates, and selling T-bills.
       d. Controlling the prime rate, trading securities, and purchasing loans.

7.44   How does the secondary mortgage market aid borrowers seeking a mortgage loan?

       a. It cycles funds back to primary lenders so they can make more loans.
       b. It issues second mortgages and sells them in the home equity market.
       c. It lends funds to banks so they can make more loans.
       d. It pays off defaulted loans made by primary mortgage lenders.

7.45   The major organizations operating in the secondary mortgage market are

       a. Fannie Mae, Freddie Mac, and Ginnie Mae.
       b. Fannie Mae, GMAC, and MGIC.
       c. Freddie Mac, FHA, and VA.
       d. Fannie Mae, Freddie Mac, and the Federal Reserve.

7.46 What is the role of Fannie Mae in the secondary mortgage market?

a. It guarantees FHA-backed and VA-backed loans.
b. It insures FHA-backed and VA-backed loans.
c. It purchases FHA-backed and VA-backed loans.
d. It originates FHA-backed and VA-backed loans.

7.47 What is the role of the Federal Housing Authority in the mortgage lending market?

a. It guarantees loans made by approved lenders.
b. It insures loans made by approved lenders.
c. It purchases loans made by approved lenders.
d. It originates loans made by approved lenders.

7.48 What is the role of the Veteran's Administration in the mortgage lending market?

a. It guarantees loans made by approved lenders.
b. It insures loans made by approved lenders.
c. It purchases loans made by approved lenders.
d. It originates loans made by approved lenders.

7.49 In a graduated payment mortgage loan,

a. loan funds are disbursed to the borrower on a graduated basis.
b. the interest rate periodically increases in graduated phases.
c. the loan payments gradually increase.
d. the loan payments gradually increase and the loan term gradually decreases.

7.50 In a buydown,

a. the lender lowers the interest rate on a loan in exchange for a prepayment of principal.
b. the borrower pays additional interest at the onset in order to obtain a lower interest rate.
c. the lender requires the borrower to buy down the price of the property by increasing the down payment.
d. the borrower pays the lender additional funds to buy down the term of the loan.

Test 8: Investments; Taxation; Ethics

8.1 When an investor has to pay a lender more to finance the investment than the investment property generates in income, the investor suffers from

a. negative amortization.
b. negative leverage.
c. a reverse mortgage.
d. a debt investment.

8.2 Cost recovery is allowed as a federal tax deduction on

a. principal residences that do not have a home office.
b. income properties.
c. land.
d. commercial properties owned by the federal government.

8.3 A homeowner paid $200,000 for a house three years ago. The house sells today for $239,000. How much has the property appreciated?

a. 8.4 %.
b. 6.5 %.
c. 19.5 %.
d. 16.3 %.

8.4 The primary tax benefit in owning a non-income property such as a residence is

a. depreciation of improvements.
b. appreciation of land.
c. a deduction for costs of operating the property.
d. a deduction for mortgage interest.

8.5 A house sold for $250,000. The seller paid a brokerage commission of six percent, legal fees of $600, and had other closing costs of $1,500. What are net proceeds from the sale?

a. $235,000.
b. $234,000.
c. $233,500.
d. $232,900.

8.6 A homeowner bought a house five years ago for $150,000. Since then, the homeowner has spent $3,000 to pave the driveway and has added a central heating/airconditioning system at a cost of $4,000. What is the homeowner's adjusted basis if the house is sold today?

a. $156,000.
b. $157,000.
c. $144,000.
d. $145,000.

8.7 A homeowner sold her house and realized a net proceeds amount of $210,000. Her adjusted basis in the home was $176,000. She immediately bought another house for $200,000. What was her capital gain?

a. $10,000.
b. $24,000.
c. $34,000.
d. None.

8.8   After five years of owner-occupancy, Simon Wilson sells his principal residence for a gain of $150,000, and the next month buys another principal residence that costs more than the adjusted sale price of the old home. Which of the following is true of the treatment of the tax on gain?

a. There is no taxable gain.
b. It must be paid in the year of the sale.
c. The homeowner may choose to pay it or defer it.
d. Tax is due on the difference between the cost of the new home and adjusted basis of the old one.

8.9   Ralph Roberts buys a small office building as an investment and participates actively in the management and operation of the building. This is an example of

a. syndication.
b. equity investment.
c. direct investment.
d. illiquidity.

8.10 Elmo Gilmore owns a small retail property that he inherited from his father. There are no mortgages or interest expenses connected with the property. Elmo takes an annual cost recovery expense of $5,000. The property has a monthly gross income of $1,500 and monthly operating expenses of $500. Elmo's taxable income from this property will be taxed at a rate of 30%. What is the tax liability for the year?

a. $2,100.
b. $3,600.
c. $3,900.
d. $7,000.

8.11 All investors desire their investments to increase in value. However,

a. the degree of return is inversely related to the degree of risk.
b. the more the investor stands to gain, the greater the risk that the investor may lose.
c. investments requiring intense management have lesser returns.
d. the more liquid an investment is, the greater the chances are that the investment will not appreciate.

8.12 Two of the financial rewards that investments offer are

a. income and tax benefits.
b. negative leverage and appreciation.
c. appreciation and taxation.
d. positive leverage and prestige.

8.13 Because a real estate investment can take a long time to sell, real estate investments are considered to be

a. management intensive.
b. insensitive to marketing.
c. vulnerable to seller's markets.
d. relatively illiquid.

8.14 Compared to a stock portfolio, a real estate investment would be considered

a. a riskier investment.
b. a more management-intensive investment.
c. a shorter-term investment.
d. a more leveraged investment.

8.15 Six investors purchase a shopping center. One investor manages the tenants and another handles the marketing and leasing. Two investors manage accounting and finance, and the remaining two run the management office. This is a possible example of

a. a general partnership.
b. a limited partnership.
c. a real estate investment trust.
d. an investment conduit.

8.16 The formula for determining taxable income produced by an income property is

a. gross income minus expenses plus land and building depreciation.
b. gross income minus expenses minus land and building depreciation.
c. gross income minus building depreciation plus land depreciation.
d. gross income minus expenses minus building depreciation.

8.17 In deriving taxable income on an investment property, it is generally legal to

a. deduct principal and interest payments from income.
b. deduct principal payments from income.
c. deduct interest payments from income.
d. deduct principal and interest payments from income and capital gain.

8.18 Jake does not use any part of his principal residence as a home office. Which of the following is true of the tax treatment of this property?

a. The owner may deduct the property's interest and principal from ordinary income.
b. The owner may depreciate the property and deduct depreciation expenses from ordinary income.
c. The owner can deduct any capital gain when the property is sold.
d. The owner may be able to avoid capital gain tax when the property is sold.

8.19 An investment property seller pays $14,000 in closing costs. These costs

a. may be deducted from personal income.
b. may be deducted from the property's income.
c. may be deducted from the sale price for gains tax purposes.
d. may be deducted from the adjusted basis for gains tax purposes.

8.20 The formula for calculating capital gain tax is the taxpayer's tax bracket multiplied by

a. the sum of the beginning basis plus gain.
b. the difference between amount realized and adjusted basis.
c. the sum of net sale proceeds and capital gain.
d. the difference between net sale proceeds and capital gain.

8.21 Which of the following entities can legally levy annual real property taxes?

a. The Internal Revenue Service.
b. A utility company.
c. A tax district.
d. A court of law.

8.22 Certain classes of property owner and types of property are exempted or immune from real property taxation in many areas. The protected categories usually include

a. recreational properties.
b. properties owned by a government agency.
c. properties that comply with the Americans with Disabilities Act.
d. properties occupied by single-parent families.

8.23 What is the purpose of an equalization factor in ad valorem taxation?

a. It modifies a local tax rate to bring it into conformity with statutory tax rates.
b. It changes the assessed value of an individual property to make it reflect the assessed values of other properties in the same neighborhood.
c. It adjusts assessments in a locality to make them more consistent with an average level for the state or other higher level jurisdiction.
d. It adjusts the amount of the homestead exemption in a certain area to make it proportionally equivalent to the average homestead exemption in other areas.

8.24 A school district's tax rate is 10 mills. The school district's required revenue from real estate taxes is $20,000,000. What is the tax base of the area?

a. $20,000,000.
b. $200,000,000.
c. $2,000,000,000.
d. $200,000,000,000.

8.25 A homeowner receives a tax bill that includes an amount for the library district, taxed at $1.00 per $1,000, and the fire protection district, taxed at $2.00 per $1,000. How much does the taxpayer have to pay for these two items if the property's taxable value is $147,000?

a. $1,567.
b. $157.
c. $1,410.
d. $441.

8.26 A town is replacing a sidewalk that serves five homes. The length of the sidewalk is 200 feet. Mary's property has 38 feet of front footage. If the cost of the project to be paid by a special assessment is $30,000, what will Mary's assessment be?

a. $6,000.
b. $5,700.
c. $789.
d. $1,579.

8.27 What is a tax deed?

a. A conveyance instrument for a property that is sold to enforce a tax lien.
b. A document recorded in title records showing that property taxes have been paid.
c. A notice to a homeowner that a tax lien has been entered against the property.
d. A document that gives a municipal authority the power to collect an individual tax bill.

8.28 If a property owner has the right to redeem his or her property after a tax sale, the owner has

a. a legal right of rescission.
b. an equitable right to acquire title.
c. a right of homestead exclusion.
d. a statutory right of redemption.

8.29 The formula for deriving a municipal jurisdiction's ad valorem tax base is

a. the jurisdiction's annual budget times the tax rate.
b. the total of all assessed values of properties minus exemptions.
c. the total amount of ad valorem taxes required by the budget.
d. the municipality's budget multiplied times the millage rate.

8.30 A homeowner's total tax bill is derived by

    a. dividing the tax requirement by the tax base.
    b. multiplying each district's tax rate times the market value of the property.
    c. multiplying each district's tax rate times the taxable value of the property.
    d. averaging the tax rate for each tax district, and multiplying the average tax rate times the assessed value.

8.31 The fair housing law that first protected people against discrimination in housing based on race was the

    a. Civil Rights Act of 1866.
    b. Civil Rights Act of 1968.
    c. Executive Order 11063 of 1962.
    d. Title VIII amendment to the Fair Housing Act.

8.32 The classes protected against discrimination by the Fair Housing Act of 1968 are

    a. race only.
    b. religion and gender only.
    c. race, color, religion, and national origin.
    d. age and gender only.

8.33 An agent is committing an act of discriminatory advertising by doing which of the following?

    a. Telling prospective buyers about the positive and negative aspects of a certain neighborhood.
    b. Telling a prospective seller that now would be a good time to put a property on the market.
    c. Advertising a property as available to individuals of a particular race.
    d. Telling a prospective buyer that the agent is too busy to show the buyer properties personally on a given day.

8.34 Which of the following is an example of blockbusting?

    a. An agent shows a minority home buyer properties located in a neighborhood where there are no other minority home owners.
    b. An agent persuades a minority home buyer to avoid looking in a neighborhood where there are no minority home owners.
    c. An agent persuades a family to put their house on the market because ethnic minority families are beginning to move into the neighborhood.
    d. An agent persuades a minority home buyer to buy a property located in an area where most of the home owners belong to minority groups.

8.35 The practice of redlining is specifically prohibited by

    a. The Home Mortgage Disclosure Act.
    b. The Real Estate Settlement Procedures Act.
    c. The Civil Rights Act of 1866.
    d. The Americans with Disabilities Act.

8.36 Title VIII of the Civil Rights Act of 1968 applies to the sale of

    a. all single-family residences.
    b. all privately owned single-family residences.
    c. privately owned single-family residences listed with a broker.
    d. privately owned single-family residences for sale by owner.

8.37 A broker signs a listing agreement to sell a home for $200,000. An immigrant couple are interested in the house and ask the agent the price. The agent states the price as $210,000. According to the fair housing laws, such an action is

    a. illegal, because the agent changed the terms of the sale to discourage this particular couple.
    b. illegal, because the agent violated the listing agreement.
    c. legal, because the quoted price increase did not exceed 10% of the listing price.
    d. legal, because the increased price does not necessarily exclude the couple.

8.38 Which of the following actions is allowed under federal fair housing laws?

    a. A broker, following the instructions of the seller, advertises the property as for sale to Christian families only.
    b. A home seller, acting without a broker, places a "for sale-- mature, single men only" sign in front of the house.
    c. The owner of four rental houses advertises one of the properties for rent to married couples, no children, no pets.
    d. The owner of a duplex who resides in one of the units refuses to rent the other unit to a non-Christian.

8.39 Cecily Longstreet believes a real estate agent has kept her from seeing a certain property for rent because she is a woman. What actions should she take if she wants legal satisfaction for her complaint?

    a. File charges of illegal discrimination with the police department that has jurisdiction over the local area.
    b. File a complaint with HUD and/or file suit against the offending parties in a state or federal court within the prescribed time period.
    c. Wait two years and then file a civil suit in federal court.
    d. Sue HUD for damages under the Civil rights Act of 1866.

8.40 George Scott hires Shannon Lang to sell his house, with the condition that he will not be the first one in the neighborhood to sell to members of a certain ethnic group. What should Shannon do about this condition?

    a. Inform Scott that the condition is illegal and that she cannot comply with it.
    b. Note the condition on the listing agreement and have Scott initial it.
    c. Pretend that she did not hear the condition and proceed to market the property to all groups.
    d. Tell Scott that she will try to discourage members of that group from looking at the property, but that she cannot control cooperating brokers.

8.41 Under federal fair housing laws, the owner of a ten-unit apartment building may legally

    a. advertise that the property is not available to anyone requiring wheelchair access.
    b. refuse to rent to aliens.
    c. require families without children to pay the same security deposit that families with children must pay.
    d. require tenants to move out when they become 62 years old.

8.42 Sam Gough wants to rent out his home, but wants to exclude families with children because of his belief that they cause damage. Under what conditions would federal fair housing laws allow Gough to rent on these terms?

    a. The owner has a consistent no-children policy in all his rental properties.
    b. The owner can prove that costs to repair damage caused by previous tenants with children exceeded the tenants' security deposit.
    c. It is a single-family house that is part of a federally-designated planned unit development.
    d. It is a single-family house, and the owner owns only one other rental home in addition to his own residence.

8.43 Which of the following laws or rulings extended discrimination to include gender, handicapped status, and family status?

a. Executive Order 11063.
b. the Civil Rights Act of 1968.
c. the Fair Housing Amendments Act of 1988.
d. Jones v Mayer.

8.44 The Wallaces, a minority family, would like to buy a home in a certain price range. Agent Ambrose shows the family all available properties in a neighborhood of families with similar backgrounds. Ambrose does not mention a number of homes in the family's price range in other neighborhoods. This agent could be liable for

a. blockbusting.
b. providing unequal services.
c. steering.
d. nothing; his services were legal and acceptable.

8.45 An agent does not like a particular minority buyer, and is very short with the person, refusing to engage in lengthy conversation or show him any properties. A second minority party visits the office the next day. The agent is very forthcoming, and shows the person five prospective properties. This agent could be liable for

a. providing unequal services.
b. steering.
c. misrepresentation.
d. nothing; both parties were minorities, and therefore no discrimination occurred.

8.46 Following the client's recommendation, an agent conceals the availability of a property from an employed but pregnant and unmarried minority woman. This agent could be liable for

a. discriminatory misrepresentation by omission.
b. steering.
c. violating fiduciary duty.
d. nothing: an agent may show or not show any property at his or her discretion.

9.1 The conditions of an escrow agreement cannot be met and the related transaction cannot be completed. In such a case, the escrow agent

    a. levies a fine against the defaulting party.
    b. assigns his or her fiduciary responsibilities to the seller's broker.
    c. returns funds to the buyer.
    d. cancels the sale contract and destroys the transaction documents.

9.2 To avoid violating the Real Estate Settlement Procedures Act, parties who are providing services to the buyer or seller in a transaction must

    a. be paid before the closing date for any service they provide.
    b. inform the closing agent of the cost of their services at least one week before the closing date.
    c. receive payment only from the funds held in escrow, not directly from buyer or seller.
    d. disclose in writing any business relationships they have with other parties involved in the transaction.

9.3 A certain item is to be prorated between a buyer and seller. If no outside party is concerned, which of the following statements is true?

    a. The item must be prorated and recorded as a debit to one party and a credit to the other party for the same amount.
    b. The item must be prorated and recorded as a debit to one party; the remainder is recorded as a credit to the other party.
    c. The party who is owed money receives a credit for the entire item and a debit for the prorated amount.
    d. The party who owes money receives a debit for the portion owed and a credit for the portion that is not owed.

9.4 An item is said to be paid in arrears if it is normally paid

    a. on a monthly or yearly basis.
    b. at some time after the expense is incurred.
    c. only after it is billed.
    d. whenever it is incurred.

9.5 A seller received a rental payment of $900 in advance. At closing, the seller has earned only $320 of this rent. What should appear on the closing statement?

    a. A debit to the seller and credit to the buyer for $320.
    b. A debit to the seller for $580 and a credit to the buyer for $320.
    c. A debit to the seller for $320 and a credit to the buyer for $900.
    d. A debit to the seller and credit to the buyer for $580.

9.6 A buyer will receive a water bill for an estimated $100 at the end of the month. At closing, the seller has used an estimated $43 in water. What should appear on the closing statement?

    a. A debit to the seller and credit to the buyer for $57.
    b. A debit to the seller and credit to the buyer for $43.
    c. A debit to the buyer and credit to the seller for $57.
    d. A debit to the buyer and credit to the seller for $43.

9.7   A sale transaction closes on April 1, the ninety-first day of the tax year. The day of closing belongs to the seller. Real estate taxes for the year, not yet billed, are expected to be $2,190. According to the 365-day method, what is the seller's share of the tax bill?

a. $1,644.00.
b. $546.00.
c. $959.30
d. $1,364.66.

9.8   A sale transaction closes on July 4. The day of closing belongs to the seller. On January 1, the seller paid a hazard insurance premium of $375 for the calendar year. According to the 12-month/30-day method, what is the seller's share of the insurance premium?

a. $183.33.
b. $187.50.
c. $189.05.
d. $191.67.

9.9   Waldo is buying Marianne's house. The closing date (day belongs to seller) of the sale transaction is September 1 (day 244 of the year). Current Year real estate taxes are $1,100 (will be billed to buyer next year). Use the 365-day method for prorating. What is Marianne's share of the real estate taxes?

a. $364.66.
b. $367.67.
c. $732.33.
d. $735.34.

9.10   Christie is buying John's house. The closing date (day belongs to seller) of the sale transaction is September 1 (day 244 of the year). Existing hazard insurance of $350 has been paid by John through December 31. Use the 365-day method for prorating. What is Christie's share of the existing hazard insurance already paid in full?

a. $116.03.
b. $117.99.
c. $232.01.
d. $233.97.

9.11   Julie is buying Florence's house. The closing date (day belongs to seller) of the sale transaction is September 1 (day 244 of the year). The buyer's loan amount is $78,750 (90%; 30 years @ 8%). The monthly payment on this loan is $577.84, with $525 going to interest in the first month. At closing, Julie must pre-pay interest for the period of Sept. 2-Sept. 30. Use the 365-day method for prorating. What is Julie's prepaid interest amount?

a. $507.50.
b. $525.00.
c. $543.10.
d. $558.58.

9.12   Melissa is buying Raymond's house. Melissa's loan amount is $88,750. She has agreed to pay 2 points at closing. How much will Melissa pay for points?

a. $157.50.
b. $177.50.
c. $1,775.00.
d. $887.50.

9.13 Tina is buying Terrell's house for $187,500. The broker's commission, to be paid by the seller, is 6%. How much will Terrell pay the broker?

  a. $31,250.
  b. $2,625.00.
  c. $4,725.
  d. $11,250.

9.14 A sale contract stipulates that a buyer is to pay the seller's transfer tax expenses. This practice is not customary in the area. In this case,

  a. the buyer and seller must amend the contract before closing.
  b. the contract is voidable, since the seller must pay the expense.
  c. the buyer may pay or not pay the expense, at his or her option.
  d. the buyer must pay the expense.

9.15 What a buyer has to pay at closing is equal to

  a. the excess of the buyer's debits over the buyer's credits.
  b. the excess of the buyer's credits over the buyer's debits.
  c. the excess of the seller's debits over the seller's credits.
  d. the excess of the seller's credits over the seller's debits.

9.16 The standard E & O policy covers damages resulting from

  a. failure to disclose an environmental condition.
  b. antitrust violations.
  c. mishandling of earnest money deposits.
  d. negligence, error or omission in carrying out professional services.

9.17 Which of the following is a common risk relating to the agency relationship?

  a. Failing to inform and disclose properly.
  b. Failing to take a personal interest in a transaction.
  c. Acting as an exclusive agent without an oral agency agreement.
  d. Forgetting to record the listing agreement.

9.18 Even after giving buyer and seller the required information about property condition disclosures, the licensee may still be subject to legal action for

  a. failing to detect customer misrepresentations.
  b. failing to disclose known adverse facts.
  c. relying on publicly available market information.
  d. advising the purchaser to exercise due diligence.

9.19 A licensee performing a comparative market analysis must be careful to

  a. use the term "market value" whenever possible in the report.
  b. show a low suggested selling price to avoid a complaint of misrepresenting the value.
  c. include the results of a certified appraisal in the analysis.
  d. avoid creating a false impression that the licensee is a certified appraiser.

9.20 One of the major risk areas in fulfilling a listing agreement is

  a. finding a buyer who turns out to be unqualified.
  b. exceeding the authority of the agreement.
  c. showing the property without the presence of the owner.
  d. cooperating with other licensees.

9.21 To reduce the risk of committing an error or omission in the contracting process, it is a good idea to

a. use a checklist of all items, contingencies, dates and responsibilities that must be met.
b. delegate some of your responsibilities to the licensee who represents the other party in the contract.
c. call the buyer and seller daily to check on progress.
d. cut the list of necessary tasks down to a few essentials and concentrate on tracking those.

9.22 Regarding contracts and forms,

a. once written and signed they cannot be changed except by a lawyer.
b. real estate licensees may alter forms but not contracts.
c. whoever originates them can make changes without the risk of unauthorized practice of law.
d. the principals may make changes as long as they sign or initial each change.

9.23 Fair housing laws are easily violated. An effective way for agents to minimize the risk of doing so is to

a. deal only with consumers who do not belong to a protected class.
b. obtain education in the content and intent of the laws.
c. make sure there is always a witness present at all meetings with consumers.
d. stay away from transactions involving public housing.

9.24 A licensee risks violating antitrust law by

a. being present at a conversation where the setting of commission rates is discussed.
b. being present at a discussion of antitrust laws.
c. charging a commission rate that happens to be the same as that charged by another firm.
d. cooperating with another firm to do market research.

9.25 How is an intentional misrepresentation penalized?

a. License discipline, fines, and possible incarceration.
b. License discipline and fines, but no incarceration.
c. License discipline only.
d. Fines only.

9.26 Of the following actions, the only one which avoids any risk of committing unintentional misrepresentation is

a. measuring and reporting property dimensions.
b. describing properties and amenities.
c. stating that a client should seek legal counsel.
d. making statements about the presence or absence of hazardous substances.

9.27 To reduce risks inherent in reporting transaction progress to a client, the licensee should

a. make reports orally only, never in writing.
b. leave progress reporting to the inspectors and other experts.
c. advise the client that it is company policy to make no progress reports until the contingency period is over.
d. avoid speculative statements in all reports

9.28 How does sharing the qualifying function with a lender protect a licensee?

a. It guarantees that a buyer will have a loan.
b. It reduces the chance of presenting an offer from an unqualified buyer.
c. It relieves the licensee of his or her due diligence responsibilities.
d. It allows the licensee to avoid asking embarrassing questions.

9.29 The area of agent activity where there is the greatest risk of failing to maintain client confidentiality is

a. trust fund handling.
b. office management.
c. the agency relationship.
d. the closing process.

9.30 The area of agent activity where there is the greatest risk of creating a false impression that the licensee is a certified appraiser is

a. performing a comparative market analysis.
b. writing property advertisements.
c. presenting written offers.
d. researching ownership documents

9.31 One of the major risk areas in advertising a listed property is that an advertisement will

a. describe the property in excessively glowing terms.
b. fail to appear at the same time in all available media.
c. omit any mention of the owner's main selling points.
d. make a substantial misrepresentation.

9.32 Property managers have a _____ relationship with the property owner.

a. non-binding
b. partnership
c. fiduciary
d. subagency

9.33 One of the property manager's fundamental responsibilities is

a. obtaining construction loans for the principal.
b. financial reporting to the principal.
c. finding a buyer for the property.
d. maintaining good standing in a managers' professional association.

9.34 Effective gross income is defined as

a. the total of scheduled rents.
b. the total of all rents and revenues generated by a property.
c. potential gross income minus debt service and reserves.
d. revenue from all sources minus losses from uncollected rents, vacancies, and evictions.

9.35 The efficiency of marketing activities can be measured in terms of

a. cost per tenant prospect generated per lease.
b. number of ads produced per marketing dollar.
c. dollars expended per square foot of vacant space.
d. percentage of reserves expended on marketing.

9.36 If a property's vacancy rate is significantly lower than market rates, it may be a sign that the manager needs to

a. lower rental rates.
b. raise rental rates.
c. find better tenants.
d. improve management quality.

9.37 What are the three kinds of maintenance a manager has to carry out for a managed property?

    a. Constructive, deconstructive, and reconstructive
    b. Routine, preventive, and corrective
    c. Scheduled, planned, and improvised
    d. Emergency, elective, and optional

9.38 The Americans with Disabilities Act requires property managers to

    a. ensure that disabled employees have the same level of access to facilities that all employees have.
    b. hire the disabled whenever possible.
    c. remove all existing barriers to the free movement of disabled persons within the property, regardless of the cost.
    d. remodel the ground floor of the property in accordance with ADA standards if it was built before 1978.

9.39 Commercial fire and hazard insurance policies usually require coverage to equal at least 80 percent of the property's

    a. replacement value.
    b. reproduction value.
    c. original cost.
    d. depreciated basis.

9.40 Trust funds to be handled by a property manager are likely to include all of the following except

    a. rents collected from tenants.
    b. cash for the management firm's operating expenses.
    c. security deposits.
    d. capital contributions from the property owner.

9.41 What kind of agency is commonly created by a management agreement?

    a. Universal
    b. Specific
    c. General
    d. Vicarious

9.42 Which of the following describes a gross lease?

    a. The tenant pays a base rent plus some or all of the operating expenses.
    b. The tenant pays a fixed rent, and the landlord pays all operating expenses.
    c. The tenant pays a base rent plus an amount based on income generated in the leased space.
    d. The tenant pays a rent that increases at specified times over the lease term.

9.43 If an apartment contains a refrigerator that is not included in the lease,

    a. the lessee is required to buy it from the landlord.
    b. the landlord is required to remove it.
    c. the lease is invalidated because of an incomplete property description.
    d. the property manager does not have to maintain it.

9.44 A basic responsibility of a landlord is to

    a. provide leased space at market rental rates.
    b. deliver a habitable property.
    c. keep the rental space freshly painted.
    d. refrain from entering the leased space at any time during the lease term.

9.45   How does a constructive eviction occur?

   a. A landlord obtains a court order to force the tenant to vacate the leased premises.
   b. A court officer forcibly removes the tenant from the premises.
   c. A tenant declares a landlord in default and vacates the leased premises.
   d. A landlord declares a tenant in default and takes possession of the leased premises.

9.46   Among the essential elements of a management plan is consideration of

   a. the competitive market for the property.
   b. the property manager's career goals.
   c. the property owner's net worth.
   d. the management firm's income goals.

10.1   A licensee sells 5/6 of an acre for $28,000, and receives a 6% commission. If she splits with her broker 50-50, what did she receive per square foot?

   a. $.023 / SF
   b. $.046 / SF
   c. $.037/ SF
   d. $.002 / SF

10.2   Lots in the South Hyde subdivision are selling for approximately $.50 / SF. The Grandersons want to build a 2,500 SF home on a 1.5 acre corner lot. The custom builder can build the home for $135 / SF. What will the completed property cost the Grandersons?

   a. $359,170
   b. $370,170
   c. $32,670
   d. $374,070

10.3   Ivan owned a 1/4 acre lot. He wanted to construct a 120' x 80' tennis court on the lot. What approximate percentage of the lot will be left over, if any, when he has completed the construction?

   a. 12%
   b. 88%
   c. 3%
   d. 15%

10.4   A developer wants to develop a 16-acre subdivision. He figures that the streets and common area will take up about 30% of this overall area. If the minimum lot size is to be 12,000 SF, how many lots can the developer have on this property?

   a. 42
   b. 487
   c. 40
   d. 57

10.5   A homeowner wants to insulate the new recreation room in her basement. She has been told that 3" of insulation would do the job. The walls are all 9' high and respectively measure 13', 13', 18', and 18' in length. How many rolls will she need if each roll measures 3" x 2' x 50'?

   a. 6
   b. 56
   c. 5
   d. 9

10.6   Maria plans to mulch the flower area around her house. The house measures 40' x 30', and she figures she'll mulch an area 8' in width to form a big rectangle all around the perimeter. What is the square footage of the resulting mulched area?

   a. 64 SF
   b. 2,576 SF
   c. 1,824 SF
   d. 1,376 SF

10.7. Calculate how many acres are in the Southeastern ¼ of the Western ½ of the Eastern ½ of Section 9.

    a. 20 acres
    b. 40 acres
    c. 60 acres
    d. 5 acres

10.8. Homeowner Savannah owns the Southeastern ¼ of the Southwestern ¼ of the Northwestern ¼ of Section 4. How many acres is that property?

    a. 4 acres
    b. 40 acres
    c. 10 acres
    d. 8 acres

10.9 Yard of Pizza has a percentage lease on its 1,800 SF space in Lincoln Shops. The terms are $1.40 / SF / month rent plus 1.75% of the store's gross income. If monthly sales averaged $41,500 last year, how much annual rent did Yard of Pizza pay last year?

    a. $38,955
    b. $43,420
    c. $30,240
    d. $21,525

10.10 A home appreciated 2 2/3% one year, then 5 1/5% the next year, then 7 1/4% the third year. What was the average appreciation over the 3-year period expressed as a decimal?

    a. 5.04%
    b. 15.24%
    c. 7.56%
    d. 4.8%

10.11 A homeowner paid $185,000 for a house three years ago. The house sells today for $239,000. How much has the property appreciated?

    a. 23 %
    b. 77 %
    c. 29 %
    d. 123 %

10.12 Seller Frank receives an offer of $290,000 on a property he listed at $308,000. How much is the offer as a percent of the listing price?

    a. 87%
    b. 91%
    c. 94%
    d. 106%

10.13 A property is being appraised using the income capitalization approach. Annually, it has potential gross income of $30,000, vacancy and credit losses of $1,500, and operating expenses of $10,000. Using a capitalization rate of 9%, what is the indicated value (to the nearest $1,000)?

    a. $206,000
    b. $167,000
    c. $222,000
    d. $180,000

10.14 If gross income on a property is $75,000, net income is $30,000 and the cap rate is 8%, the value of the property using the income capitalization method is

a. $625,000
b. $375,000
c. $3,750,000
d. $937,500

10.15 The roof of a property cost $16,000. The economic life of the roof is 20 years. Assuming the straight-line method of depreciation, what is the depreciated value of the roof after 3 years?

a. $16,000
b. $13,600
c. $18,400
d. $12,000

10.16 Lee had to report his home office depreciation for the tax year. He has a 2,500 SF home and a 500 SF office area. Lee paid $280,000 for his home, and he figures the land portion carries about 25% of that value. If Lee depreciates on a 39-year basis, how much can he write off for his home office depreciation per year?

a. $1,077
b. $1,436
c. $5,384
d. $2,108

10.17 A property is being appraised by the cost approach. The appraiser estimates that the land is worth $40,000 and the replacement cost of the improvements is $175,000. Total depreciation from all causes is $27,000. What is the indicated value of the property?

a. $148,000
b. $228,000
c. $162,000
d. $188,000

10.18 An apartment owner paid $500,000 for her complex 5 years ago. An appraiser at that time valued the land @ $100,000, but land has appreciated 25% over this period. The investor has used a 40-year straight-line depreciation method to depreciate the property. What is its current value using the cost approach?

a. $437,500
b. $462,500
c. $475,000
d. $546,875

10.19 An apartment building that recently sold for $400,000 had monthly gross rent receipts of $3,200. What is its monthly gross rent multiplier?

a. 80
b. .01
c. 110
d. 125

10.20 A rental home has monthly gross income of $1,100. A suitable gross income multiplier derived from market data is 14.7. What estimated sale price (to the nearest $1,000) is indicated?

a. $99,000
b. $162,000
c. $194,000
d. $173,000

10.21 Amy obtains a 75% LTV loan on her new $200,000 home with an annual interest rate of 6%. What is the first month's interest payment?

a. $900
b. $250
c. $1,000
d. $750

10.22 Emily has an interest-only home equity loan at an annual interest rate of 5.3%. If her monthly payment is $790, how much is the loan's principal balance (to the nearest $1,000)?

a. $222,000
b. $179,000
c. $95,000
d. $146,000

10.23 The loan officer at Sixth Fourth Bank tells Amanda she can afford a monthly payment of $1,000 on her new home loan. Assuming this is an interest-only loan, and the principal balance is $249,000, what interest rate is Amanda getting?

a. 4.82%
b. 5.03%
c. 6.25%
d. 3.69%

10.24 The Keegans obtain a fixed-rate amortized 30-year loan for $280,000 @ 6.25% interest. If the monthly payments are $1,724, how much interest do the Keegans pay in the second month of the loan?

a. $1,748.33
b. $1,456.95
c. $1,458.33
d. $1724.00

10.25 A lender offers the Greys two alternative loan packages for their $60,000 home equity application. One option is an interest-only loan for 5 years @ 6.5% interest with no points, and the second, a 6.25% interest-only loan for 5 years with 1 point to be paid at closing. Which loan will cost the Greys less total interest, and by how much?

a. The first option, by $150.
b. The second option, by 150.
c. The second option, by $750.
d. Both options charge the same amount of interest.

10.26 Jose recently obtained a 90% loan on his $410,000 home, and he had to pay $6,150 for points. How many points did he pay?

a. 1.4 points
b. 1.67 points
c. 2.48 points
d. 1.5 points

10.27 Mack is buying Roy's house for $500,000. Mack's loan amount is $325,000. He has agreed to pay 1.5 points at closing. How much will Mack pay for points?

a. $450
b. $4,500
c. $4,875
d. $7,500

10.28 A lender determines that a homebuyer can afford to borrow $130,000 on a mortgage loan. The lender requires an 80% loan-to-value ratio. How much can the borrower pay for a property and still qualify for this loan amount?

a. $138,000
b. $104,000
c. $162,500
d. $170,000

10.29 Home buyer Janet pays $1,600 / month for the interest-only loan on her new house. The loan's interest rate is 6.75%. If she obtained a 75% loan, what was the purchase price?

a. $313,333
b. $31,604
c. $379,259
d. $256,000

10.30 Loan applicant Taylor has an annual gross income of $76,000. How much will a lender allow Taylor to pay for monthly housing expense to qualify for a loan if the lender uses an income ratio of 30%?

a. $2,160
b. $1,900
c. $1,215
d. $4,433

10.31 An investor paid $80,000 for a lot and $600,000 to have an apartment building constructed on it. He has depreciated the property for the past 10 years on a 39-year straight-line schedule. If he sells the property this year and realizes $780,000, what is his capital gain?

a. $253,846
b. $274,000
c. $100,000
d. $179,000

10.32. A homeowner bought a house five years ago for $250,000. Since then, the homeowner has spent $2,000 to build a screened porch and has added a central air-conditioning system at a cost of $5,000. What is the homeowner's adjusted basis if the house is sold today?

a. $256,000
b. $257,000
c. $244,000
d. $245,000

10.33 A homeowner sold her house and had net proceeds of $265,000. Her adjusted basis in the home was $231,000. She immediately bought another house for $301,000. What was her capital gain?

a. $265,000
b. $36,000
c. $34,000
d. None

10.34 Debra bought a home for $120,000, paying $24,000 down and taking a mortgage loan of $96,000. The following year she had a new roof put on, at a cost of $5,000. What is Debra's adjusted basis in the house if she now sells the house for $150,000?

a. $29,000
b. $96,000
c. $101,000
d. $125,000

10.35 A certain investor wants an 11% return on investment from any real estate investment. A property priced at $360,000 has gross income of $60,000 and expenses of $22,000. Approximately how much too high or too low is the price of this property for the investor to obtain her desired return exactly?

a. $1,000 overpriced.
b. $8,000 underpriced.
c. $15,000 overpriced.
d. $16,000 underpriced.

10.36 An office building investor sees a listing of an office building which is priced at $2 million. He loves the property, but he knows he needs to make a return of at least 8% to satisfy his partners. If the building is 25,000 SF, rents for $10/SF per year, has 5% vacancy, and annual expenses of $70,000, should he buy it? What is his return?

a. No, since he will yield 2.00%.
b. Yes, since he will yield 8.375%.
c. Yes, since he will yield 8%.
d. Yes, since he will yield 9.125%.

10.37 Chad owns a small retail property that he inherited from his father. There are no mortgages or interest expenses connected with the property. Chad takes an annual cost recovery expense of $7,000. The property has a monthly gross income of $1,650 and monthly operating expenses of $600. Chad's taxable income from this property will be taxed at a rate of 30%. What is the tax liability for the year?

a. $1,680
b. $5,940
c. $2,100
d. $7,000

10.38 A property has a net income of $150,000, interest payments of $105,000, principal payments of $30,000, and annual cost recovery of $7,000. The property's tax rate is 28%. What is the property's annual tax on income?

a. $14,550
b. $40,040
c. $10,640
d. $2,240

10.39 An investor bought 4 oversized lots in order to subdivide. He paid $70,000 for the lots. After subdividing, the investor was able to sell each lot for $23,000. Excluding commissions and closing costs, what per cent profit did the investor realize?

a. 0%
b. 45%
c. 23.9%
d. 31.4%

10.40 A school district's tax rate is 10 mills. The school district's required revenue from taxes is $10,000,000. What is the tax base of the area?

a. $10,000,000
b. $100,000,000
c. $1,000,000,000
d. $100,000,000,000

10.41 A homeowner's residence has an assessed valuation of $140,000, and a market value of $170,000. The homestead exemption is $25,000. Tax rates for the property are 7 mills for schools; 3 mills for the city; 2 mills for the county; and 1 mill for the local community college. What is the homeowner's tax bill?

a. $1,495
b. $1,820
c. $1,150
d. $2,210

10.42 The village of Goodsprings has an annual budget requirement of $8,000,000 to be funded by property taxes. Assessed valuations are $400,000,000, and exemptions total $25,000,000. What must the tax rate be to finance the budget?

a. 2.00%
b. 2.13%
c. 1.32%
d. 21.33%

10.43 A property has sold for $127,000. The listing agreement calls for a commission of 7%. The listing broker and selling broker agree to share the commission equally. What will the listing agent receive if the agent is scheduled to get a 40% share from his broker?

a. $4,445
b. $3,556
c. $2,667
d. $1,778

10.44 Kevin, who works for selling broker Paul, sells a house listed by listing broker Adams. The house sells for $325,000. The co-brokerage split between Paul and Adams is 50-50. Kevin is on a 65% commission schedule with Paul. If the total commission rate is 6.5%, what is Kevin's commission?

a. $6,866
b. $5,282
c. $10,563
d. $13,731

10.45. A sale transaction closes on April 1, the ninety-first day of the tax year. The day of closing belongs to the seller. Real estate taxes for the year, not yet billed, are expected to be $3,150. According to the 365-day method, what should appear on the closing statement?

a. A debit to the buyer and credit to the seller for $2,364.62
b. A debit to the buyer and credit to the seller for $785.34
c. A credit to the buyer and debit to the seller for $785.34
d. A credit to the buyer and debit to the seller for $2,364.62

10.46 Alexis is buying Jack's house. The closing date (day belongs to seller) of the sale transaction is September 1 (day 244 of the year). Her loan has a monthly payment of $577.84, with $525 going to interest in the first month. At closing, Alexis must pre-pay interest for the period of Sept. 2-Sept. 30. Use the 365-day method for prorating. What is her prepaid interest amount?

a. $507.50
b. $525.00
c. $543.10
d. $558.58

10.47 A sale transaction on rental property closes on December 16. The landlord received the December rent of $1,380 on December 1. Assuming the closing day is the buyer's, and that the 365-day method is used for prorating, which of the following entries would appear on the settlement statement?

a. Debit seller $667.74.
b. Credit seller $1,380.00.
c. Debit buyer $712.26.
d. Credit buyer $712.26.

10.48 A home sells for $322,600 in Primm County. Here, transfer taxes are set at $1.00 per $500 of the sale price. Title insurance runs $450, and the attorney costs $550. The agent's commission is 7%, and the mortgage balance is $210,000. Annual real estate taxes are estimated to be $4,000, half of which will have to be charged to the seller. If the seller pays all of these expenses, what will she net at closing?

a. $86,873
b. $88,371
c. $81,372
d. $86,372

10.49 A farmer wants to net at least $5,000/acre on the sale of his 300-acre property. If he allows for 10% commissions and closing costs, and to allow for negotiating room, he wants to get 95% of the listing price as the selling price, what should his listing price be per acre?

a. $5,750
b. $5,882
c. $4,250
d. $5,848

10.50. The Wildes have purchased a $740,000 home. The land is worth 25%, and they insure the improvements @ 75% of their replacement value. If the Wildes suffer damage estimated at $500,000, and they have an 80% co-insurance clause, what will their recovery be from the policy?

a. Zero
b. $531,915
c. $500,000
d. $468,750

10.51 The Uptons carry a $140,000 property insurance policy which covers 75% of the replacement cost of their insurable property, valued at $190,000. They have an 80% co-insurance requirement in the policy. If the family incurs a $150,000 loss, what if any amount will the Uptons recover?

a. $159,999
b. $140,625
c. $140,000
d. $187,500

Section V: Arizona Specific Practice Tests

Test 11: Arizona Law; Arizona Licensing Laws; Easements; Encumbrances; Ownership; Conveyances

11.1   Article 26 of the Arizona State Constitution authorizes licensed real estate salespeople and brokers to

   a. practice law without a law license.
   b. prepare any and all documents incidental to a real estate transaction.
   c. draft legal contracts and legal documents on a freelance basis.
   d. write contracts for personal property sales.

11.2   Law based on customs and traditions is

   a. statutory law.
   b. administrative law.
   c. common law.
   d. civil law.

11.3   The Arizona Real Estate Commissioner

   a. is elected every four years and can serve two terms.
   b. is appointed by the state congress.
   c. is hired as a state employee.
   d. is appointed by the governor.

11.4   The real estate advisory board is made up of how many members?

   a. 6
   b. 8
   c. 9
   d. 12

11.5   Which of the following may engage in real estate activities but is exempt from holding a real estate license?

   a. A cemetery salesperson
   b. A person selling or renting her or his own property
   c. A timeshare salesperson
   d. A membership camping salesperson

11.6   To successfully apply for an Arizona real estate license, a candidate must be

   a. 18 years of age and meet no state residency requirement.
   b. 18 years of age and a resident of Arizona for three of the last five years.
   c. 21 years of age and meet no residency requirement.
   d. 21 years of age and a current resident of Arizona.

11.7 The requirements for applying for a broker's state real estate license are the same as those for salesperson applicants, except that candidates must

    a. be at least 21 years of age as the result of needing at least three years of experience as a real estate salesperson.
    b. have three years of full time real estate experience in the past five years.
    c. live in the state at time of application.
    d. pay Arizona income tax and have a valid Arizona driver's license.

11.8 Which is a required real estate course for continuing education that an active licensee must complete every two years?

    a. Buyer Due Diligence
    b. Fair Housing
    c. Legal Land Description
    d. Real Estate Marketing

11.9 When a salesperson is employed by a brokerage and has an active license, where is her or his official copy of the license?

    a. With ADRE in Phoenix
    b. In the licensee's possession
    c. With the employing broker's designated broker
    d. There is no physical license.

11.10 Two temporary real estate licenses are allowed in Arizona. They are the temporary broker's license and the

    a. temporary timeshare salesperson license.
    b. provisional salesperson license.
    c. part-time property manager certificate.
    d. temporary cemetery salesperson license.

11.11 Statutory law allows real estate brokers and salespersons to perform broker price opinions as long as they

    a. do not call it an appraisal.
    b. have studied appraisal in the 90-hour salesperson pre-licensing course.
    c. are accompanied to the property by a licensed appraiser.
    d. have at least six hours of credit toward an appraiser's license.

11.12 An aggrieved member of the public may seek damages against a licensee via the Arizona Real Estate Recovery Fund only after

    a. proving damages.
    b. adjudication of the lawsuit.
    c. *lis pendens*.
    d. ADRE administrative hearings.

11.13 An easement which benefits corporations and individuals as opposed to "the land" is

    a. appurtenant.
    b. illegal by state statute.
    c. an easement in gross.
    d. never found in Arizona.

11.14 In Arizona, married couples who do not specify how they wish to hold title to property default to which of the following?

   a. Community property
   b. Community property with right of survivorship
   c. Joint tenancy
   d. Tenancy in severalty

11.15 Arizona is a

   a. dower and curtsey state.
   b. tenancy in the entireties state.
   c. community property state.
   d. Mexican land grant state.

11.16 In Arizona, a manufactured home on a rental pad

   a. may be sold as real property as long as it hasn't been moved after original transportation to a site.
   b. may be sold like any other real property with the aid of salesperson with a valid license.
   c. is personal property.
   d. is real property just like any other home.

11.17 Cooperatives are

   a. freehold estates.
   b. leasehold estates.
   c. special forms of condominiums.
   d. the same as communes.

11.18 The Arizona Code of Real Estate is

   a. a voluntary guide to professional behavior.
   b. statutory law.
   c. administrative law.
   d. a code developed and implemented by the Arizona Association of Realtors®.

11.19 Arizona licensee Frank uses his knowledge of real estate to write contracts and other contractual documents for his friends who are selling their homes without a brokerage for a small flat fee. He is violating

   a. A.R.S. Title 32, Chapter 20.
   b. Arizona administrative law.
   c. Article 26 of the state constitution.
   d. no Arizona case laws.

11.20 Arizona's legislature enacted which of the following methods of holding interests in real property in 1994-95?

   a. Community property
   b. Tenancy in common
   c. Community property with right of survivorship
   d. Joint tenancy with grand incident right

11.21 Which of the following entails stock ownership?

   a. Timeshares
   b. Cooperatives
   c. Manufactured homes
   d. Condominiums

11.22 An action considered a type of easement which allows the right to remove soil, minerals, fruit, timber or other land product with compensation to the land owner is called

a. adverse possession.
b. emblements.
c. profit *a prende.*
d. *fructus industrialis.*

11.23 An action taken by ADRE to immediately stop a licensee's activities which endanger the public health, safety and welfare is called a

a. summary suspension.
b. consent order.
c. letter of concern.
d. surrender of license.

11.24 Which state office is charged with protecting the public from consumer fraud as well as anti-competitive behavior?

a. The Arizona Corporation Commission
b. The Arizona Fair Trade Commission
c. The Office of the Arizona Attorney General
d. The Arizona Office of Consumer Affairs

11.25 What prevents Arizona real estate licensees from functioning as transactional brokerage?

a. ADRE
b. Article 26 of the State Constitution
c. Agency law
d. AAR

11.26 Arizona salespeople who fail to renew their licenses on time are

a. suspended.
b. revoked.
c. given a 30-day grace period to complete renewal.
d. required to take an additional six hours of continuing education courses.

11.27 In Arizona, which of the following appraisers require the greatest number of classroom hours and hours of supervised experience for licensure?

a. The certified general appraiser
b. The certified residential appraiser
c. The licensed residential appraiser
d. The Arizona master appraiser

11.28 A delay in homeowners taking action against violations of homeowner usage rules is called

a. CC&Rs.
b. laches.
c. deed restrictions.
d. specific performance.

11.29 Which of the following is a voluntary, specific lien?

a. An IRS lien
b. A mortgage lien
c. A mechanic's lien
d. A property tax lien

11.30 If the state of Arizona takes real property through escheat, how long must the state search for legitimate heirs of the decedent?

    a. No search is required.
    b. 1 year
    c. 7 years
    d. There is no time limit.

11.31 As forms of encumbrance, light, smells, and noise are

    a. common forms of nuisances.
    b. not significant enough to be actionable.
    c. examples of sensory trespass.
    d. intangible unlawful entry.

11.32 In Arizona, a contract for the purchase of real property signed by a minor is

    a. allowable only if the minor is not emancipated.
    b. automatically void unless the minor is emancipated.
    c. acceptable if the minor is of sound mind.
    d. valid if the minor signs with a fictitious name.

11.33 The most common deed used for voluntary transfer of title to real property as the result of a sale in Arizona is

    a. a warranty deed.
    b. a sheriff's deed.
    c. a trustee's deed.
    d. a tax deed.

11.34 Which of the following is a bargain and sale deed used in involuntary alienation?

    a. A warranty deed
    b. A quit claim deed
    c. A treasurer's deed
    d. A correction deed

11.35 A person receiving a property in a real estate transaction is called the

    a. grantor.
    b. grantee.
    c. lienor.
    d. optionee.

11.36 The wording in Arizona warranty deeds reads, "For the amount of $10 or more…" The $10 referred to is called

    a. down payment.
    b. earnest money.
    c. nominal consideration.
    d. a lien.

11.37 The deed that may be executed so that one spouse in a marriage may hold title separately from her or his spouse is called a(n)

    a. special warranty deed.
    b. sheriff's deed.
    c. unrecorded deed.
    d. disclaimer deed.

11.38 Which of the following is a monetary encumbrance?

   a. Trespass
   b. CC&Rs
   c. A lien
   d. Deed restrictions

11.39 In construction terminology, a stand-alone garage is called

   a. an attached garage.
   b. a semi-attached garage.
   c. a detached garage.
   d. a tandem garage.

11.40 Which of the following is an example of "good" consideration in real estate contracts?

   a. A gift
   b. Earnest money
   c. A down payment
   d. Nominal consideration

11.41 The promise that a grantor will defend a grantee's deed against all claims made by third parties is the covenant

   a. of further assurance.
   b. of quiet enjoyment.
   c. against encumbrances.
   d. of seisen.

11.42 The federal internal revenue service bases its tax policies regarding timeshares on the idea that

   a. they are pre-paid vacations in real estate.
   b. they are not deeded, so deductions on loan interest are not allowed.
   c. all expenses related to owning a timeshare are deductible.
   d. income made by timeshare sales associates is not taxable.

11.43 The authorization of government agencies to enact rules and regulations along with the power to enforce them is

   a. Constitutional law.
   b. statutory law.
   c. civil law.
   d. administrative law.

Test 12: Land; Environmental Law; Disclosure & Consumer Protection; Regulated Activity and Relationships

12.1   Material which is ignitable, corrosive, reactive or toxic is called

a. sludge.
b. contamination.
c. hazardous waste.
d. effluent.

12.2   A material placed by humans for use in construction and insulation which might be a potentially hazardous substance in a dwelling is

a. radon.
b. asbestos.
c. mold.
d. copper.

12.3   In Arizona, all legal land descriptions determined by a government rectangular survey end with

a. G&SRBM.
b. a section number.
c. a township designation.
d. the smallest portion of a quarter of a section.

12.4   The legal land description used most often to identify parcels in subdivisions is

a. metes and bounds.
b. government rectangular survey.
c. lot, block, and tract.
d. monuments and markers.

12.5   How many baselines and meridians divide Arizona?

a. 1
b. 2
c. 4
d. 5

12.6   In construction, headers above doors and windows are called

a. beams.
b. joists.
c. studs.
d. sills.

12.7   Which of the following is not required information in an ADRE subdivided land questionnaire?

a. True condition of title
b. Location of the nearest public schools
c. Utilities
d. Size of houses to be built

12.8   Subdivision law is also considered

   a. common law.
   b. case law.
   c. disclosure law.
   d. family law.

12.9   Which of the following is true regarding a subdivision purchaser's right of rescission?

   a. There is no right of rescission except in special circumstances.
   b. There is no right of rescission, but there is a right of redemption.
   c. Purchasers have seven days after signing the contract; six months if the buyers haven't seen the property; and up to three years if promised access is not delivered.
   d. Purchasers can rescind any time prior to close of escrow.

12.10 Unsubdivided land consists of parcels

   a. 36 acres or less.
   b. more than 36 acres but less than 160.
   c. more than 160 acres.
   d. which cannot be subdivided.

12.11 Arizona isn't considered a mandatory disclosure state, but which of the following is, in fact, mandatory disclosure?

   a. When the same licensee or brokerage is representing both the buyer and seller in a transaction
   b. The presence of sex offenders in a neighborhood
   c. A home's reputation for being haunted
   d. Excessive incoming water pressure in a neighborhood

12.12 Part of buyer due diligence is the responsibility to make a physical inspection of a property which is known as

   a. a home inspection.
   b. an appraisal.
   c. actual notice.
   d. constructive notice.

12.13 Which of the following is true regarding subdivision disclosure laws?

   a. They are examples of consumer protection laws.
   b. They are unnecessarily rigid.
   c. They are federal rather than state laws.
   d. They apply only to parcels larger than 160 acres.

12.14 The major concern with illegally growing marijuana in Arizona residential homes is

   a. marijuana growers have too many pot parties which create nuisances.
   b. marijuana growing is equally destructive to a structure as a meth lab.
   c. selling marijuana out of a home is operating a business out of a home which is prohibited by many HOAs and municipal codes.
   d. excessive watering of plants can cause mold, and growers often reroute water and electricity to growing areas in violation of building codes and structural safety.

12.15 The purpose of a Phase I environmental study in Arizona is to

   a. determine if a Phase II study is needed.
   b. use ground-penetrating radar to detect underground storage tanks.
   c. fully test soil, air, and water for contaminants.
   d. test for radon, asbestos, and mold.

12.16 Which of the following regulatory entities inspects and verifies the subdivision application?

   a. ADRE
   b. ADEQ
   c. The State Attorney General's Office
   d. The Arizona Corporation Commission

12.17 An Arizona agency disclosure and election form

   a. hires a brokerage to represent a principal in the purchase or sale of real property.
   b. creates legal agency.
   c. disavows agency requirements.
   d. discloses how a client will be represented by a brokerage.

12.18 Which of the following is not a program area of the Arizona Department of Environmental Quality?

   a. Water quality
   b. Air Quality
   c. Waste
   d. Wetlands

12.19 While finder's fees are generally prohibited by law in Arizona, referral fees are allowed because

   a. they are broker-to-broker payments.
   b. the law allows licensed salespeople to share commissions with unlicensed people.
   c. once a licensee earns a commission, he or she can do anything he or she wants with it.
   d. it is allowed by administrative law.

12.20 According to Arizona water laws, the state's interior watersheds, defined as non-Colorado River water, are governed by

   a. the riparian doctrine.
   b. the doctrine of prior appropriation
   c. the Arizona Department of Water Quality.
   d. the state legislature.

12.21 When groundwater is pumped out in greater quantities than is replaced by nature, the result is called

   a. overdraft.
   b. subsistence.
   c. allocation.
   d. withdrawal.

12.22 Which of the following is a navigable waterway in Arizona?

   a. The Salt River
   b. The Verde River
   c. The Colorado River
   d. The Gila River

12.23 Permission to pump water for non-irrigation uses in AMAs is obtained via

   a. withdrawal permits.
   b. service area rights.
   c. the ADWQ.
   d. lawsuits by property owners.

12.24 In Arizona, water rights are

    a. first in time, first in use.
    b. determined by property owners who own the water.
    c. federal.
    d. authorized by the U.S. Army Corps of Engineers.

12.25 Within a brokerage, who is charged with the responsibility for supervising all licensee advertising?

    a. The employing broker
    b. The designated broker
    c. The office manager
    d. The advertising manager

12.26 According to Arizona administrative law, the term "acre" can only be used when referring to

    a. vacant land.
    b. an area of land representing 43,560 square feet.
    c. farm and ranch land.
    d. water volume.

12.27 In Arizona, the employing broker's name must be clear and prominent in all advertising except

    a. There is no exception.
    b. small classified ads consisting of all type and no photos.
    c. billboard and banner advertising.
    d. car and yard signs.

12.28 Which of the following will address civil complaints or mediate disputes regarding earnings, splitting, or non-payment of licensee compensation?

    a. The Arizona Department of Real Estate
    b. The Arizona Corporation Commission
    c. The Arizona State Attorney General's office
    d. The Arizona Association of Realtors®

12.29 ADRE requires all official files to be maintained

    a. in a locked drawer or file cabinet of the individual salesperson.
    b. off-site in a facility separate from the main brokerage office.
    c. at the ADRE storage facility in Phoenix.
    d. in the main brokerage office.

12.30 Which of the following is not required by Arizona agency regarding statutory requirements for fiduciary duty?

    a. Confidentiality
    b. Courtesy
    c. Reasonable care and due diligence
    d. Obedience

12.31 How much brokerage money can be kept in a broker trust account?

    a. $250
    b. $1,500
    c. $3,000
    d. An unlimited amount

12.32 An example of stigmatized property is

    a. one in which the survey boundaries are in doubt.
    b. where an overpriced property for sale lingers on the market for years and years.
    c. a property reputed to be haunted.
    d. a property with significant environmental damage.

12.33 Which of the following state agencies should a homeowner consider to complain about the actions of an HOA?

    a. HUD
    b. ADRE
    c. The Arizona Corporation Commission
    d. CERCLA

12.34 Which of the following documents is used to hire a brokerage to enter into an agency relationship with a principal?

    a. A listing agreement
    b. A purchase agreement
    c. An agency disclosure and election form
    d. An ADRE agency application

12.35 Agency, in real estate brokerage practice, is primarily regulated by

    a. codes of ethics.
    b. voluntary compliance.
    c. brokerage enforcement.
    d. law.

12.36 With regard to advertising, which of the following is not included in the state rules?

    a. Brokerage versus licensee telephone numbers in ads
    b. Clear and prominent brokerage identification in all advertising
    c. The definition of an acre
    d. Including the designated broker's name in all advertising

12.37 Upon the death of designated broker Vince, his daughter Sandra wants to take over Vince's clients. To do so, she must

    a. inform ADRE of her intent to take over the clients.
    b. renegotiate all the listings on behalf of the brokerage.
    c. hope Vine willed all the listings to her in his will.
    d. wait for a probate court to assign Vince's assets.

13.1   A promissory note is

    a. a security instrument in a financed loan. ✔
    b. evidence of debt, promise to repay, and terms of repayment.
    c. evidence of transfer of title.
    d. the same as a mortgage.

13.2   What is the length of the statutory redemption period in a deed of trust loan in Arizona?

    a. There is no redemption period but a reinstatement period instead.
    b. 6 months
    c. 270 days
    d. 1 year

13..3   A judicial foreclosure proceeding is

    a. a mortgage foreclosure.
    b. a deed of trust foreclosure.
    c. a vendor/vendee forfeiture.
    d. a reserve bid.

13.4   In Arizona, property tax payers who owe less than $100

    a. are exempt from paying such a small amount.
    b. are allowed to let their taxes accumulate and then pay every three years.
    c. must pay in full on October 1 of each year.
    d. are required to pay a minimum of $250 regardless.

13.5   The purpose of the Arizona Residential Landlord and Tenant Act (ARLTA) is to

    a. protect tenants.
    b. protect landlords.
    c. protect landlords and tenants.
    d. protect rental investors.

13.6   Which of the following is exempt from the ARLTA?

    a. Industrial and commercial rentals
    b. Residential rental complexes of more than 12 units
    c. Residential rentals of one year of less
    d. Rental homes

13.7   A distraint clause

    a. is a residential lease provision that allows landlords to lock out residential tenants.
    b. allows commercial tenants to be locked out of their units and their property confiscated in case of default.
    c. speeds up rent payments to the end of a residential lease in case of default.
    d. is a commercial lease provision that allows tenants to withhold rent in case of disagreements with their landlords

13.8 According to the ARLTA, security deposits may not be equivalent to what portion of the periodic monthly rent amount?

a. 100%
b. 150%
c. 200%
d. There is no limit.

13.9 A valid lease must be signed by

a. both the landlord and property owner.
b. the lessee only.
c. the lessor only.
d. the lessee and lessor.

13.10 Which of the following is not conveyed in a business opportunity sale?

a. Training and non-compete agreements
b. Inventory
c. "Blue sky"
d. The building housing the business

13.11 A business in a commercial transaction transfers with a

a. deed.
b. bill of sale.
c. title binder.
d. defeasance clause.

13.12 The Uniform Commercial Code and bulk sales laws

a. deal primarily with personal property conveyed in commercial or business opportunity sales.
b. regulate commercial and industrial leasing.
c. are related to timeshare sales.
d. are vital to subdivision sales.

13.13 According to the ARLTA, rental dwellings may not be used

a. to operate a home-based business.
b. for anything unlawful.
c. to house special needs residents.
d. for more than one family.

13.14 A letter of intent is most often found in what type of real estate transaction?

a. A residential lease
b. Timeshare sales
c. Cemetery plot sales
d. A commercial or business opportunity sale

13.15 Which of the following is an optional clause in a property management agreement?

a. a mutually agreeable cancellation policy
b. automatic renewal provisions
c. agreement start and end date
d. amount of management company compensation

13.16 A multiple listing service (MLS) is

    a. developed and implemented by every state brokerage independently.
    b. a statewide listing of residential properties for sale or lease.
    c. a computerized listing of local or regional real estate inventory for sale or lease.
    d. a nationwide collection of real estate inventory.

13.17 When a real estate designated broker sets a rigid policy for commission ranges, the broker is

    a. in violation of the federal Sherman Anti-Trust Act.
    b. in violation of Arizona state anti-trust laws.
    c. in violation of both state and federal anti-trust laws.
    d. not in violation of anti-trust laws.

13.18 With regard to partial rent payments made by a tenant to a landlord, the ARLTA specifies

    a. landlords are required to take partial payments until 10 days after the due date of rent.
    b. landlords do not have to accept partial payments.
    c. landlords do not have to accept partial payments less than 50% of the amount of total monthly rent.
    d. landlords must accept all partial payments by law.

13.19 If a landlord fails to comply with a term of a lease which may impact tenant health and safety, the tenant may

    a. withhold rent until the problem is resolved.
    b. deliver notice of the failure and intent to terminate the lease within 5 days of the event.
    c. immediately terminate the lease even if the tenant or tenant guest caused the problem.
    d. fine the landlord three times the daily rent amount for every day the problem is not resolved.

13.20 In counting days to be credited to parties in a real estate transaction in proration, the day of closing for a buyer and first day of rent for a renter is credited to the

    a. vender and vendee.
    b. seller or landlord.
    c. buyer or tenant.
    d. lender.

Section VI: Arizona License Examination Sample Test

Arizona Practice Exam

S 1. A farmer temporarily installs produce coolers in a leased farm stand in order to prevent spoilage. The coolers would be considered which of the following?

a. Trade fixtures that are real property.
b. Trade fixtures that are personal property.
c. Temporary real property.
d. Emblements.

S 2. Property can be converted from real to personal property and from personal property to real property by means of which processes, respectively?

a. Assemblage and plottage.
b. Application and dissolution.
c. Severance and affixing.
d. Planting and harvesting.

S 3. The highest form of ownership interest one can acquire in real estate is the

a. legal life estate.
b. conventional life estate.
c. defeasible fee simple estate.
d. absolute fee simple estate.

S 4. The distinguishing feature of a defeasible fee simple estate is that

a. it can be passed on to heirs.
b. it has no restrictions on use.
c. the estate may revert to a grantor or heirs if the prescribed use changes.
d. it is of unlimited duration.

S 5. Maria acquires a property from her uncle Alfonso. When Maria dies, the estate will pass to Alfonso's other niece, Serena. The type of estate that Maria has in the property is a

a. conventional life estate.
b. legal life estate.
c. fee simple defeasible estate.
d. tenancy by the entireties.

S 6. One difference between a cooperative estate and a condominium estate is that

a. a condominium owner owns a unit of air space whereas the co-op owner owns a proprietary lease.
b. a condominium sale adversely affects other unit owners.
c. the coop owner owns stock and a freehold real estate interest whereas the condominium owner simply a proprietary lease.
d. the condominium owner owns the common elements and the airspace whereas the coop owner only owns the apartment.

S 7.   Who are the essential parties involved in an estate in trust?

    a.   Owner, trustor and lawyer.
    b.   Owner, trustor and trustee.
    c.   Trustee, title company, and beneficiary.
    d.   Trustor, trustee and beneficiary.

S 8.   A condominium owner enjoys a

    a.   share in an association that owns one's apartment.
    b.   tenancy in common interest in airspace and common areas of the property.
    c.   fee simple ownership of the airspace in a unit and an undivided share of the entire property's common areas.
    d.   fee simple ownership of a pro rata share of the entire property.

S 9.   With various types of junior liens, the order of payment priority is generally established according to

    a.   the date of recordation.
    b.   what form of tax is in question.
    c.   the order of disbursement.
    d.   whether the lien was subordinated.

S 10.   What is a lien-theory state in contrast to a title-theory state?

    a.   A state in which liens are given priority over other encumbrances.
    b.   A state in which a mortgagor retains title to the property when a mortgage lien is created.
    c.   A state in which the holder of a mortgage lien receives title to the mortgaged property until the debt is satisfied.
    d.   A state in which liens must be recorded to be enforceable.

S 11.   A property owner has an easement appurtenant on her property. One day the property is sold to another party who is opposed to the easement. Following the closing, this particular form of easement

    a.   terminates.
    b.   transfers with the property.
    c.   transfers with the owner to a new property.
    d.   becomes a license on the property.

S 12.   What fundamental legal purpose is fulfilled by title records?

    a.   Keeping the county apprised of tax payments.
    b.   Preventing identity theft.
    c.   Giving constructive notice of one's rights and interests in the property.
    d.   Assembling all relevant documents in a single place.

S 13.   What is "chain of title?"

    a.   The list of all parties who have ever owned real estate.
    b.   The bundle of rights linked to the recorded title to a parcel.
    c.   A chronology of successive owners of record of a parcel of real estate.
    d.   Involuntary conveyance of title by statutory rules of descent.

S 14.   Which of the following provides the strongest evidence of marketable title?

    a.   A general warranty deed.
    b.   A title certificate.
    c.   Title insurance.
    d.   An attorney's opinion.

S 15. A store owner enters into a lease that charges rent per square foot, a common area fee, and a portion of the store owner's gross income from the property. This kind of lease is a

    a. triple charge, or triple net lease.
    b. proprietor's lease.
    c. percentage lease.
    d. retailer's gross lease.

S 16. An owner leases a property to a business in exchange for rent. The tenant is required to pay all operating expenses as well. This is an example of a

    a. proprietary lease.
    b. percentage lease.
    c. gross lease.
    d. net lease.

S 17. A lease automatically terminates under which of the following circumstances?

    a. The tenant fails to pay rent.
    b. The leased property is foreclosed.
    c. The tenant goes out of business.
    d. The landlord cancels the lease.

S 18. A county or municipal authority usually grants a certificate of occupancy for new construction only after

    a. all contractors' work has been inspected.
    b. all work has been completed for at least sixty days.
    c. the construction conforms to building codes.
    d. the tax assessor has valued the improvement.

S 19. A property owner is precluded by deed restriction from developing a thirty foot boat dock. The limitation prompts the owner to sell to another party. The new owner

    a. is free to build the dock since the next door neighbor built a similar dock two weeks later.
    b. takes title subject to the same restriction.
    c. can build the dock with special permission from the zoning board.
    d. may build, since the restriction is extinguished by the sale.

S 20. Emily sells Rycole a property containing a deed condition. The condition stipulates that the forested portion of the property must never be razed for development. Three months later, Rycole proceeds to harvest the trees and turn the area into an executive golf course. What recourse, if any, does Emily have under the deed condition?

    a. She has the right to re-possess the property because the grantee has violated the condition.
    b. The condition has ceased to apply because she allowed the violation to continue for a certain period of time.
    c. She can claim the proceeds from the harvested trees.
    d. She can force Rycole to sell the property to a new owner who agrees to comply with the condition.

S 21. What is the essential purpose of legal descriptions of real property?

    a. To create a consistent, unchanging standard for uniquely locating a property.
    b. To enable courts and attorneys to calculate property size accurately.
    c. To comply with common law for real property.
    d. To eliminate cumbersome metes and bounds descriptions.

S 22. Which of the following characterizes metes and bounds descriptions?

    a. They use meridians and base lines.
    b. They identify an enclosed area, beginning and ending at the same point.
    c. They use lot and block numbers.
    d. They incorporate elevation into the descriptions.

S 23. A buyer agrees to all terms of a seller's offer except the length of time for a contingency to procure financing. The buyer extends the financing period in the offer by one week, signs the form, and mails it back to the seller. At this point, the seller's offer

    a. is void.
    b. becomes an executory contract.
    c. becomes a counteroffer.
    d. has been accepted, since the modification was a contingency.

S 24. Real estate contracts that are not personal service contracts

    a. may be assigned.
    b. are not assignable.
    c. must be in writing.
    d. are exempt from the statute of frauds.

S 25. Which of the following contracts must be in writing to be enforceable?

    a. A parol contract.
    b. A six-month lease.
    c. A two-year lease.
    d. An executory contract.

S 26. Agent Bob, who works for Broker Bill, obtains an owner listing to lease a building. Bill's other agent, Sue, locates a tenant for Bob's listing. Broker Bill in this instance is

    a. an implied agent.
    b. a dual agent.
    c. a single agent.
    d. a subagent.

S 27. A transaction broker should disclose his or her agency relationship to prospective buyers and sellers

    a. upon first substantive communication.
    b. upon completion of the listing agreement.
    c. immediately following completion of any offer.
    d. immediately prior to closing.

S 28. A transaction facilitator in a residential transaction represents

    a. the seller.
    b. the buyer.
    c. both seller and buyer.
    d. neither seller nor buyer.

S 29. A principal instructs an agent to inform minority buyers that the property for lease was just leased an hour ago and is no longer available. The agent refuses to comply. In this case,

    a. the agent should exercise caution until the listing expires, then decline to renew it.
    b. the principal has proposed an illegal act, which should not be obeyed.
    c. the agent is liable for breaching the listing terms.
    d. the agent may sue the principal for discrimination and misrepresentation.

S 30. The amount of a real estate broker's commission is established by

    a.   agreement among competing brokers.
    b.   negotiation with clients.
    c.   the local Board of Realtors®.
    d.   state real estate license law.

S 31. A client revokes an exclusive right-to-sell listing two months prior to expiration. The reason stated: the client is too busy to meet with the agent. In this case,

    a.   the client is criminally liable for negligence.
    b.   the client may be liable for a commission and marketing expenses.
    c.   the agent can sue the client for specific performance, even if no customer had been located.
    d.   the agent must accept the revocation without the possibility of damage recovery.

S 32. A protection period clause in an exclusive listing provides that

    a.   the owner is protected from all liabilities arising from the agent's actions performed within the agent's scope of duties.
    b.   the agent has a claim to a commission if the owner sells or leases to a party within a certain time following the listing's expiration.
    c.   agents are entitled to extend a listing agreement's term if a transaction is imminent.
    d.   an owner is not liable for a commission if a prospective customer delays in completing an acceptable offer.

S 33. Real estate advertising must conform to regulatory standards and requirements. One requirement is

    a.   a broker may only place blind ads in social media outlets.
    b.   a broker must have all advertising approved by the local real estate board.
    c.   the advertising must not be deceptive.
    d.   sales agents may only advertise in their own name.

S 34. The three principal brokerage firms in a market agree to pay sales agents 15% more than any other competitor currently in practice. This is an example of

    a.   collusion.
    b.   price fixing.
    c.   allocation of markets.
    d.   steering.

S 35. Two leading agencies jointly agree to raise commissions charged to residential sellers to 7.5% of the sales price. Which of the following is true?

    a.   This is a perfectly legitimate business practice.
    b.   The brokers have illegally fixed prices.
    c.   The brokers have allocated markets.
    d.   The brokers have engaged in legal collusion.

S 36. A sale contract contains an open-ended financing contingency: if the buyer cannot obtain financing within a reasonable time, the deal is off. Six months later, the buyer still cannot secure financing. Which of the following is true?

    a.   The seller may cancel the contract, since it can be ruled invalid.
    b.   The buyer can continue indefinitely to seek financing, and the seller's property must remain off the market, since "reasonable" is not defined.
    c.   The escrow agent is entitled to the buyer's deposit.
    d.   The seller can force a lender to commit to a loan under fair financing laws.

S 37. In the event of a buyer's default, a provision for liquidated damages in a sale contract enables a seller to

    a. sue the buyer for specific performance.
    b. force the buyer to quitclaim equitable title.
    c. sue the buyer for the broker's marketing expenses.
    d. claim the deposit as compensated damages for the buyer's failure to perform.

S 38. Which of the following is true of an option-to-buy agreement?

    a. The potential buyer, the optionee, is obligated to buy the property once the option agreement is completed.
    b. The optionor must perform if the optionee takes the option, but the optionee is under no obligation to do so.
    c. The contract can be executed at no cost to the optionee.
    d. It is a bilateral agreement.

S 39. If a manufacturer that is the major employer in a small city moves its operations to another city, it is reasonable to expect

    a. a fall in housing demand, but no other changes in the real estate market.
    b. a decline in demand for all types of real estate in the real estate market.
    c. an immediate fall in the demand for industrial real estate, but no other changes in the real estate market.
    d. an immediate decline in the prices for industrial and office real estate, but no impact on the residential market.

S 40. If a commercial real estate market is undersupplied, it is likely that

    a. rental prices in that market will fall.
    b. rental prices in that market will rise.
    c. rental prices will remain stable until equilibrium is reached.
    d. construction will increase to the point of equilibrium.

S 41. The amount of available property that becomes occupied over a period of time is called

    a. vacancy.
    b. absorption.
    c. equilibrium.
    d. occupation.

S 42 The roof of a property cost $20,000. The economic life of the roof is 20 years. Assuming the straight-line method of depreciation, what is the depreciated value of the roof after 3 years?

    a. $20,000.
    b. $17,000.
    c. $14,000.
    d. $3,000.

S 43. The income capitalization approach to appraising value is most applicable for which of the following property types?

    a. Single family homes.
    b. Apartment buildings.
    c. Undeveloped land.
    d. Churches.

S 44. In the income capitalization approach, an appraiser

    a.   estimates gross income and multiplies times the gross income multiplier.
    b.   estimates effective income, subtracts tax, and applies a capitalization rate.
    c.   estimates net income and applies a capitalization rate to it.
    d.   estimates potential income and applies a capitalization rate to it.

S 45. Net operating income is equal to

    a.   potential income minus expenses minus debt service.
    b.   effective gross income minus potential income.
    c.   potential gross income minus vacancy and credit loss minus expenses.
    d.   effective gross income minus vacancy and credit loss.

S 46. If net income on a property is $40,000 and the cap rate is 10%, the value of the property using the income capitalization method is

    a. $100,000.
    b. $400,000.
    c. $1,000,000.
    d. $4,000,000.

S 47. The key feature of an adjustable mortgage loan is that

    a.   the interest rate may vary.
    b.   the monthly payment increases over the life of the loan.
    c.   the principal balance does not amortize.
    d.   the loan term can be shortened or lengthened.

S 48. Why is a wraparound mortgage loan potentially interesting to a home seller as an investment?

    a.   It is a senior loan that can be easily subordinated for additional debt.
    b.   A wraparound lender can profit when the interest rate of the wraparound exceeds that of the underlying mortgage.
    c.   The underlying loan is retired early.
    d.   The second mortgage borrower may make payments directly to the first mortgage lender.

S 49. A builder is required to secure a loan with mortgages on three properties. This is an example of

    a.   a participation mortgage loan.
    b.   a blanket mortgage loan.
    c.   a permanent mortgage loan.
    d.   a bridge loan.

S 50. Which of the following is true of a loan with negative amortization?

    a.   The interest rate on the loan increases as the principal balance decreases.
    b.   Payments are not sufficient to retire the loan.
    c.   The loan balance is diminishing, or going negative.
    d.   Additional interest is being added to the monthly payment.

S 51. The loan-to-value ratio is used as an underwriting mechanism because

    a.   the LTV determines the profitability of the loan.
    b.   the loan amount needs to be less than the property's value.
    c.   borrowers tend to inflate the true value of the property.
    d.   a full-price loan overfinances the borrower.

S 52. In the past, borrowers were often surprised by unexpected or undisclosed borrowing fees and expenses at closing. This phenomenon has been largely corrected through disclosure requirements mandated by which of the following laws?

a. Equal Credit Opportunity Act
b. Truth-in-Lending laws
c. National Disclosure Procedures Act
d. Federal Fair Housing Laws

S 53. Which of the following is an important function of the secondary mortgage market?

a. Participants borrow funds from banks so the banks can make more loans.
b. Participants issue tax certificates and sell them to primary lenders.
c. Participants purchase pools of defaulted loans from lenders to keep them solvent.
d. Participants sell mortgage-backed securities in order to buy pools of loans.

S 54. Cash flow is a measure of how much pre-tax or after-tax cash an investment property generates. To derive cash flow it is therefore necessary to exclude

a. cost recovery expense.
b. interest expense.
c. loan principal payments.
d. net operating income.

S 55. The method for deriving an investor's return on investment, or ROI, is by

a. dividing net operating income by cash flow.
b. multiplying the required yield times after-tax cash flow.
c. dividing net income by the price paid for the property.
d. multiplying cash flow times the price paid for the property.

S 56. Which of the following items would affect a homeowner's adjusted basis?

a. Installing a higher capacity air conditioning and purifying system.
b. Replacing a washing machine.
c. Stripping and staining hardwood floors.
d. Replacing a broken picture window.

S 57. Which of the following is true with respect to real property taxation by the federal government?

a. It imposes ad valorem property taxes and capital gain tax.
b. It may not impose property taxes or tax liens.
c. There are no federal ad valorem taxes on real property.
d. It imposes ad valorem tax, but not capital gain tax.

S 58. Ad valorem taxes are based on

a. the replacement value of property.
b. the assessed value of property.
c. the millage value of property.
d. the broker's estimate of value.

S 59. A retirement facility prohibits ownership of any unit by persons under 55 years of age. The association claims it has made the prohibition properly. Which of the following is true?

a. They are violating the Civil Rights Act of 1866.
b. They are violating the Fair Housing Amendments Act of 1988.
c. They are guilty of age discrimination.
d. The prohibition may be legal if performed correctly.

S 60. An owner suddenly pulls a property off the market after hearing from the agent on the phone that the agent had received a full-price offer from a minority party. The agent then informs the offeror that the home has been removed from the market and is unavailable. Which party or parties, if any, have violated fair housing laws?

   a. The agent only.
   b. The owner only.
   c. The agent and the owner.
   d. Neither agent nor owner.

S 61. Which of the following are examples of closing items not prorated between buyer and seller?

   a. Taxes.
   b. Inspection fees.
   c. Utilities.
   d. Condominium assessments.

S 62. Which of the following activities is not allowed under the Real Estate Settlements and Procedures Act?

   a. A broker having any business relationship with an insurance company that is involved in the broker's transaction.
   b. A broker pre-qualifying a buyer for a mortgage loan.
   c. A lender requiring a deposit from a borrower for a tax and insurance escrow account.
   d. A lender paying a fee to a broker for referring a borrower to the lender.

S 63. Which of the following communication records must (as opposed to should) be kept?

   a. Notes on every conversation.
   b. Copies of required communications to principals.
   c. Notes from company training sessions.
   d. Business cards of licensees one meets at open houses.

S 64. To minimize the risk of violating fair housing laws, a licensee should

   a. refuse to use terms that refer to or describe any of the classes of persons protected by the laws.
   b. avoid working in neighborhoods that are predominantly occupied by a single ethnic group.
   c. make discriminatory or derogatory remarks in conversation only, never in writing.
   d. give better service to members of a protected class than is standard for other clients or customers.

S 65. What are "tenant improvements?"

   a. Modifications to a rental suite to conform to a tenant's usage specifications
   b. Marketing programs that yield a higher quality of tenant
   c. Increased revenue resulting from a rise in rental rates
   d. Increased occupancy resulting from a population increase in the market area

S 66. For the proper handling of client and owner monies, a property manager is generally required to

   a. deposit all funds every month in the management firm's central operating account.
   b. employ a notary to witness and record every deposit or payment received.
   c. maintain a special trust account in a qualified financial depository.
   d. disburse all funds to their legal owners on a weekly basis.

S 67. Jennifer advised her clients they needed to paint their living room before showing the property. The walls of these rooms were all 8' high. The wall lengths were 14', 18', 16', and 18'. If a gallon of paint covers 200 SF, how many whole gallons would the homesellers have to buy?

    a.   1
    b.   2
    c.   3
    d.   6

S 68. An investor just purchased a rectangular 2-acre retail lot for $250 a frontage foot. If she paid $100,000 total, what was the depth of the lot?

    a.   400'
    b.   250
    c.   871'
    d.   218'

S 69. Andra can afford to spend $5,000 in closing costs to refinance her home. The lender quotes closing costs of $800 plus 2 points. The house appraised out at $240,000, and she can get an 80% loan. Can Annika afford to refinance?

    a.   No, she is short by $64.
    b.   No, she is short by $1,600.
    c.   Yes, with $360 left over.
    d.   Yes, she in fact breaks even.

S 70. A lender offers an investor a maximum 70% LTV loan on the appraised value of a property. If the investor pays $230,000 for the property, and this is 15% more than the appraised value, how much will the investor have to pay as a down payment?

    a. $93,150
    b. $79,350
    c. $90,000
    d. $69,000

S 71. A house is being appraised using the sales comparison approach. The house has three bedrooms, two bathrooms, and a patio. The appraiser selects a comparable house that has three bedrooms, 2.5 bathrooms, and no patio. The comparable house just sold for $100,000. A half-bath is valued at $5,000, and a patio at $1,000. Assuming all else is equal, what is the adjusted value of the comparable?

    a. $100,000
    b. $104,000
    c. $96,000
    d. $106,000

S 72. A family purchased a $90,000 lot to build a custom home. At the date of closing, the lot was assessed at $84,550 and the tax rate was $1.91 / $100 assessed valuation. When they completed the home, the assessment increased by $235,000 to include the new construction. If the monthly tax escrow is based on the assessed value, what will the monthly tax escrow be?

    a. $517
    b. $6096
    c. $508
    d. $367

S 73. The James family purchased a home for $180,000 five years ago and obtained an 80% LTV loan. Now the property has appreciated 25%. In addition, the loan has been paid down $11,000. What is the James's current equity in the home?

    a. $47,000
    b. $81,000
    c. $45,000
    d. $92,000

S 74. George and Mary have owned a rental house for 10 years. They bought it for $240,000 and estimated the land value @ 25%. If the property is depreciated on a 39-year schedule, and appreciation totals 50% over the period, what is their gain if they sell the property today?

    a. $159,230
    b. $166,150
    c. $181,538
    d. $120,000

S 75. Adelpha's home is valued at $250,000. She has insurance coverage of $160,000 with an 80% co-insurance clause. If Adelpha has a damage claim amounting to $100,000, how much will she receive from her policy?

    a. $32,000
    b. $60,000
    c. $80,000
    d. $100,000

S 76. Tom's neighbor knows Tom is an active real estate licensee and offers him $1,500 to prepare contracts and related forms for the neighbor's "for sales by owner" transaction. Which of the following is true?

    a.   Tom cannot accept the offer because he does not represent the neighbor in the transaction.
    b.   Tom can accept the offer as long as he accepts $500 or less.
    c.   Tom is free to accept any freelance paperwork preparation work as long as his broker isn't involved.
    d.   Tom can accept the assignment as long as he works for an Arizona transactional brokerage.

S 77. A.R.S. Title 32, Chapter 20 is also known as

    a.   Article 26.
    b.   Arizona Case Law.
    c.   Arizona's Code of Real Estate.
    d.   the Arizona Department of Real Estate.

S 78. The seller buys title insurance for the buyer, and the buyer buys it for the lender at close of escrow. This is a matter of what type of law?

    a.   Constitutional law
    b.   Statutory law
    c.   Administrative law
    d.   Common law

S 79. Article XXVI of the Arizona State Constitution authorizes real estate licensees to

    a.   perform appraisal services.
    b.   work as real estate loan originators.
    c.   engage in the limited practice of law.
    d.   represent both buyers and sellers in a real estate transaction.

S 80. Mary is an unlicensed administrative assistant for a real estate team within a brokerage. What is her legal status?

    a. She is considered a team member but cannot help the team market.
    b. Mary is not legally part of the team because she is unlicensed.
    c. Mary can only be a legal part of the team if the team members are from different brokerages.
    d. She can be a legal part of the team if 50% of the team members are also unlicensed.

S 81. Larry gives Susan, an active Arizona licensee, the names of four new people being relocated to his company and suggests she contact them to help them find homes. What can Susan give Larry in return?

    a. A warm smile and hearty "thank you"
    b. An unlimited portion of her commission on each sale for each buyer on the list
    c. No more than 5% of her commission on the buyer sales
    d. A monetary reward defined as "reasonable" by ADRE

S 82. The primary purpose of Arizona licensing and regulation is to

    a. generate fee income for ADRE.
    b. protect the public.
    c. restrict the number of new licensees entering the profession.
    d. prevent property owners from representing themselves in real estate transactions.

S 83. How many members of the Real Estate Advisory Board must have residential brokerage experience within five years of appointment?

    a. Two
    b. Four
    c. Six
    d. Nine

S 84. Which of the following is true regarding requirements for obtaining an Arizona real estate license?

    a. Despite requiring three years of real estate experience in the last five years for broker candidates, salespeople and brokers both must be at least 18 years of age.
    b. All candidates for licensure must be residents of Arizona.
    c. Candidates are required to pass a state licensing examination but not a school test.
    d. Future real estate licensees may complete 90 hours of classroom education from an approved or unapproved school.

S 85. James is given a $1,000 "tip" over and above the earned commission by his buyer client for doing such a good job helping the buyer locate and purchase a new home. Can James accept the tip?

    a. Yes, because it is considered a gratuity rather than earned income
    b. No, because only a designated broker can accept money from the public for real estate services in Arizona .
    c. Yes, but only if James spends it quickly before his broker and ADRE find out about it
    d. No, because tips are prohibited as a form of finder's fee

S 86. Which of the following broker licensees is not required to complete nine hours of broker management clinics for license renewal?

    a. A self-employed broker
    b. A sole proprietorship
    c. A broker who might be appointed as a temporary designated broker
    d. An associate broker with no additional responsibilities

S 87. Exaggerated or superlative comments which are not intended to be fact are

    a.   prohibited in real estate marketing by ADRE.
    b.   considered misrepresentations or fraudulent in Arizona real estate marketing.
    c.   called puffing.
    d.   always investigated by the Arizona State Attorney General's Office.

S 88. All easements in Arizona are

    a.   appurtenant.
    b.   non-possessory rights which are written and recorded.
    c.   to prevent land from being land-locked.
    d.   personal easements or easements in gross.

S 89. An easement is terminated by a merger of the dominant and servient properties. That means

    a.   either the dominant or servient owns both parcels.
    b.   the easement was abandoned.
    c.   the easement was terminated illegally.
    d.   the easement was converted from an appurtenant to personal easement..

S 90. Farmer Brown continues to have legal access to a pond where he enjoys fishing on a section of land he recently sold. It is an easement, and it is most likely the result of

    a.   reservation in deed.
    b.   adverse possession.
    c.   easement by necessity.
    d.   a prescription easement.

S 91. Bill and Sharon are a legally married couple in Arizona who hold interest in their home as community property. Sharon decides that upon her death, she would like her three children to inherit her share of the home. Can she will her half to her children?

    a.   No, community property has an automatic survivorship right for Bill
    b.   No, community property's survivorship right will defeat Sharon's will
    c.   Yes, community property as a way, manner, or mode of holding interest in property in Arizona allowing a husband or wife in a marriage to will one's share to a third party
    d.   Yes, but Arizona law allows Sharon to will to only one party other than her husband, not three

S 92. Arizona is a community property state because some of its real property laws are modeled after

    a.   French feudal property law.
    b.   English common law.
    c.   Spanish land grant law.
    d.   dower and curtsey laws.

S 93. A cooperative is a

    a.   freehold interest.
    b.   leasehold interest.
    c.   condominium.
    d.   commune.

S 94. For a real estate professional to represent a single or doublewide manufactured home on a rental pad, the real estate professional must

    a.   hold a valid Arizona real estate license.
    b.   hold a personal property sales certification from the Arizona Department of Real Estate.
    c.   register with the Registrar of Contractors.
    d.   have a "dealer's" license from the Arizona Department of Fire, Building and Safety.

S 95. Water which seeps through the earth but is not part of a defined underground waterway is called

    a.   avulsion.
    b.   alluvion.
    c.   percolated water.
    d.   erosion.

S 96. According to the Groundwater Management Code, the lowest level of water management is

    a.   Irrigation Non-expansion Areas (INAs).
    b.   Active Management Areas.
    c.   general provisions that apply statewide.
    d.   exempt domestic wells.

S 97. Groundwater withdrawn under a Type 2 right can only be used for

    a.   grandfathered irrigation.
    b.   domestic uses.
    c.   cities, towns, and private water companies.
    d.   non-irrigation purposes including industry, livestock watering, and golf courses.

S 98. Wetlands account for how much of Arizona land?

    a.   0%
    b.   1%
    c.   3%
    d.   18%

S 99. The state agency regulating the environment is the

    a.   EPA.
    b.   ADEQ.
    c.   ADWR.
    d.   Army Corps of Engineers.

S 100. Sara has an accepted purchase contract on an eight-year-old subdivision home. She is notified that there was a meth lab located in the premises two years ago. What option does she have regarding the purchase?

    a.   She cannot cancel the purchase contract but may have additional inspections done on the property.
    b.   She has five days from acknowledging the notice to cancel the contract.
    c.   She may not cancel the contract if notice is accompanied by a Certificate of Remediation.
    d.   She may cancel the contract only if remediation was not done by a registered drug lab remediation firm.

S 101. After an illegal drug lab has been removed from a dwelling, within what period of time must the site be remediated?

    a.   180 days
    b.   Nine months
    c.   Twelve months
    d.   There is no mandated time period.

S 102. In Arizona, a hazardous substance coming into a home via air is

   a. radon.
   b. asbestos.
   c. mold.
   d. groundwater contamination.

S 103. Why did original government rectangular survey surveyors choose the confluence of the Gila and Salt Rivers as Arizona's initial point?

   a. Surveyors sought natural monuments which wouldn't change in the future.
   b. The confluence was located as near to the center of the state as could be determined.
   c. Surveyors did not choose the confluence; Arizona's initial point is in Phoenix.
   d. The survey team spend several weeks at the confluence due to adverse weather conditions.

S 104. What is true about the Navajo Meridian?

   a. It no longer exists.
   b. It is located partially in Arizona, New Mexico, Colorado and Utah.
   c. It is a second principal baseline and meridian in Arizona.
   d. It is one of three principal baselines and meridians in Arizona along with the G&SRBM and San Bernardino principal baseline and meridian.

S 105. How many acres are there in SE4, NW4; E2?

   a. 5
   b. 16
   c. 40
   d. 360

S 106. How many rods are there in 5,280 feet?

   a. 320
   b. 80
   c. 66
   d. 16.5

S 107. What must be obtained before a sale of subdivided land can be completed and title transferred?

   a. A Commissioner's Public Report (CPR)
   b. Lot reservations for unimproved parcels numbering at least 50% of all available lots
   c. 20% conditional sales contracts and 20% lot reservations
   d. Conditional sales contracts for parcels accounting for at least 50% of all available parcels

S 108. How long after execution can purchase contracts be voided on unsubdivided land?

   a. Seven days after signing the contract
   b. Up to six months if the buyer(s) have not personally inspected the property
   c. Up to three years
   d. Up to three years if promised access hasn't been delivered

S 109. The Arizona lien in first position and which takes precedence over all other liens is

   a. the home mortgage loan
   b. an IRS lien
   c. property taxes
   d. a mechanic's lien

S 110. Jennifer has a mechanic's lien against her home. The lien is

    a.   voluntary and general.
    b.   involuntary and specific.
    c.   voluntary and specific.
    d.   involuntary and general.

S 111. With regard to mechanic's liens in Arizona,

    a.   a general contractor's lien enjoys priority over a subcontractor's lien.
    b.   mechanic's liens are not lawful.
    c.   suppliers of building and repair materials cannot lien.
    d.   unlicensed contractors and handypersons cannot lien.

S 112. John's grandfather died intestate, and John did not learn of his death until two years after his passing. The state sold the property via escheat. If John can prove he is a legitimate heir, the state will

    a.   disallow his claim because he had one year to appear.
    b.   buy back the property for John.
    c.   return the sales price of the property to John after recovering it via a special appropriation.
    d.   do nothing.

S 113. Deed restrictions are similar to

    a.   CC&Rs.
    b.   encroachments.
    c.   nuisances.
    d.   trespass.

S 114. Sam receives a violation notice from his neighborhood's HOA for $35 for a trash can violation. He does not pay it. What can the HOA do to Sam?

    a.   Foreclose
    b.   Put a lien on his property
    c.   Discontinue his trash removal services
    d.   Nothing

S 115. Which of the following is an example of a bargain and sale deed from involuntary alienation?

    a.   A general warranty deed
    b.   A special warranty deed
    c.   A trustee's deed from deed of trust foreclosure
    d.   A quit claim deed

S 116. Grandpa Jones drafts a deed to his property in the name of his infant grandson, puts it in a safe, and instructs his relatives to open the safe upon his death. One year after he dies, his son opens the safe and finds the deed. The property has already been sold to a new buyer to settle grandpa's estate. What is the status of the grandson's deed?

    a.   It is void because the grandson is under the age of majority in Arizona (18).
    b.   It is valid and competes with the new buyer's deed, but has lesser validity because it was never legally delivered.
    c.   It is void because it was never recorded.
    d.   The grandson is guaranteed the property because of the grandfather's intent.

S 117. Steve and Mary have a homestead exemption on their house in Prescott. They buy a new home in Tucson and turn the Prescott home into a second home for vacations. What is the status of the homestead exemption?

    a.   The homestead exemption remains on the Prescott home because they still own it.
    b.   The homestead exemption is transferred to their new home in Tucson.
    c.   They will now have two homestead exemptions, one each on the Prescott and Tucson homes.
    d.   They will have not homestead exemption on either because they own two homes.

S 118. In Arizona property disclosure, a material fact is

    a.   one which materially impacts the value or desirability of a property.
    b.   one which is obvious and readily apparent.
    c.   a latent defect.
    d.   one which does not have to be disclosed by law

S 119. Jennifer askes Sharon, who holds an active Arizona real estate license, to aid her in selling her home, and Sharon accepts. What is Sharon's relationship to Jennifer?

    a.   None, because Sharon does not have a signed, on-paper, employment agreement with Jennifer
    b.   None, because only Sharon's broker can establish formal real estate relationships with members of the public
    c.   Jennifer and Sharon do not have any formal relationship because Sharon has not provided any real estate services.
    d.   Jennifer and Sharon have an agency relationship.

S 120. With regard to real estate financing, Arizona is primarily

    a.   a deed of trust and lien theory state.
    b.   a mortgage state.
    c.   a title theory state.
    d.   a Torrens system state.

S 121. Raymond is the buyer of a resale home whose financing includes a deed of trust. Raymond is the

    a.   mortgagee.
    b.   mortgagor.
    c.   beneficiary.
    d.   trustor.

S 122. Elizabeth pays the second half of this year's property taxes on April 28 of the following year. What is the status of her tax payment?

    a.   It is on time.
    b.   It is late because it is due within the same year.
    c.   It is delinquent because it was due in February of the following year.
    d.   It is late because it was due October 1 of the current year.

S 123. According to the ARLTA, if Jake fails to pay his rent in time, his landlord can legally

    a.   issue a five-day pay or quit notice or otherwise initiate eviction action.
    b.   lock out Jake until his rent is paid.
    c.   both lock Jake out and confiscate Jake's property.
    d.   give Jake a pay or quit notice but must allow Jake 30 days to pay.

S 124. Emma and Malinda live in a sorority house adjacent to a state university campus. What is their status under the ARLTA?

    a. They have the same rights as any other renter in the state.
    b. They only have ARLTA rights if the living unit is actually on state university property.
    c. They have no rights under ARLTA because it exempts fraternal and social organization housing.
    d. Their rights are the same as people living in cooperatives.

S 125. Which type of deed offers the greatest responsibility and liability for the grantor, and highest level of protection for the grantee?

    a. A quit claim deed
    b. A warranty deed
    c. A sheriff's deed
    d. A treasurer's deed

Section VII : Answer Key

NATIONAL TEST 1: Rights; Interests and Estates; Ownership

1.1 (a) Wells, driveways, and signs on a parcel of land.
The legal concept of real estate encompasses land and all man-made structures that are "permanently" attached to the land. The phrase "permanently attached" refers primarily to one's intention in attaching the item. Obviously, very few if any man-made structures can be permanently attached to the land in the literal sense. But if a person constructs a house with the intention of creating a permanent dwelling, the house is considered real estate. By contrast, if a camper affixes a tent to the land with the intention of moving it to another camp in a week, the tent would not be considered real estate.

1.2 (c) A chicken coop permanently attached to land.
Improvements to real estate include such things as fences, streets, buildings, wells, sewers, sidewalks and piers. Modifications to land or a developer's preparations of a parcel of land can include such activities as grading or clearing, neither of which are considered to be "improvements" in this sense of the word.

1.3 (b) The center of the earth and infinite space above the earth.
The legal concept of land encompasses the surface area of the earth; everything beneath the surface of the earth extending downward to its center; all natural things permanently attached to the earth; and the air above the surface of the earth extending outward to infinity. Land, therefore, includes minerals beneath the earth's surface, water on or below the earth's surface, and the air above the surface.

1.4 (a) enjoyed by the owner of a property.
This group of rights includes the right to Possess, Use, Transfer, Encumber, and Exclude others from using the property. (Remember: "PUTEE") Transfer rights include the right to sell, rent, donate, assign, or bequeath. The owner may also encumber the item by mortgaging it as collateral for debt.

1.5 (b) Any item of property that is not definable as real property.
Personal property is any owned item which is not real estate, and the rights associated with owning the personal property item. Items of personal property are also called chattels or personalty.

1.6 (b) pledge the property as collateral for debt..
The right to encumber the property essentially means the right to mortgage the property as collateral for debt. There may be restrictions to this right, such as a spouse's right to limit the degree to which a homestead may be mortgaged.

1.7 (a) transfer of a portion of the bundle of rights.
An ordinary lease is a common example of the transfer of a portion of one's bundle of rights. The owner relinquishes the right to possess portions of the surface, perhaps a building, in return for rent. The tenant enjoys the rights to possess and use the building over the term of the lease, after which these rights revert to the landlord. During the lease term, the tenant has no rights to the property's subsurface or airspace other than what the building occupies. Further, the tenant does not enjoy any of the other rights in the bundle of rights: he or she cannot encumber the property or transfer it. To a limited degree, the tenant may exclude persons other than the legal owner from the property.

1.8 (d) Yes. The drones infringe on his air rights.
Air rights apply to the space above the surface boundaries of the parcel, as delineated by imaginary vertical lines extended to infinity. Since the advent of aviation, property owners' air rights have been curtailed to allow aircraft to fly over one's property provided the overflights do not interfere with the owner's use and enjoyment of the property. The issue of violation of air rights for the benefit of air transportation is an ongoing battle between aircraft owners, airlines, airports, and nearby property owners.

1.9 (c) Navigable lakes, seas, and oceans.
Littoral rights concern properties abutting bodies of water that are not moving, such as lakes and seas. Owners of properties abutting a navigable, non-moving body of water enjoy the littoral right of use, but do not own the water nor the land beneath the water. The legal premise underlying the definition of littoral

rights is that a lake or sea is a navigable body of water, therefore, public property owned by the state. By contrast, a body of water entirely contained within the boundaries of an owner's property is not navigable. In such a case, the owner would own the water as well as unrestricted rights of usage.

1.10 (a) the high water mark of the body of water at the shoreline.
Ownership extends to the high-water mark of the body of water. The low water mark would imply that the owner owned the water itself at times of high water levels!

1.11 (d) They transfer with the property when the property is sold.
Littoral rights attach to the property. When the property is sold, the littoral rights transfer with the property to the new owner.

1.12 (c) Streams and rivers.
Riparian rights concern properties abutting moving water such as streams and rivers. If a property abuts a stream or river, the owner's riparian rights are determined by whether the water is navigable or not navigable. If the property abuts a non-navigable stream, the owner enjoys unrestricted use of the water and owns the land beneath the stream to the stream's midpoint. If the waterway in question is navigable, the waterway is considered to be a public easement. In such a case, the owner's property extends t the water's edge as opposed to the midpoint of the waterway.

1.13 (b) An item of personal property that has been converted to real property.
A personal property item that has been converted to real property by attachment to real estate is called a fixture. Typical examples are chandeliers, toilets, water pumps, septic tanks, and window shutters. The owner of real property inherently owns all fixtures belonging to the real property. When the owner sells the real property, the buyer acquires rights to all fixtures.

1.14 (a) the owner originally intended to remove it after a period of time.
One's original intention can override the test of movability in determining whether an item is a fixture or not. If someone attached an item to real property, yet intended to remove it after a period of time, the article may be deemed personal property. If a person intended an article to be a fixture, even though the item is easily removable, the article may be deemed a fixture. For example, an apartment renter installs an alarm system, fully intending to remove the system upon lease expiration. Here, the alarm system would be considered personal property.

1.15 (c) Fifty percent of the estate consisting of the indivisible whole of the real property.
An undivided interest is an owner's fractional interest in an entire (undivided) estate, but not in a physical portion of the real property itself. An owner who has an undivided equal interest with another cannot exercise exclusive rights over a portion of the real estate, which is an indivisible whole.

1.16 (a) an estate in land.
Interests are principally distinguished by whether they include possession. If the interest-holder enjoys the right of possession, the party is considered to have an estate in land, or, familiarly an estate. Freehold and leasehold estates in land are further distinguished by whether the duration of the owner's rights can be determined.

1.17 (a) a public interest.
Public entities may own or lease real estate, in which case they enjoy an estate in land. However, government entities also have non-possessory interests in real estate which act to control land use for the public good within the entity's jurisdiction. The prime example of public interest is police power, or the right of the local or county government to zone. Another example of public interest is the right to acquire ownership through the power of eminent domain.

1.18 (c) a freehold estate.
In a freehold estate, the duration of the owner's rights cannot be determined: the rights may endure for a lifetime, for less than a lifetime, or for generations beyond the owner's lifetime. By contrast, leasehold estates have expirations.

1.19 (d) that the estate is limited by a lease term.
A leasehold estate is distinguished by its specific duration, as represented by the lease term. Further, leasehold tenants only enjoy limited property rights: use; temporary possession, and limited exclusion.

1.20 (d) Fee simple defeasible.

The defeasible fee estate is perpetual, provided the usage conforms to stated conditions. Essential characteristics are that the property must be used for a certain purpose or under certain conditions, and, if the use changes or if prohibited conditions are present, the estate reverts to the previous grantor of the estate.

1.21 (c) An ordinary life estate.

A life estate is limited in duration to the life of the owner or other named person. Upon the death of the owner (ordinary life estate) or other named individual (pur autre vie life estate), the estate passes to the original owner (a reversionary interest) or another named party (a remainder interest). Thus with the life estate, the owner enjoys full ownership rights during the estate period, and holders of the future interest own either a reversionary or a remainder interest.

1.22 (b) a legal life estate.

Homestead, dower, and curtesy are legal life estates. A legal life estate is created by state law as opposed to being created by a property owner's agreement. The focus of a legal life estate is defining and protecting the property rights of surviving family members upon the death of the husband or wife.

1.23 (b) The boat, house, and motorcycle.

Separate property consists of: property owned by either spouse at the time of the marriage; property acquired by either spouse through inheritance or gift during the marriage; property acquired with separate-property funds; and income from separate property. Community property consists of all other property earned or acquired by either party during the marriage. A spouse owns separate property free and clear of claims by the other spouse. He or she can transfer it without the other spouse's signature. Upon the death of the separate property owner, the property passes to heirs by will or laws of descent. Community property cannot be transferred or encumbered without the signatures of both spouses. Upon the death of either spouse, half of the deceased's community property passes to the surviving spouse, and the other half passes to the decedent's heirs.

1.24 (d) The right to possess and use the premises.

Leasehold tenants are entitled to possess and use the leased premises during the lease term in the manner prescribed in the lease. They also have restricted rights to exclusion.

1.25 (a) the tenant makes, and landlord accepts, regular rent payments.

In an estate from period-to-period, also called a periodic tenancy, the tenancy period automatically renews as long as the tenant pays rent in a timely manner and the landlord accepts it. At the end of a tenancy period, if the landlord accepts another regular payment of rent, the leasehold is considered to be renewed for another period. A conveyance of leased property does not cancel a leasehold interest.

1.26 (c) terminates on the death of lessor or lessee.

The estate at will, also called a tenancy at will, has no definite expiration date and hence no "renewal" cycle. The landlord and tenant agree that the tenancy will have no specified termination date, provided rent is paid on time and other lease conditions are met. For example, a son leases a house to his father and mother "forever," or until they want to move. The estate at will is terminated by proper notice, or by the death of either party.

1.27 (a) an estate at sufferance.

In an estate at sufferance, a tenant occupies the premises without consent of the landlord or other legal agreement with the landlord. Usually such an estate involves a tenant who fails to vacate at the expiration of the lease, continuing occupancy without any right to do so. For example, a tenant violates the provisions of a lease and is evicted. The tenant protests and refuses to leave despite the eviction order.

1.28 (b) Estate from period to period.

In an estate from period-to-period, also called a periodic tenancy, the tenancy period automatically renews for an indefinite period of time, subject to timely payment of rent. At the end of a tenancy period, if the landlord accepts another regular payment of rent, the leasehold is considered to be renewed for another period.

1.29 (a) tenancy in severalty.
If a single party owns the fee or life estate, the ownership is a tenancy in severalty. Synonyms are sole ownership, ownership in severalty, and estate in severalty.

1.30 (c) tenancy in common.
The tenancy in common, also known as the estate in common, is the most common form of co-ownership when the owners are not married (though tenants in common can be married). The defining characteristics are: two or more owners; identical rights; interests individually owned; electable ownership shares; no survivorship; and no unity of time. With "identical rights", co-tenants share an indivisible interest in the estate, i.e., all have equal rights to possess and use the property subject to the rights of the other co-tenants.

1.31 (a) Parties must acquire respective interests at the same time.
To create a joint tenancy, all owners must acquire the property at the same time, use the same deed, acquire equal interests, and share in equal rights of possession. These are referred to as the four unities.

1.32 (b) cannot will their interest to a party outside the tenancy. The survivorship feature of joint tenancy presents an advantage to tenancy in common, in that interests pass without probate proceedings. On the other hand, joint tenants relinquish any ability to will their interest to parties outside of the tenancy.

1.33 (c) Legal life estate.
A legal life estate is created by state law as opposed to being created by a property owner's agreement. The focus of a legal life estate is defining and protecting the property rights of surviving family members upon the death of the husband or wife.

1.34 (a) A homestead interest cannot be conveyed by one spouse.
A homestead is one's principal residence. Homestead laws protect family members against losing their homes to general creditors attempting to collect on debts. Homestead laws generally provide that: the homestead interest cannot be conveyed by one spouse; both spouses must sign the deed conveying homestead property.

1.35 (a) sell or transfer his interest without the consent of the other tenants in common.
All tenants in common have distinct and separable ownership of their respective interests. Co-tenants may sell, encumber, or transfer their interests without obstruction or consent from the other owners. A co-tenant may not, however, encumber the entire property.

1.36 (c) Income derived from community property
If an income-producing property has been defined as community property, the revenue accruing from the investment is likewise community property.

1.37 (c) The beneficiary
A land trust allows the trustor to convey the fee estate to the trustee and to name himself or herself the beneficiary. The land trust applies only to real property, not to personal property. The agreement, or deed in trust, grants the beneficiary the rights to possess and use the property, and to exercise control over the actions of the trustee.

1.38 (c) The Buick and the second property
Community property laws define property rights of legal spouses before, during, and after their marriage, as well as after the death of either spouse. Community property law distinguishes real and personal property into categories of separate and community property. Separate property belongs to one spouse; community property belongs to both spouses equally. Separate property is that property which is acquired prior to the marriage, by gift or inheritance during the marriage, property acquired by separate-property funds, or income from separate property.

1.39 (a) A cooperative may hold an owner liable for the unpaid operating expenses of other tenants.
Since the corporation owns an undivided interest in the cooperative property, debts and financial obligations apply to the property as a whole, not to individual units as in a condominium.

1.40 (b) The owners enjoy an indivisible interest.
The tenancy in common, also known as the estate in common, is the most common form of co-ownership when the owners are not married (though tenants in common can be married). The defining characteristics

are: two or more owners; identical rights; interests individually owned; electable ownership shares; no survivorship; and no unity of time. With "identical rights," co-tenants share an indivisible interest in the estate, i.e., all have equal rights to possess and use the property subject to the rights of the other co-tenants.

1.41 (a) sell her interest to a third party without the consent of Robert
All tenants in common have distinct and separable ownership of their respective interests. Co-tenants may sell, encumber, or transfer their interests without obstruction or consent from the other owners. A co-tenant may not, however, encumber the entire property.

1.42 (d) It passes by probate to the deceased tenant's heirs.
A deceased co-tenant's estate passes by probate to the decedent's heirs and devisees rather than to the other tenants in common. Any number of heirs can share in the ownership of the willed tenancy.

1.43 (c) The tenants have an equal and indivisible ownership interest.
In a joint tenancy, two or more persons collectively own a property as if they were a single person. Rights and interests are indivisible and equal: each has a shared interest in the whole property which cannot be divided up. Joint tenants may only convey their interests to outside parties as tenant-in-common interests. One can not convey a joint tenant interest.

1.44 (a) there is a single title to the property.
Whereas tenants in common hold separate title to their individual interests, joint tenants together hold a single title to the property. This is referred to as unity of ownership.

1.45 (a) the new owner becomes a tenant in common with the other owners, who continue to hold a joint tenancy with each other and a tenancy in common with the new owner.
A joint tenant may transfer his or her interest in the property to an outside party, but only as a tenancy in common interest. Whoever acquires the interest co-owns the property as a tenant in common with the other joint tenants. The remaining joint tenants continue to own an undivided interest in the property, less the new co-tenant's share.

1.46 (d) It passes to the surviving joint tenants.
In most states, joint tenants enjoy rights of survivorship: if a joint tenant dies, all interests and rights pass to the surviving joint tenants free from any claims of creditors or heirs. When only one joint tenant survives, the survivor's interest becomes an estate in severalty, and the joint tenancy is terminated.

1.47 (c) If they are married.
Tenancy by the entireties is a form of ownership reserved exclusively for husband and wife. It features survivorship, equal interests, and limited exposure to foreclosure.

1.48 (c) The trustee.
In an estate in trust, a fee owner-- the grantor or trustor-- transfers legal title to a fiduciary-- the trustee-- who holds and manages the estate for the benefit of another party, the beneficiary. The trust may be created by a deed, will, or trust agreement.

1.49 (a) sell or mortgage the unit without impediment from individual owners of neighboring units.
Condominium units can be individually sold, mortgaged, or otherwise encumbered without interference from other unit owners. An owner may not sell interests in the apartment separately from the interest in the common elements. Unit owners exclusively possess their apartment space, but must share common areas with other owners.

1.50 (b) the unit's pro rata share of the property value as defined in the declaration.
The unit's pro rata share of the property's ownership as defined in the declaration determines the amount of a unit owner's assessment. For example, if a unit represents a 2% share of the property value, that unit owner's assessment will be 2% of the property's common area expenses.

1.51 (a) shares in a corporation or association and a proprietary lease in a physical unit.
In a cooperative, or co-op, one owns shares in a non-profit corporation or cooperative association, which in turn acquires and owns an apartment building as its principal asset. Along with this stock, the shareholder acquires a proprietary lease to occupy one of the apartment units.

1.52 (d) the corporate entity of the cooperative association.
The corporate entity of the cooperative association is the only party in the cooperative with a real property interest. The association's interest is an undivided interest in the entire property. There is no ownership interest in individual units, as with a condominium.

1.53 (a) undivided interests in the property as tenants in common.
In a freehold time-share, or interval ownership estate, tenants in common own undivided interests in the property. Expense prorations and rules governing interval usage are established by separate agreement when the estate is acquired.

NATIONAL TEST 2: Encumbrances; Liens; Title Transfer and Recording; Leases

2.1 (c) A third party's interest in a real property that limits the interests of the freehold property owner.
An encumbrance is an interest in and right to real property that limits the legal owner's freehold interest. In effect, an encumbrance is another's right to use or take possession of a legal owner's property, or to prevent the legal owner from enjoying the full bundle of rights in the estate.

2.2 (a) They involve the property that contains the easement and a non-owning party. An easement is an interest in real property that gives the holder the right to use portions of the legal owner's real property in a defined way. One cannot own an easement over one's own property. Easement rights may apply to a property's surface, subsurface, or airspace, but the affected area must be defined. An easement may be affirmative, allowing a use, such as a right-of-way, or negative, prohibiting a use, such as an airspace easement that prohibits one property owner from obstructing another's ocean view.

2.3 (d) An easement appurtenant.
An easement appurtenant gives a property owner a right of usage to portions of an adjoining property owned by another party. The property enjoying the usage right is called the dominant tenement, or dominant estate. The property containing the physical easement itself is the servient tenement, since it must serve the easement use.

2.4 (c) easement by necessity.
An easement by necessity is an easement appurtenant granted by a court of law to a property owner because of a circumstance of necessity, most commonly the need for access to a property. Since property cannot be legally landlocked, or without legal access to a public thoroughfare, a court will grant an owner of a landlocked property an easement by necessity over an adjoining property that has access to a thoroughfare.

2.5 (b) an unauthorized physical intrusion of one property into another.
An encroachment is the unauthorized, physical intrusion of one owner's real property into that of another. Examples of encroachments are: a tree limb extending into the neighbor's property, violating his or her airspace; a driveway extending beyond the lot line onto the neighbor's land; and a fence built beyond the property line.

2.6 (c) a trespasser has been using an owner's property for a certain period with the owner's knowledge but without permission.
If someone uses another's property as an easement without permission for a statutory period of time and under certain conditions, a court order may give the user the easement right by prescription, regardless of the owner's desires. For a prescriptive easement order to be granted, the following circumstances must be true: the use has been occurring without permission or license; the owner knows or is presumed to have known of the use; and the use has been generally uninterrupted over the statutory prescriptive period.

2.7 (d) how a property may be used and what improvements may be built on it.
A deed restriction is a limitation imposed on a buyer's use of a property by stipulation in the deed of conveyance or recorded subdivision plat. A deed restriction may apply to a single property or to an entire subdivision. A developer may place restrictions on all properties within a recorded subdivision plat. Subsequent re-sales of properties within the subdivision are thereby subject to the plat's covenants and conditions.

2.8 (c) the creditor's claim against the property as collateral security for the loan.
A lien is a creditor's claim against personal or real property as security for a debt of the property owner. If the owner defaults, the lien gives the creditor the right to force the sale of the property to satisfy the debt. For example, a homeowner borrows $5,000 to pay for a new roof. The lender funds the loan in exchange for the borrower's promissory note to repay the loan. At the same time, the lender places a lien on the property for $5,000 as security for the debt. If the borrower defaults, the lien allows the lender to force the sale of the house to satisfy the debt.

2.9 (d) An equitable interest.
A lienor generally has an equitable interest in the property, but not legal ownership. The exception is a mortgage lien on a property in a title-theory state. In these states, the mortgage transaction conveys legal title to the lender, who holds it until the mortgage obligations are satisfied. During the mortgage loan period, the borrower has equitable title to the property.

2.10 (a) Payment of the debt that is the subject of the lien and recording of the satisfaction.
A lien terminates on payment of the debt and recording of documents. Payment of the debt and recording of the appropriate satisfaction documents ordinarily terminate a lien. If a default occurs, a suit for judgment or foreclosure enforces the lien. These actions force the sale of the property.

2.11 (d) involuntary general lien.
A general lien is one placed against any and all real and personal property owned by a particular debtor. An example is an inheritance tax lien placed against all property owned by the heir. A specific lien attaches to a single item of real or personal property and does not affect other property owned by the debtor. In addition, judgment liens are junior, involuntary liens.

2.12 (a) Real estate tax lien.
The category of superior, or senior, liens ranks above the category of inferior, or junior, liens, meaning that superior liens receive first payment from the proceeds of a foreclosure. The superior category includes liens for real estate tax, special assessments, and inheritance tax. Other liens, including income tax liens, mortgage liens and judgment liens, are inferior.

2.13 (d) subordinate the lien.
A lienor can change the priority of a junior lien by voluntarily agreeing to subordinate, or lower, the lien's position in the hierarchy. This change is often necessary when working with a mortgage lender who will not originate a mortgage loan unless it is senior to all other junior liens on the property. The lender may require the borrower to obtain agreements from other lien holders to subordinate their liens to the new mortgage.

2.14 (c) A proceeding to enforce a lien by forcing the sale or transfer of a secured property.
All liens can be enforced by the sale or other transfer of title of the secured property, whether by court action, operation of law, or through powers granted in the original loan agreement. The enforcement proceedings are referred to as foreclosure. Note that lienors already possess equitable title, so they do not need to undertake a legal proceeding to establish this.

2.15 (b) file a foreclosure suit.
Judicial foreclosure occurs in states that use a two-party mortgage document (borrower and lender) that does not contain a "power of sale" provision. Lacking this provision, a lender must file a foreclosure suit and undertake a court proceeding to enforce the lien.

2.16 (a) strict foreclosure. Strict foreclosure is a court proceeding that gives the lender title directly, by court order, instead of giving cash proceeds from a public sale. On default, the lender gives the borrower official notice. After a prescribed period, the lender files suit in court, whereupon the court establishes a period within which the defaulting party must repay the amounts owed. If the defaulter does not repay the funds, the court orders transfer of full, legal title to the lender.

2.17 (d) A license, which terminates upon the owner's death.
A license is a personal right that a property owner grants to another to use the property for a specific purpose (to reach the kindergarten school bus). Unlike a personal easement in gross, which terminates only on the death of the grantee (Betty Luanne, in this instance), a license is revocable at any moment, is not

transferable and does not attach to the land. It ceases on the death of either party, or on the sale of the property.

2.18 (d) Dominant tenement.
An easement appurtenant gives a property owner a right of usage to portions of an adjoining property owned by another party. The property enjoying the usage right is called the dominant tenement, or dominant estate. The property containing the physical easement itself is the servient tenement, since it must serve the easement use.

2.19 (b) a deed restriction.
A private party who wants to control the quality and standards of a property can establish a deed restriction. Deed restrictions take precedence over zoning ordinances if they are more restrictive.

2.20 (a) It involves a monetary claim against the value of a property.
A lien is a creditor's claim against personal or real property as security for a debt of the property owner. If the owner defaults, the lien gives the creditor the right to force the sale of the property to satisfy the debt. Liens do not necessarily alter the property value. Liens can be involuntary as well as voluntary. Finally, liens attach to the property, but so do other encumbrances.

2.21 (d) It is knowledge received or imparted through direct experience.
The term "notice" is synonymous with "knowledge." A person who has received actual notice has actual knowledge of something. Receiving actual notice means learning of something through direct experience or communication. Thus, a document in itself cannot be actual notice. It is the seeing of the document that makes it actual notice.

2.22 (b) It is knowledge one could have or should have obtained.
Constructive notice, or legal notice, is knowledge of a fact that a person could have or should have obtained. The foremost method of imparting constructive notice is by recordation of ownership documents in public records, specifically, title records. Since public records are open to everyone, the law generally presumes that when evidence of ownership is recorded, the public at large has received constructive notice of ownership.

2.23 (a) grant, deed, and will.
Voluntary transfer, or voluntary alienation, is an unforced transfer of title by sale or gift from an owner to another party. If the transferor is a government entity and the recipient is a private party, the conveyance is a public grant. If the transferor is a private party, the conveyance is a private grant. A living owner makes a private grant by means of a deed of conveyance, or deed. A private grant that occurs when the owner dies is a transfer by will.

2.24 (c) It gives constructive notice of ownership.
Recording is not necessary to make a deed valid. However, it is in the grantee's best interests to do so. Recording the deed gives the public constructive notice of the grantee's ownership.

2.25 (b) granting clause.
The granting, or premises, clause is the only required clause. It contains the conveyance intentions; names the parties; describes the property; and indicates a nominal consideration.

2.26 (a) general warranty deed.
The general warranty deed, or warranty deed for short, contains the fullest possible assurances of good title and protection for the grantee. The deed is technically a bargain and sale deed in which the grantor promises to defend against any and all claims to the title. The overall general warranty covenant is: "I own and will defend."

2.27 (d) To have an encumbrance removed if the lienholder cannot prove its validity.
Where there is a possibility that prior errors in deeds or other recorded documents might cloud (encumber) the title, the relevant parties execute a quitclaim deed to convey "any and all" interest to the grantee. If a party responsible for encumbering title refuses to quitclaim the interest, the owner may file a quiet title suit. This requires the lienor to prove the validity of an interest. If the defendant is unable to do so, the court removes the cloud by decree.

2.28 (a) A transfer tax based on the price of the property being conveyed.
State law usually requires payment of a documentary stamp tax on a conveyance of real property. The tax is based on the actual price of the property conveyed, thus enabling taxing authorities to ascertain current market value for ad valorem tax purposes. Payment of the tax is evidenced on the deed.

2.29 (b) probate.
A court proceeding called probate generally settles a decedent's estate, whether the person has died testate (having left a valid will) or intestate (having failed to do so).

2.30 (a) It will escheat to the state or county.
If an intestate decedent has no heirs, the estate escheats, or reverts, to the state or county after all claims and debts have been validated and settled.

2.31 (d) Eminent domain.
Various government and public entities can transfer private property to the public sphere by the power of eminent domain. The transfer is involuntary, even though the owner receives compensation. For example, a city government wants to widen a highway to accommodate growth. The government uses eminent domain to condemn and purchase all properties abutting the thoroughfare in order to complete the construction project.

2.32 (a) openly possessing and claiming the property without the owner's consent.
To claim legal title, the adverse possessor must be able to show a claim of right or color of title as reason for the possession; have notorious possession, which is possession without concealment; maintain a consistent claim of hostile possession, which is a claim to ownership and possession regardless of the owner's claims or consent; occupy the property continuously for a statutory period of time; in some states, pay taxes.

2.33 (c) The buyer.
Title records protect the buyer by revealing whether a property has marketable title, one free of undesirable encumbrances. The buyer is legally responsible for knowing the condition of title, since it is a matter of public record.

2.34 (a) a clouded title.
Chain of title refers to the succession of property owners of record dating back to the original grant of title from the state to a private party. If there is a missing link in the chronology of owners, or if there was a defective conveyance, the chain is said to be broken, resulting in a clouded title to the property.

2.35 (b) standard owner's title insurance policy.
An owner's policy may have standard coverage or extended coverage. Standard coverage protects against title defects such as incompetent grantors, invalid deeds, fraudulent transaction documents, and defects in the chain of title. Extended coverage protects against liabilities that may not be of public record, including fraud, unrecorded ownership claims, unintentional recording errors, and unrecorded liens.

2.36 (a) voluntary alienation.
Voluntary alienation is an unforced transfer of title by sale or gift from an owner to another party.

2.37 (d) A quitclaim deed.
A quitclaim deed transfers real and potential interests in a property, whether an interest is known to exist or not. The grantor makes no claim to any interest in the property being conveyed and offers no warrants to protect the grantee. Where there is a possibility that prior errors in deeds or other recorded documents might cloud (encumber) the title, the relevant parties execute a quitclaim deed to convey "any and all" interest to the grantee.

2.38 (a) pass to the heirs by the laws of descent and distribution.
In this circumstance, the estate, including real property, will pass to lawful heirs according to the state's laws of descent and succession or distribution. These laws apportion the estate without regard to the wishes of the heirs or the intentions of the decedent. Escheat, by which the state takes the property, applies only if there are no legal heirs.

2.39 (d) declined because possession was secretive.
One of the preconditions for a claim of ownership based on adverse possession is notorious possession, or possession without concealment. Even if the length of possession in this case meets the statutory requirement, the drifter's secretiveness would invalidate the claim.

2.40 (b) free of undisclosed defects and encumbrances.
Marketable title is, by definition, one that is free and clear of undesirable and unknown encumbrances, claims, clouds, or other defects. Attorney's abstracts and title certificates do not guarantee that a title is marketable.

2.41 (c) Estate at will.
Three of the four principal types of leasehold estate are: the estate for years, which has a specific lease term; the estate from period-to-period, where the lease term of a specific period automatically renews; and the estate at will, which has no specified lease term. The fourth principal type, the estate at sufferance, is a tenancy without consent that therefore also has no specific term.

2.42 (b) for specified reasonable purposes.
A tenant has the sole right to occupy and use the premises without interference from outside parties, including the landlord. The landlord may enter the premises for specified purposes such as inspections, but the interference must be reasonable and limited. In addition, the landlord can do nothing outside of the lease's express provisions that would impair the tenant's enjoyment of income deriving from use of the premises.

2.43 (a) compliance with the rules and regulations of the building.
The lease defines the tenant's obligations, which principally are to pay the rent on time; maintain the property's condition; and comply with the rules and regulations of the building.

2.44 (b) providing required building support and services.
The lease defines the landlord's obligations, which principally are to provide the necessary building support and services, and maintain the condition of the property. It is the tenant's responsibility to obtain insurance and to determine the fairness of the rent.

2.45 (d) the tenant's estate is still obligated under the lease.
A valid lease creates obligations that survive the death of the landlord or tenant, with certain exceptions. A tenant's estate remains liable for payment of rent if the tenant dies; the landlord's estate remains bound to provide occupancy despite the landlord's death.

2.46 (a) The remaining tenant is responsible for the full rent obligation.
Multiple tenants who sign a single lease are jointly and severally responsible for fulfilling lease obligations. Thus, if one renter abandons an apartment, the other renters remain liable for rent.

2.47 (c) sublease.
Subletting (subleasing) is the transfer by a tenant, the sublessor, of a portion of the leasehold interest to another party, the sublessee, through the execution of a sublease. The sublease spells out all of the rights and obligations of the sublessor and sublessee, including the payment of rent to the sublessor. The sublessor remains primarily liable for the original lease with the landlord. The subtenant is liable only to the sublessor.

2.48 (d) net lease.
A net lease requires a tenant to pay for utilities, internal repairs, and a proportionate share of taxes, insurance, and operating expenses in addition to rent. In effect, the landlord "passes through" actual property expenses to the tenant rather than charging a higher rent level. Net leases vary as to exactly what expenses the tenant is responsible for. The purest form of net lease requires tenants to cover all expenses, including major repairs and property taxes.

2.49 (a) gross lease.
A gross lease, or full service lease, requires the landlord to pay the property's operating expenses, including utilities, repairs, and maintenance, while the tenant pays only rent. Rent levels under a gross lease are higher than under a net lease, since the landlord recoups expense outlays in the form of added rent.

2.50 (b) An owner-developer wants to retain ownership of the land portion of the improved real property.
Ground leases are primarily used when an owner wishes to lease raw land to an agricultural or mining interest; when unimproved property is to be developed and the owner wants to retain ownership of the land; when the developer or future users of the property do not want to own the land; or when the owner of an improved property wishes to sell an interest in the improvements while retaining ownership of the underlying land.

2.51 (a) either party giving proper notice.
In the absence of an explicit term with beginning and ending date, a court will generally construe the lease to be a tenancy at will, cancelable upon proper notice.

2.52 (b) a tenancy from period-to-period.
URLTA sets standards for improving oral, vague, or unbalanced lease agreements. In the case of an unclear lease expiration date, the lease is generally deemed to be a periodic tenancy.

2.53 (a) a hotel.
State laws based on URLTA generally do not apply to transient occupancies, such as hotel and motel rentals, proprietary leases in cooperatives, or to occupancy in a residence that is under a contract for deed.

2.54 (c) a temporary possessory interest.
A lease is both an instrument of conveyance and a contract between principal parties to uphold certain covenants and obligations. As a conveyance, a lease conveys an interest, called the leasehold estate, but does not convey legal title to the property. For this reason, a leasehold is also called a less-than-freehold estate.

2.55 (d) A leased fee estate.
In conveying the leasehold estate, the landlord acquires a leased fee estate, which entails the rights to: receive rent; re-possess the property following the lease term; and monitor the tenant's obligations to maintain the premises.

2.56 (c) occupy the property.
The legal essence of a valid lease is that it conveys an exclusive right to use and occupy a property for a limited period of time in exchange for rent and the return of the property after the lease term is over.

2.57 (a) The buyer acquires title subject to the lease, which remains in effect.
The landlord may sell, assign, or mortgage the leased fee interest. However, transferring and encumbering the leased property do not extinguish the obligations and covenants of a lease. Buyers and creditors, therefore, must take their respective interests subject to the terms of the lease.

2.58 (c) When either party gives proper notice.
In the absence of an explicit term with beginning and ending date, a court will generally construe the lease to be a tenancy at will, cancelable upon proper notice.

2.59 (c) a five-year lease must be in writing to be enforceable.
Generally, a lease for a period exceeding one year cannot be oral but must be in writing to be enforceable because of the statute of frauds.

2.60 (b) The original tenant retains primary responsibility for performance of the original lease contract.
In a sublease-- a transfer of a portion of the leasehold-- the sublessor (original tenant) remains primarily liable for the original lease with the landlord. The subtenant is liable only to the sublessor.

NATIONAL TEST 3: Land Use Regulation & Control; Legal Descriptions; Contract Law

3.1 (d) Zoning ordinances are a primary means of keeping land use in harmony with the master plan.
The master plan fuses state and regional land use laws with local land use objectives that correspond to the municipality's social and economic conditions. The completed plan becomes the overall guideline for creating and enforcing zones, building codes, and development requirements.

3.2 (c) specify usage for every parcel within the zoning authority's jurisdiction.
The intent of zoning ordinances is to specify land usage for every parcel within the jurisdiction. In some areas, state laws permit zoning ordinances to apply to areas immediately beyond the legal boundaries of the city or county.

3.3 (b) To separate land uses so that they do not interfere with each other.
One of the primary applications of zoning power is the separation of residential properties from commercial and industrial uses. Proper design of land use in this manner preserves the aesthetics and value of neighborhoods and promotes the success of commercial enterprises through intelligently located zones. Six common types of zone are: residential; commercial; industrial; agricultural; public; and planned unit development (PUD).

3.4 (c) The public interest
The principal forms of exceptions to a conforming use is legal nonconforming use (grandfathered in); variance based on hardship; and special exception based on the public interest.

3.5 (d) The area of a commercial or industrial facility in relation to the size of the site.
Commercial zoning regulates intensity of usage by limiting the area of store or office per site area. Intensity regulation is further achieved by minimum parking requirements, setbacks, and building height restrictions.

3.6 (c) It requires that multiple tracts of land be developed according to a single design.
Planned unit development zoning restricts use to development of whole tracts that are designed to use space efficiently and maximize open space. A PUD zone may be for residential, commercial, or industrial uses, or combinations thereof.

3.7 (a) A homeowner in a residential zone converts her residence to a private school.
A legal nonconforming use can be illustrated as follows. A motel is situated in a residential area that no longer allows commercial activity. The zoning board rules that the motel may continue to operate until it is sold, destroyed or used for any other commercial purpose. An illegal nonconforming use is one that conflicts with ordinances that were in place before the use commenced. For instance, if the motel in the previous example is sold, and the new owner continues to operate the property as a motel, the motel is now an illegal, nonconforming use.

3.8 (b) A variance is granted by the zoning board if the owner has a justifiable reason.
A nonconforming use is one that clearly differs from current zoning and is subject to change upon conveyance. A zoning variance allows a use that differs from the applicable ordinance for a variety of justifiable reasons.

3.9 (c) certificate of occupancy.
Building inspectors inspect a new development or improvement for code compliance. If the work complies, the municipality or county issues a certificate of occupancy which officially clears the property for occupation and use.

3.10 (c) It conveys legal title to the acquiring entity.
Eminent domain allows a government entity to purchase a fee, leasehold, or easement interest in privately owned real property for the public good, regardless of the owner's desire to sell or otherwise transfer any interest. In exchange for the interest, the government pays the owner a "just" compensation. To acquire a property, the public entity initiates a condemnation suit. Transfer of title extinguishes all existing leases,

liens, and other encumbrances on the property.

3.11 (d) parties responsible for improper disposal of hazardous waste could be charged for the cleanup costs.
Under CERCLA and the Superfund Amendment of 1986, current landowners as well as previous owners of a property may be held liable for environmental violations, even if "innocent" of a violation. Sellers often carry the greatest exposure, and real estate licensees may be held liable for improper disclosure.

3.12 (a) Individual property rights and the public's interest.
The optimum management of real property usage must take into account both the interests of the individual and the interests of the surrounding community. While maintaining the value of an individual estate is important, the owner of an estate must realize that unregulated use and development can jeopardize the value not only of the owner's estate but of neighboring properties.

3.13 (c) police power.
At the local level, county and city governments control land use through the authority known as police power. The most common expressions of police power are county and municipal zoning.

3.14 (d) The owner must sell the property in exchange for market-value compensation.
Eminent domain allows a government entity to purchase a fee, leasehold, or easement interest in privately owned real property for the public good, regardless of the owner's desire to sell or otherwise transfer any interest. In exchange for the interest, the government pays the owner a "just" compensation.

3.15 (a) reasonably promote community health, safety and welfare.
Local planners do not have unlimited authority to do whatever they want. Their zoning ordinances must be clear in import, apply to all parties equally, and promote health, safety, and welfare of the community in a reasonable manner.

3.16 (d) To ensure that improvements comply with codes.
Local governments enforce zoning ordinances by issuing building permits to those who want to improve, repair, or refurbish a property. To receive a permit, the project must comply with all relevant ordinances and codes.

3.17 (b) To regulate the density of dwellings in the residential zone.
Residential zoning regulates density, by limiting the number and size of dwelling units and lots in an area.

3.18 (a) a special exception.
A special exception grant authorizes a use that is not consistent with the zoning ordinance in a literal sense, yet is clearly beneficial or essential to the public welfare and does not materially impair other uses in the zone.

3.19 (c) a legal nonconforming use.
An illegal nonconforming use is one that conflicts with ordinances that were in place before the use commenced. For instance, if a motel that was allowed as a legal nonconforming use is sold, and the new owner continues to operate the property as a motel, the motel is now an illegal, nonconforming use.

3.20 (b) a plat of subdivision.
In addition to complying with zoning ordinances, a developer of multiple properties in a subdivision must meet requirements for subdivisions, including submission of a plat of subdivision.

3.21 (a) accurately identifies the boundaries of the property as distinct from all other properties.
A legal description of real property is one which accurately locates and identifies the boundaries of the subject parcel to a degree acceptable by courts of law in the state where the property is located. The general criterion for a legal description is that it alone provides sufficient data for a surveyor to locate the parcel. A legal description identifies the property as unique and distinct from all other properties.

3.22 (c) reference points, angles, and distances.
A metes and bounds description identifies the boundaries of a parcel of real estate using reference points, distances, and angles. The description always identifies an enclosed area by starting at an origination point, called point of beginning, or POB, and returning to the POB at the end of the description.

3.23 (b) two consecutive common meridians.
The "vertical" area between consecutive meridians is called a range. A range is identified by its relationship to the principal meridian. All ranges are six miles wide.

3.24 (c) two consecutive parallels.
The "horizontal" area between two parallels is called a tier, or a township strip. A tier is identified by its relationship to the base parallel. All tiers are six miles wide.

3.25 (b) Six miles by six miles, or 6 miles square.
A township is the area enclosed by the intersection of two consecutive meridians and two consecutive parallels. Since the parallels and meridians are six miles apart, a township is a square with six miles on each side. Its area is therefore 36 square miles. Remember to differentiate square miles from miles square: 4 square miles is a measure of area (2 miles x 2 miles); 4 miles square is a representation of the sides of a square (4 miles by 4 miles).

3.26 (d) 1/64.
The size in acres of a subsection of a township is a fraction of 640 acres, since there are 640 acres in a section. Thus ten acres is 10/640, or 1/64th of a section.

3.27 (d) properties in a subdivision.
The recorded plat method, also called the lot and block system, is used to describe properties in residential, commercial, and industrial subdivisions. Under this system, tracts of land are subdivided into lots. The entire group of lots comprises the subdivision. In a large subdivision, lots may be grouped together into blocks for ease of reference.

3.28 (c) Metes and bounds.
A metes and bounds description identifies the point of beginning and describes the distance and direction from that point to the first monument, and thence to subsequent monuments and back to the beginning to define the property's enclosed perimeter.

3.29 (d) Thirty-six.
The rectangular survey system divides a township into thirty-six sections.

3.30 (a) 640.
Each side of a section is one mile in length. Thus the area of a section is one square mile, or 640 acres.

3.31 (c) something of value traded in exchange for something of value.
A contract must contain a two-way exchange of valuable consideration as compensation for performance by the other party. The contract is not valid or enforceable if just one party provides consideration. Valuable consideration may be something of tangible value, such as money, or something the party promises to do. It may also be something intangible that a party must give up.

3.32 (a) contain a legal description of the property.
In addition to satisfying the requirements of a valid contract in general, a contract that conveys an interest in real estate must be in writing, contain a legal description of the property, and be signed by one or more of the parties.

3.33 (d) A reasonable time, or until the expiration date on the offer.
If an offer contains an expiration date and the phrase "time is of the essence," the offer expires at exactly the time specified. In the absence of a stated time period, the offeree has a "reasonable" time to accept an offer.

3.34 (b) The buyer's death terminated the offer.
Any of the following actions or circumstances can terminate an offer: acceptance; rejection; revocation; lapse of time; counteroffer; or death or insanity of either party.

3.35 (c) A contract for the sale of undeveloped land.
A real estate contract that is not a personal contract for services can be assigned to another party unless the terms of the agreement specifically prohibit assignment. Listing agreements, for example, are not

assignable, since they are personal service agreements between agent and principal. Sales contracts, however, are assignable, because they involve the purchase of real property rather than a personal service.

3.36 (b) the parties act is if there is a contract.
An implied contract is an unstated or unintentional agreement that may be deemed to exist when the actions of any of the parties suggest the existence of an agreement.

3.37 (b) A sale contract before closing.
An executory contract is one in which performance is yet to be completed. A sales contract prior to closing is executory: while the parties have agreed to buy and sell, the buyer has yet to pay the seller and the seller has yet to deed the property to the buyer.

3.38 (a) both parties promise to do something in exchange for the other party's performance.
A bilateral contract is one in which both parties promise to perform their respective parts of an agreement in exchange for performance by the other party. An example of a bilateral contract is an exclusive listing: the broker promises to exercise due diligence in the efforts to sell a property, and the seller promises to compensate the broker when and if the property sells.

3.39 (c) The broker may have a claim for marketing expenses expended during the listing term.
The damaged party may elect the following legal remedies: rescission; forfeiture; suit for damages; or suit for specific performance. However, the broker must show that the seller has breached the contract.

3.40 (d) the failure of a party to perform according to the terms of the contract.
A breach of contract is a failure to perform according to the terms of the agreement.

3.41 (b) The act of declaring that a contract is no longer in effect for a given party.
Parties to a contract may rescind a contract by mutual consent, or a damaged party may rescind the contract unilaterally. This act of rescission cancels the contract and returns the parties to their pre-contract condition, including the refunding of any monies already transferred.

3.42 (a) reflect a mutual understanding or agreement.
Mutual consent, also known as offer and acceptance and meeting of the minds, requires that a contract involve a clear and definite offer and an intentional, unqualified acceptance of the offer.

3.43 (c) unenforceable.
A valid contract that is in writing is enforceable within a statutory time period. A valid contract that is made orally is also generally enforceable within a statutory period, with the exception that some contracts are enforceable only if they are in writing. These laws apply in particular to the transfer of interests in real estate. A void or voidable contract was not a truly valid contract.

3.44 (b) is possibly valid and enforceable.
Incompetent parties, or parties of "unsound mind," may not enter into enforceable contracts. However, during the period of one's incompetency, a court may appoint a guardian who may act on the incompetent party's behalf with court approval.

3.45 (c) a counteroffer.
By changing any of the terms of an offer, the offeree creates a counteroffer, and the original offer is void. At this point, the offeree becomes the offeror, and the new offeree gains the right of acceptance. If accepted, the counteroffer becomes a valid contract provided all other requirements are met.

3.46 (d) valuable consideration.
Valuable consideration can be something of tangible value, such as money, or something a party promises to do or not do. For example, a home builder may promise to build a house for a party as consideration for receiving money from the home buyer.

3.47 (c) is void.
The content, promise, or intent of a contract must be lawful. A contract that proposes an illegal act is void.

3.48 (a) must act within a statutory period.
The statute of limitations restricts the time period for which an injured party in a contract has the right to

rescind or disaffirm the contract. A party to a voidable contract must act within the statutory period.

3.49 (b) require certain conveyance-related contracts to be in writing.
The statute of frauds requires that certain contracts must be in writing to be enforceable. Real estate contracts that convey an interest in real property fall in this category, with the exception that a lease of one year's duration or less may be oral.

3.50 (b) The buyer has no obligations to the seller whatsoever.
The mutual consent required for a valid contract is reached through the process of offer and acceptance. If the offeree accepts all terms without amendment, the offer becomes a contract. The exact point at which the offer becomes a contract is when the offeree gives the offeror notice of the acceptance. If an offer contains an expiration date and the phrase "time is of the essence," the offer expires at exactly the time specified.

NATIONAL TEST 4: Agency; Listing Agreements

4.1 (b) the laws of agency, or in some states, by statute.
In every state, a body of law, generally called the law of agency, defines and regulates the legal roles of this relationship. While the relationship is subject to contract law, agency law dictates how the relationship will achieve its purposes, regardless of what the listing contract states.

4.2 (c) The relationship is independent of any compensation arrangement.
It is important to understand that the agency relationship does not require compensation or any form of consideration. Nor does compensation define an agency relationship: a party other than the principal may compensate the agent.

4.3 (c) The defaulting party may have a financial consequence.
Involuntary termination of the relationship may create legal and financial liability for a party who defaults or cancels. For example, a client may renounce an agreement but then be held liable for the agent's expenses or commission.

4.4 (b) present all offers to the principal regardless of their amount.
A conventional listing agreement does not authorize an agent to obligate the client to contracts, and it does not allow the agent to conceal offers to buy, sell, or lease coming from a customer or another agent. Further, since a client relies on a broker's representations, a broker must exercise care not to offer advice outside of his or her field of expertise.

4.5 (c) confidentiality.
The confidentiality standard is one of the duties that extends beyond the termination of the listing: at no time in the future may the agent disclose confidential information.

4.6 (d) comparable to that of other practitioners in the area.
The agent is hired to do a job, and is therefore expected to do it with diligence and reasonable competence. Competence is generally defined as a "standard of practice" equal to the level of real estate marketing skills and knowledge of other practitioners in the area.

4.7 (c) disclose the information to the seller.
An agent has the duty to inform the client of all material facts, reports, and rumors that might affect the client's interests in the property transaction. This includes: the agent's opinion of the property's condition; information about the buyer's motivations and financial qualifications; discussions between agent and buyer regarding the possibility of the agent's representing the buyer in another transaction.

4.8 (a) the Andersons.
Since Gerry executed an agency agreement with the Andersons, they become the client and the Lincolns the customer, regardless of who pays the commission.

4.9 (c) a broker who has an agency relationship with a client.
In a subagency, a broker or licensed salesperson works as the agent of a broker who is the agent of a client.

Subagents might include a cooperating licensed broker, that broker's licensed salespeople, and the listing broker's licensed salespeople, all of whom agree to work for the listing broker on behalf of the client.

4.10 (b) One agent represents both sides in a transaction.
Dual agency means representing both principal parties to a transaction. The agent represents both buyer and seller or tenant and owner.

4.11 (c) disclosing material facts that affect the value of the property to both parties.
In the role of facilitator, the broker's only fiduciary duties and standards of conduct are those of accounting; skill, care, and diligence; honesty and fair dealing; and disclosure to both parties of all material facts in residential sale transactions affecting the property's value. Some states do not allow for this form of relationship in a real estate transaction.

4.12 (a) The agent is showing the client's property to a prospective buyer.
Agency disclosure must occur upon "substantive contact" between the listing agent and a customer. Examples of substantive contact include: showing the prospect a property; eliciting confidential information from a prospect regarding needs, motivation, or financial qualification; and executing a contractual offer to sell or lease.

4.13 (d) trust, confidence, and good faith.
The essence of the agency relationship is trust, confidence, and mutual good faith. The principal trusts the agent to exercise the utmost skill and care in fulfilling the authorized activity, and to promote the principal's best interests. The agent undertakes to strive in good faith to achieve the desired objective, and to fulfill the fiduciary duties.

4.14 (b) general.
In a general agency, the principal delegates to the agent ongoing tasks and duties within a particular business or enterprise. Such delegation may include the authority to enter into contracts.

4.15 (b) special.
Under a special agency agreement, the principal delegates authority to conduct a specific activity, after which the agency relationship terminates. In most cases, the special agent may not bind the principal to a contract. Real estate brokerage is commonly based on a special agency.

4.16 (c) a party creates an agency relationship outside of an express agreement.
An agency relationship can arise by implication, intentionally or unintentionally. Implication means that the parties act as if there were an agreement. For example, if an agent promises a buyer to do everything possible to find a property at the lowest possible price, and the buyer accepts the proposition, there may be an implied agency relationship even though there is no specific agreement.

4.17 (a) Condemnation of the property
An agency relationship may terminate contrary to the wishes of the parties by reason of: death or incapacity of either party; abandonment by the agent; condemnation or destruction of the property; renunciation; breach; bankruptcy; or revocation of the agent's license.

4.18 (a) The agent has violated the duty of confidentiality.
An agent may not disclose any information that would harm the client's interests or bargaining position, or anything else the client wishes to keep secret. The confidentiality standard is one of the duties that extends beyond the termination of the listing: at no time in the future may the agent disclose confidential information.

4.19 (b) the agent has not violated fiduciary duty.
Since it is illegal to refuse to show buyers the property based on where the buyers live, the agent has not violated fiduciary duty. The duty of obedience only applies to legal activities.

4.20 (d) inform the seller.
An agent has the duty to inform the client of all material facts, reports, and rumors that might affect the client's interests in the property transaction.

4.21 (a) prior to completing a listing agreement.
An agent who intends to represent a seller or owner must disclose the import of the proposed agency relationship in writing before the listing agreement is executed.

4.22 (c) Whenever substantive communication is made beyond casual conversation.
A listing agent must disclose in writing to a buyer or tenant that the agent represents the owner in the transaction. This disclosure must occur before or at the first "substantive contact" with the customer prospect. In some states, buyer representatives must disclose the agency relationship to sellers or their agents upon initial contact.

4.23 (b) upon initial contact.
A buyer agent must disclose the agency relationship to the seller or seller's agent on first contact. Substantive contact is assumed to occur immediately in this circumstance.

4.24 (a) may not represent one party's interests to the detriment of the other.
A dual agent's first duty is to disclose the agency relationship to both principal parties or to withdraw from one side of the duality. After disclosing, the agent must obtain the written consent of both parties. If both parties accept the dual agency, the agent owes all the fiduciary duties to both parties except full disclosure, undivided loyalty, and exclusive representation of one principal's interests.

4.25 (d) practicing law without a license.
An agent should not act or speak outside the agent's area of expertise. A customer may rely on anything an agent says, and the agent will be held accountable. For example, an agent represents that a property will appreciate. The buyer interprets this as expert investment advice and buys the property. If the property does not appreciate, the buyer may hold the agent liable.

4.26 (a) Fiduciary and contractual obligations with the client.
A listing agreement establishes an agency relationship between agent and client that commits the agent to the full complement of fiduciary duties to the client in fulfilling the agreement.

4.27 (d) market, sell and show the property.
Special agency limits the scope of the broker's authority to specific activities, generally those which generate customers and catalyze the transaction. A special agency agreement usually does not authorize a broker to obligate the client to a contract as a principal party. Normally, principals do not delegate the authority to negotiate price to an agent in a residential transaction.

4.28 (b) An implied agency may have been created, with obligations to perform for both seller and agent.
Clients and agents may also create an implied agency listing based on substantive actions rather than on an express agreement. For example, if a seller allows a broker to undertake certain activities toward effecting a transaction without a specific authorization, but with full knowledge and consent, an implied agency may have been created.

4.29 (a) The agent cannot assign the listing agreement.
Since a listing agreement is a personal service contract, it is not assignable. In particular, a broker cannot assign a listing to another broker.

4.30 (b) exclusive right to sell.
The exclusive right to sell listing, or "exclusive," gives the agent the most control over the property and the greatest likelihood of being compensated for his or her marketing efforts.

4.31 (c) A listing that is entered in a multiple listing service to enable cooperation with member brokers.
Though not a distinct type of listing agreement, multiple listing is a significant feature of brokerage practice. Multiple listing is an authorization to enter a listing in a multiple listing service.

4.32 (b) The customer must be legally competent to undertake the transaction.
Effecting a completed transaction means finding a customer who is not only ready, willing, and able, but one who makes an acceptable offer. A ready, willing, and able customer is one who is: amenable to the terms of the transaction (ready and willing), and is financially capable of paying the price and legally

capable of completing the transaction (able).

4.33 (a) obtain and distribute compensation.
In the normal course of business, a listing broker delegates marketing responsibilities to salespeople. A salesperson may not, however, seek compensation directly from a client. Only the broker can obtain and disburse the compensation.

4.34 (c) Perry, since he found the customer.
The two principal determinants of procuring cause are being first to find the customer, and being the one who induces the customer to complete the transaction.

4.35 (d) It may be terminated against the agent's will.
A listing may terminate on grounds of: performance; infeasibility; mutual agreement; revocation; abandonment; breach; lapse of time; invalidity of the contract; incapacitation of either party; destruction of the property; or, in this case; involuntary title transfer.

4.36 (b) Sue the broker for money damages.
If the broker cancels the listing or otherwise defaults, the client may sue the broker for money damages.

4.37 (b) exclusive agency agreement.
An exclusive agency listing authorizes a single broker to sell the property and earn a commission, but leaves the owner the right to sell the property without the broker's assistance, in which case no commission is owed.

4.38 (c) open listing.
An open listing is a non-exclusive authorization to sell or lease a property. The owner may offer such agreements to any number of brokers in the marketplace. With an open listing, the broker who is the first to perform under the terms of the listing is the sole party entitled to a commission.

4.39 (d) net listing.
A net listing is one in which an owner sets a minimum acceptable amount to be received from the transaction and allows the broker to have any amount received in excess as a commission, assuming the broker has earned a commission according to the other terms of the agreement.

4.40 (a) the client.
Generally, buyer and tenant representation agreements are subject to the same laws and regulations as those applying to owner listings. The only difference is the client and his or her transaction expectations.

4.41 (a) To list the owner's property in a multiple listing service.
A multiple listing is not a distinct listing contract but rather a provision in an exclusive listing authorizing the broker to place the listing into a multiple listing service. A multiple listing service is an organization of member brokers who agree to cooperate in the sale of properties listed by other brokers in exchange for a share of the broker's resulting commission.

NATIONAL TEST 5: Brokerage Business; Sale Contracts

5.1 (d) Non-profit corporation.
A non-profit corporation is a corporate entity which is not legally entitled to generate profit. A non-profit organization may not broker real estate.

5.2 (c) are properly licensed.
A joint venture is a partnership formed to complete a specific business endeavor, such as a real estate development. Individuals, general and limited partnerships, and corporations may participate. A joint venture may broker real estate, provided the co-venturers are duly licensed.

5.3 (b) a single employing broker who has an active broker's license.
Only a broker with an active broker's license can hire and employ a licensed salesperson. A licensed salesperson may work only for the employing broker and may not work for or receive direct compensation from any other broker.

5.4 (c) Offer a property for lease on behalf of the employing broker.
A sales agent is only authorized to represent a broker and carry out such duties as the broker may legitimately delegate. Thus a sales agent does not directly represent the client in a transaction but is rather the agent of the broker and subagent of the client.

5.5 (d) The employing broker.
Agents can only receive compensation from their employing brokers. Co-op commissions, referral fees, and other compensations always flow through the broker to the sales agent.

5.6 (d) $4,940.
First calculate the total commission, then the co-brokerage splits, then the agent-broker split. Thus: $380,000 x 6.5% = $24,700 total commission. ($24,700 x 50%) = $12,350 total listing broker share. ($12,350 x 40% = $4,940 agent's share.

5.7 (c) $4,278.
The total commission is ($245,000 x 3%) = $7,350. The agent gets (65% x $7,350) - $500, which equals $4,278.

5.8 (c) complete the signing of the listing.
Once the seller signs the listing, the next critical task is to get it signed, thereby making the listing a contract. Some states allow a salesperson to do this and in other states, the listing must be given to the broker for signing. This result will set in motion the process of marketing the property. The agency disclosures must take place prior to the execution of the agreement.

5.9 (b) Present the offer to the seller at the earliest possible moment.
When a buyer or tenant makes an offer, the agent must present it to the seller or landlord at the earliest possible moment. If the terms of the offer are unacceptable, the agent may assist the seller in developing a counteroffer.

5.10 (c) The broker has illegally converted security funds for business use.
Conversion is the act of misappropriating escrow funds for the broker's business or personal use. Conversion carries serious consequences, including license revocation.

5.11 (d) Never.
All advertising must reveal the identity of the broker; licensed brokers and agents may not use blind ads that conceal their identities.

5.12 (a) fair trade and anti-trust laws.
Brokerage companies, like other businesses, are subject to anti-trust laws designed to prevent monopolies and unfair trade practices. In real estate brokerage, the primary manifestations of unfair trade practice are collusion, price fixing and market allocation. In this instance the brokers are price fixing.

5.13 (b) Outside brokers assist a listing agent in procuring a buyer.
Most listing agreements provide for brokerage cooperation in the multiple listing clause. A transaction involving a cooperating subagent is called co-brokerage. In a co-brokered transaction, the listing broker splits the commission with the "co-broker," typically on a 50-50 basis.

5.14 (d) Only members of the National Association of Realtors®.
The term Realtor® is a protected trade name of the National Association of Realtors®. Only members of this organization may use the term to refer to themselves.

5.15 (a) represent their employing broker in procuring clients and customers.
Agents may only act on behalf of their broker. They may not assume responsibilities for other listings since listings are not transferable.

5.16 (a) The IC is responsible for his or her own taxes; the broker does not withhold.
Generally, a broker has limited control over the actions of a contractor. Specifically: a broker can require performance results, but is limited in demanding how a contractor performs the work; and the broker does not take responsibility for a contractor's income and social security taxes.

5.17 (b) competitive conditions.
Commission structures are negotiated between the agent and employing broker as a function of competitive market conditions.

5.18 (c) avoid disclosing what price the owner will accept.
An agent must be extremely careful at this point to abide by fiduciary obligations to the client, whoever that party may be. Discussions of price are particularly delicate: whether the client is buyer or seller, the agent's duty is to uphold the client's best interests. Thus it is not acceptable to suggest to a customer what price the client will or will not accept.

5.19 (d) mixing escrow funds with the broker's operating funds.
Commingling, a prohibited activity, is the act of mixing the broker's personal or business funds with escrow funds.

5.20 (a) There is insufficient evidence of anything other than a normal business practice.
Charging identical commission rates in itself is legitimate. Price-fixing occurs when competitors have in fact colluded together to set prices.

5.21 (c) all the obligations and promises are performed and the transaction is closed.
An executory contract is one for which the signatories have yet to perform their respective obligations and promises. Upon closing, the sale contract is fully performed and no longer exists as a binding agreement.

5.22 (a) Use a standard contract promulgated by a state agency or a real estate board.
It is advisable, and legally required in most states, for a broker to use a standard contract form promulgated by state agencies or real estate boards, as such forms contain generally accepted language. This relieves the broker of the dangers of creating new contract language, which can be construed as a practice of law for which the broker is not licensed.

5.23 (b) be written.
A contract for the sale of real estate is enforceable only if it is in writing. A buyer or seller cannot sue to force the other to comply with an oral contract for sale, even if the contract is valid.

5.24 (a) The contract has been legitimately cancelled and is null and void.
To be valid, a contract must meet the criteria of: competent parties, voluntary act of good faith, mutual consent, legal purpose, and valuable consideration. The buyer broke the mutual consent requirement by opting out before being told of the seller's acceptance. Thus, there is no valid contract.

5.25 (c) An offer and acceptance.
A contract of sale is created by full and unequivocal acceptance of an offer. Offer and acceptance satisfy the mutual consent requirement for a valid contract. The offeree must accept the offer without making any changes whatsoever.

5.26 (d) Equitable title.
A sale contract gives the buyer an interest in the property that is called equitable title, or ownership in equity. If the seller defaults and the buyer can show good faith performance, the buyer can sue for specific performance, that is, to compel the seller to transfer legal title upon payment of the contract price.

5.27 (b) a condition that, if unmet, renders the contract unenforceable.
A contingency is a condition that must be met before the contract is enforceable. If one party cannot meet a contingency condition by a specified deadline, the other party may cancel the contract.

5.28 (c) The buyer may be able to have the contract canceled.
The termite inspection clause is a contingency clause. If one party cannot meet a contingency condition by a specified deadline, the other party may cancel the contract. Did the clause state that the inspector had to be properly licensed? If so, the buyer has a good case for cancellation.

5.29 (a) Until the seller communicates acceptance of the offer.
An offeror may revoke an offer for any reason prior to communication of acceptance by the offeree.

5.30 (b) Fred has entered into contracts with both Jack and Sally to sell the same property.
Jack's acceptance of Fred's offer creates a valid contract, just as Fred's acceptance of Sally's offer creates a valid contract. Fred should have revoked his offer to Jack before accepting Sally's offer.

5.31 (d) agency relationships and property condition.
It is common for the seller to disclose the property condition requiring the buyer to acknowledge receipt of the disclosure. The broker discloses the applicable agency relationships in the transaction and names the party who must pay the brokerage commission.

5.32 (b) valuable consideration and a right to buy.
An option-to-buy is an enforceable contract in which a potential seller, the optionor, grants a potential buyer, the optionee, the right to purchase a property before a stated time for a stated price and terms. In exchange for the right of option, the optionee pays the optionor valuable consideration.

5.33 (a) Schmidt must sell to Carboy for $10,000.
Mary's option-to-buy contract is enforceable, assuming she paid a consideration for it.

5.34 (d) It is always assignable unless the contract prohibits assignment.
A real estate contract that is not a personal service contract can be assigned to another party unless the terms of the agreement specifically prohibit assignment. An option-to-buy is therefore assignable in the absence of such a prohibiting clause.

5.35 (c) At the end of the contract period, the vendor conveys legal title, provided the vendee has fulfilled all obligations.
A contract for deed is a bilateral agreement between a seller, the vendor, and a buyer, the vendee, in which the vendor defers receipt of some or all of the purchase price of a property over a specified period of time. At the end of the period, the buyer completes payment to the vendor of the full purchase price and the vendor deeds legal title to the vendee.

5.36 (b) the parties have completed a verbal, executory contract.
As a sale contract created by an offer and acceptance, the parties have an executory contract: the parties have yet to perform their respective obligations and promises. However, as a contract for the sale of real estate, this verbal contract is not enforceable. An enforceable real estate sale contract must be in writing.

5.37 (c) The assignor has completed a legal action.
Either party to a sale transaction can assign the sale contract to another party, subject to the provisions and conditions contained in the agreement.

5.38 (d) any conveyance may trigger an acceleration of any loans secured by the property.
The mortgage agreement may or may not state that the seller's loan will be accelerated by the lender and called due on sale. The due-on-sale clause in the sale contract merely stipulates that the buyer and seller recognize the possibility that loans that survive the closing may be called due.

5.39 (d) The option is expired, and the tenant has no rightful claim to money paid for the option.
The option automatically expires at the end of the option period. The landlord has no obligation, either to sell the property or to return the consideration, after the expiration date.

5.40 (c) the seller retains legal title while the buyer makes partial payments until the contract is fully executed.
In a contract for deed, the seller, or vendor, defers receipt of some or all of the purchase price of a property over a specified period of time. During the period, the vendor retains legal title and the vendee acquires equitable title. At the end of the period, the buyer pays the vendor the full purchase price and the vendor deeds legal title to the vendee.

NATIONAL TEST 6: Economics; Appraisal

6.1 (b) demand for the item is increasing in relation to supply of the item.
In a market economy, the primary interactions between supply, demand and price are: if supply increases

relative to demand, price decreases; if supply decreases relative to demand, price increases; if demand increases relative to supply, price increases; and if demand decreases relative to supply, price decreases.

6.2 (d) Supply and demand are equal, and price and value are equal.
A market tends toward a state of equilibrium in which supply equals demand, and price, cost, and value are identical. According to this principle, market demand moves to meet supply, and supply moves to meet demand. If there is an extreme shortage of an item for which there is normally a strong demand, suppliers will rush to increase production to close the gap. If inventories of an item are very high, suppliers will stop production until the oversupply has been depleted.

6.3 (c) the uniqueness of every parcel.
In comparison with other economic products and services, real estate has certain unique traits. Traits of real estate include: inherent product value; uniqueness of every property; demand must come to the supply; illiquidity; slow to respond to changes; and a decentralized local market.

6.4 (d) Prices rise.
If demand is increasing and a moratorium slows supply, demand will begin to outpace supply, forcing prices to rise as the product becomes scarcer in relation to demand.

6.5 (b) an increase in demand for all types of real estate.
New businesses will arise to support the new company. They will hire new employees, some from out of town. The new employees will need housing. Hence the demand for residential real estate, as well as for commercial and industrial, will intensify, and it will also stimulate new construction.

6.6 (d) The number of available units that become occupied over a period of time.
Absorption is the amount of available property that becomes occupied over a period of time.

6.7 (a) rising prices.
Within the business cycle of real estate, declining vacancy indicates a combination of increasing demand which "fills up" supply which in turn decreases. As space becomes scarcer, rents for available space increase.

6.8 (b) desire, utility, scarcity, and purchasing power.
The value of something is based on the answers to four questions: how much do I desire it; how useful is it; how scarce is it; and am I able to pay for it.

6.9 (b) will increase.
If there is no longer a supply to meet the increasing demand of a growing population, prices for existing supply will rise.

6.10 (d) the market tending toward equilibrium.
A market tends toward a state of equilibrium in which supply equals demand, and price, cost, and value are identical. Thus if supply is scarce, construction will increase to stabilize the imbalance.

6.11 (c) the market is over-supplied.
Falling prices indicate an oversupply of commercial properties in relation to demand. In this case, construction of new supply will also slow down.

6.12 (a) have been increasing.
A rise in prices is a market signal that there is an undersupply of product in relation to demand. As the market moves toward equilibrium, builders construct more buildings to meet the unmet demand.

6.13 (c) It is often difficult to convert to cash.
Since real estate is often a large, long-term investment that has no exact duplicate, the process of a buyer's evaluating and choosing the right property is long and complex; hence, finding a buyer at a desired price can take a long time.

6.14 (b) The number of persons employed in base industries in an area
Base employment is the number of persons employed in the base industries that represent the economic foundation of an area. It is the driving component of total employment, which includes secondary and

support industries, and which creates demand for all types of real estate.

6.15 (d) The total existing space of a certain type that is unoccupied at a given time
Vacancy is the amount of total real estate inventory of a certain type that is unoccupied at a given time. It is often stated as a percentage of total inventory, the vacancy rate for that property type.

6.16 (a) local government influencing the real estate market, regardless of demand.
Local governments sometimes declare a moratorium on new construction because of present or projected inadequacies of the infrastructure—water, sewer, power, roads, etc.—or because of the desire to conform to a master plan. The result may be to drive up prices, as supply cannot freely increase to meet demand.

6.17 (c) In- and out-migrations of major employers
Changes in employment numbers in a local market area, especially in major industries, have a direct impact on real estate demand in the area. Money supply, interest rates, and trade imbalances also have an impact, but they are regional or national factors rather than strictly local.

6.18 (b) Vacancy rises and prices fall.
New construction generally occurs to meet an excess of demand. By adding supply, it tends to increase vacancy and lower prices until supply-demand equilibrium is achieved.

6.19 (d) Residential
While all types of users may have these needs, they are most prominent for residential users because of concerns for family comfort and safety. Retail users are more concerned with competitive features of the trade area; office users care more about occupancy costs and suitability for the business; industrial users care more about such features as functionality, accessibility, and the labor pool.

6.20 (c) its susceptibility to swings in the local economy.
Because a real property cannot be transferred to a large, central real estate marketplace, its marketability is closely tied to local conditions. Investors and users must come to the product, unlike other types of economic product that can be moved to a place in search of greater demand.

6.21 (b) anticipation.
Anticipation is the value principle that a buyer will pay a price based on the benefits the buyer expects to derive from a property over a holding period. For example, if an investor anticipates an annual rental income from a leased property to be one million dollars, this expected sum has a direct bearing on what the investor will pay for the property.

6.22 (b) A homeowner adds a third bathroom to a house and thereby increases the appraised value by $10,000.
The principle of contribution focuses on the degree to which a particular improvement affects market value of the overall property. In essence, the contribution of the improvement is equal to the change in market value that the addition of the improvement causes. For example, adding a bathroom to a house may contribute an additional $15,000 to the appraised value. Thus the contribution of the bathroom is $15,000.

6.23 (a) assemblage.
Assemblage, or the conjoining of adjacent properties, sometimes creates a combined value that is greater than the values of the unassembled properties. The excess value created by assemblage is called plottage value.

6.24 (d) Market value is an estimate; market price is the price at which a property sold.
Market value is an estimate of the price at which a property will sell at a particular time. The market price, as opposed to market value, is what a property actually sells for. Market price should theoretically be the same as market value if all the conditions essential for market value are present. Market price, however, may not reflect the analysis of comparables and of investment value that an estimate of market value includes.

6.25 (d) define the appraisal problem and the purpose of the appraisal.
The first step in the process is to define the appraisal problem and the purpose of the appraisal. This involves identifying the subject property by legal description; specifying the interest to be appraised; specifying the purpose of the appraisal; specifying the date for which the appraisal is valid; and identifying

233

the type of value to be estimated.

6.26 (c) weighing the applicability of the approaches and considering the quality of data supporting each approach.
The final step in the appraisal process is to reconcile the value estimates produced by the three approaches to value into a final value estimate. To do this, an appraiser must weigh the appropriateness of a particular approach to the type of property being appraised and take into account the quality and quantity of data obtained in each method.

6.27 (b) Make dollar adjustments to the sale prices of comparable properties to account for competitive differences with the subject. The sales comparison approach consists of comparing sale prices of recently sold properties that are comparable with the subject, and making dollar adjustments to the price of each comparable to account for competitive differences with the subject. After identifying the adjusted value of each comparable, the appraiser weights the reliability of each comparable and the factors underlying how the adjustments were made. The weighting yields a final value range based on the most reliable factors in the analysis.

6.28 (d) takes into account the competitive value of specific amenities of the subject property.
The sales comparison approach is widely used because it takes into account the subject property's specific amenities in relation to competing properties. In addition, because of the currency of its data, the approach incorporates present market realities.

6.29 (a) adds value to a comparable that is inferior to the subject property.
If the comparable is inferior to the subject in some characteristic, an amount is added to the price of the comparable. If the comparable is better than the subject in some characteristic, an amount is deducted from the sale price of the comparable. This neutralizes the comparable's competitive advantage or disadvantage in an adjustment category. For example, a comparable has a swimming pool and the subject does not. To equalize the difference, the appraiser deducts an amount, say $6,000, from the sale price of the comparable.

6.30 (b) requires the fewest and smallest adjustments.
As a rule, the fewer the total number of adjustments, the smaller the adjustment amounts, and the less the total adjustment amount, the more reliable the comparable.

6.31 (c) $195,000.
Since the comparable has an extra bath, it is adjusted downward to equalize with the subject. Conversely, since it has no patio, the appraiser adds value to the comparable. Thus, $200,000 minus $7,000 plus $2,000 equals $195,000.

6.32 (d) Add the estimated land value and cost of improvements and subtract the accrued depreciation of the improvements.
The cost approach consists of estimating the value of the land "as if vacant;" estimating the cost of improvements; estimating and deducting accrued depreciation; and adding the estimated land value to the estimated depreciated cost of the improvements.

6.33 (b) is very accurate for a property with new improvements that represent the highest and best use.
The strengths of the cost approach are that it: provides an upper limit for the subject's value based on the undepreciated cost of reproducing the improvements. It is also very accurate for valuing a property with new improvements which are the highest and best use of the property.

6.34 (c) a property loses the same increment of value each year over the economic life of the property.
All property improvements have an economic life, which becomes incrementally shorter year after year as physical deterioration takes its toll. The property as a whole does not lose value, since land itself does not depreciate. Similarly, an improvement can regain value if it is repaired or updated. Finally, not all properties lose value from economic obsolescence.

6.35 (d) $115,000.
To appraise value using the cost approach, add the land value to the value of the depreciated improvement. Thus you have $30,000 + ($95,000 - 10,000), or $115,000.

6.36 (b) Divide the income a property generates by a rate of return.
An appraiser obtains an indication of value from the income capitalization method by dividing the estimated net operating income for the subject by the rate of return, or capitalization rate. The formula is: NOI / Cap rate = Value.

6.37 (c) uses a method that is also used by investors to determine how much they should pay for an investment property.
The strength of the income approach is that it is used by investors themselves to determine how much they should pay for a property. Thus, in the right circumstances, it provides a good basis for estimating market value. The approach, however, does not project what an income property's future income will be. Moreover, it is not an applicable method for estimating value if the subject is a non-income producing property.

6.38 (a) $370,000.
First, identify net income by subtracting out vacancy and expenses. Then divide by the capitalization rate. Thus, ($60,000 –3,000 – 20,000) ÷ 10% = $370,000.

6.39 (d) 150.
The monthly gross rent multiplier for a property is equal to the price divided by the monthly rent. Thus, ($450,000 ÷ $3,000) = 150.

6.40 (c) $203,000.
Multiply the monthly gross income times 12 to derive annual income. Multiply annual income times the gross income multiplier to derive the estimate of price. Thus, $1,200 times 12 equals $14,400. This times 14.1 equals $203,040, or $203,000 rounded.

6.41 (c) the state in which the appraiser operates.
A state-certified appraiser is one who has passed the necessary examinations and competency standards as established by each state in conformance with the federal standards.

6.42 (a) The Financial Institutions Reform, Recovery and Enforcement Act (FIRREA).
Title XI of FIRREA requires that competent individuals whose professional conduct is properly supervised perform all appraisals used in federally-related transactions. As of January 1, 1993, such federally-related appraisals must be performed only by state-certified appraisers.

6.43 (a) if two similar properties are for sale, a buyer will purchase the cheaper of the two.
According to the principle of substitution, a buyer will pay no more for a property than the buyer would have to pay for an equally desirable and available substitute property. For example, if three houses for sale are essentially similar in size, quality and location, a potential buyer is unlikely to choose the one that is priced significantly higher than the other two.

6.44 (a) is physically and financially feasible, legal, and the most productive.
This valuation principle holds that there is, theoretically, a single use for a property that produces the greatest income and return. A property achieves its maximum value when it is put to this use. The use must however be legal.

6.45 (d) $200,000. Market value is an opinion of the price that a willing seller and willing buyer would probably agree on for a property at a given time if: the transaction is for cash; the property is exposed on the open market for a reasonable period; buyer and seller have full information about market conditions ; there is no abnormal pressure on either party; it is an "arm's length" transaction; title is marketable; and the price does not include hidden influences such as special financing deals. The amount Lynne actually paid is the market price. The previous listing price and Ken's offer might be interesting data for the appraiser, but the appraisal must also consider other market data, such as comparable sales.

6.46 (a) there may be no recent sale price data in the market.
The sales comparison approach is limited in that every property is unique. As a result, it is difficult to find good comparables, especially for special-purpose properties. In addition, the market must be active; otherwise, sale prices lack currency and reliability.

6.47 (c) selects comparable properties, adjusts the comparables, and estimates the value.
The steps are to first identify comparable sales; then compare comparables to the subject and make adjustments to comparables; then, finally, weigh values indicated by adjusted comparables for the final value estimate of the subject.

6.48 (b) the seller offers below-market seller financing.
The principal factors for comparison and adjustment are time of sale, location, physical characteristics, and transaction characteristics. An adjustment may be made for such differences as mortgage loan terms, mortgage assumability, and owner financing.

6.49 (b) weights the comparables.
The last step in the approach is to perform a weighted analysis of the indicated values of each comparable. The appraiser, in other words, must identify which comparable values are more indicative of the subject and which are less indicative. However, all comparables are taken into account, not simply the nearest comparable.

6.50 (b) market value is not always the same as what the property cost.
The limitations of the cost approach are that: the cost to create improvements is not necessarily the same as market value; and depreciation is difficult to measure, especially for older buildings.

6.51 (b) replacement cost.
Reproduction cost is the cost of constructing, at current prices, a precise duplicate of the subject improvements. Replacement cost is the cost of constructing, at current prices and using current materials and methods, a functional equivalent of the subject improvements.

6.52 (d) functional obsolescence.
Functional obsolescence occurs when a property has outmoded physical or design features which are no longer desirable or acceptable to current users.

6.53 (b) incurable economic obsolescence.
Economic (or external) obsolescence is the loss of value due to adverse changes in the surroundings of the subject property that make the subject less desirable. Since such changes are usually beyond the control of the property owner, economic obsolescence is considered an incurable value loss.

6.54 (c) depreciation.
Depreciation is the loss of value in an improvement over time. The loss of an improvement's value can come from any cause, such as deterioration, obsolescence, or changes in the neighborhood.

6.55 (a) estimates depreciation, subtracts depreciation from cost, and adds back the land value.
The steps in the costs approach are: (1) estimate land value; (2) estimate reproduction or replacement cost of improvements; (3) estimate accrued depreciation; (4) subtract accrued depreciation from reproduction or replacement cost; and (5) add land value to depreciated reproduction or replacement cost.

NATIONAL TEST 7: Finance

7.1 (b) A state in which a mortgagee has equitable title to a secured property.
States differ in their interpretation of who owns mortgaged property. Those that regard the mortgage as a lien held by the mortgagee (lender) against the property owned by the mortgagor (borrower) are called lien-theory states. Those that regard the mortgage document as a conveyance of ownership from the mortgagor to the mortgagee are called title-theory states.

7.2 (d) It is evidence of the borrower's debt to the lender.
A valid mortgage or trust deed financing arrangement requires a note as evidence of the debt.

7.3 (a) trust deed or mortgage.
The mortgage or trust deed is evidence of the collateral pledge of the purchased property as security for the loan.

7.4 (b) mortgagor.
The mortgagor is the borrower and the mortgagee is the lender. As a memory aid, notice that "lender" and "mortgagee" both have two "e"s. "Mortgagor" and "borrower" both have two "o"s.

7.5 (d) $1,000.
Multiply the rate times the loan amount and divide by 12 to calculate monthly interest. Thus, ($200,000 x 6%) ÷ 12 = $1,000.

7.6 (b) $100,000.
The equation for the loan amount is (annual interest divided by the interest rate) = loan amount. Thus, ($500 x 12) ÷ .06 = $100,000.

7.7 (a) 7.5%.
The equation for the interest rate is (annual payment / loan amount) = interest rate. Thus ($3750 / $50,000) = 7.5%.

7.8 (b) $2,000.
A discount point is one percent of the loan amount. Thus, one point on a $100,000 loan equals ($100,000 x 2%) or ($100,000 x .02), or $2,000.

7.9 (b) Part of each periodic payment is applied to repayment of the loan balance in advance and part is applied to payment of interest in arrears.
In an amortizing loan, part of the principal is repaid periodically along with interest, so that the principal balance decreases over the life of the loan. The annual interest is never the same, since the principal balance to which the interest rate applies changes every year. Interest on a loan is always paid in arrears, not in advance.

7.10 (b) private mortgage insurance.
Mortgage insurance protects the lender against loss of a portion of the loan (typically 20-25%) in case of borrower default. Private mortgage insurance generally applies to loans that are not backed by the Federal Housing Administration (FHA) or Veterans Administration (VA) and that have a down payment of less than 20% of the property value. The FHA has its own insurance requirement for loans with a down payment of less than 20%.

7.11 (d) The fraction of the appraised value of the property offered as collateral which the lender is willing to lend.
The relationship of the loan amount to the property value, expressed as a percentage, is called the loan-to-value ratio, or LTV. If the lender's loan to value ratio is 80%, the lender will lend only $80,000 on a home appraised at $100,000. The difference between what the lender will lend and what the borrower must pay for the property is the amount the borrower must provide in cash as a down payment.

7.12 (c) buyer's down payment.
Price less loan is the down payment. This is also the buyer's initial equity.

7.13 (a) refusing a loan because the borrower does not match the lender's target market.
The Equal Credit Opportunity Act (ECOA) requires a lender to evaluate a loan applicant on the basis of that applicant's own income and credit rating, unless the applicant requests the inclusion of another's income and credit rating in the application. In addition, ECOA has prohibited a number of practices in mortgage loan underwriting, including refusing a loan based on an applicant's demographic characteristics.

7.14 (b) $1680.
Monthly income qualification is derived by multiplying monthly income by the income ratio. Thus (72,000 / 12) x .28 = $1680. Remember to first derive the monthly income.

7.15 (b) adjust the applicant's debt ratio calculation and lower the loan amount.
Since a lender lends only part of the purchase price of a property according to the lender's loan-to-value ratio, a lender will verify that a borrower has the cash resources to make the required down payment. If someone is lending an applicant a portion of the down payment with a provision for repayment, a lender will consider this another debt obligation and adjust the debt ratio accordingly. This can lower the amount

a lender is willing to lend.

7.16 (c) All loans secured by a residence.
Regulation Z applies to all loans secured by a residence. It does not apply to commercial loans or to agricultural loans over $25,000. Its provisions cover the disclosure of costs, the right to rescind the credit transaction, advertising credit offers, and penalties for non-compliance with the act.

7.17 (d) the borrower has a limited right to cancel the transaction within a certain period.
A borrower has a limited right to cancel the credit transaction, usually within three days of completion of the transaction. The right of rescission does not apply to "residential mortgage transactions," that is, to mortgage loans used to finance the purchase or construction of the borrower's primary residence. It does, however, apply to refinancing of mortgage loans, and to home equity loans. State law may require a rescission period and notice on first mortgage loan transactions as well.

7.18 (b) ask the buyer/borrower about his/her religion or national origin.
ECOA prohibits discrimination in extending credit based on race, color, religion, national origin, sex, marital status, age, or dependency upon public assistance. A creditor may not make any statements to discourage an applicant on the basis of such discrimination or ask any questions of an applicant concerning these discriminatory items. A real estate licensee who assists a seller in qualifying a potential buyer may fall within the reach of this prohibition.

7.19 (d) not FHA-insured or VA-guaranteed.
A conventional mortgage loan is a permanent long-term loan that is not FHA-insured or VA-guaranteed. FNMA does not "back" loans; FHA only insures FHA loans; and the VA, not GNMA guarantees loans.

7.20 (b) limited by when the loan was originated.
Rules for assumability vary according to when the FHA-insured loan was originated and whether the original loan was for an investment property or an owner-occupied principal residence. Loans originated before December 1, 1986, are generally assumable without restriction. Loans originated after December 1, 1986, require that the assumer show creditworthiness. Some mortgages executed from 1986 through 1989 contain language that is not enforced as a result of later Congressional action. Mortgages from that period are now freely assumable, despite any restrictions stated in the mortgage.

7.21 (c) how much of a loan the VA will guarantee.
A veteran must apply for a Certificate of Eligibility to find out how much the VA will guarantee in a particular situation.

7.22 (d) Zero.
If a loan is fully amortizing, its loan balance is zero at the end of the loan term.

7.23 (b) The buyer gives the seller a mortgage and note as part of the purchase price of the property.
With a purchase money mortgage, the borrower gives a mortgage and note to the seller to finance some or all of the purchase price of the property. The seller in this case is said to "take back" a note, or to "carry paper," on the property.

7.24 (c) hypothecation.
The process of securing a loan by pledging a property without giving up ownership of the property is called hypothecation.

7.25 (a) The borrower gives the lender a note and a mortgage in exchange for loan funds.
When a borrower gives a note promising to repay the borrowed money and executes a mortgage on the real estate for which the money is being borrowed as security, the financing method is called mortgage financing.

7.26 (c) The trustor conveys title to a trustee in exchange for loan funds from the beneficiary.
A deed of trust conveys title to the property in question from the borrower (trustor) to a trustee as security for the loan. The trustee is a third party fiduciary to the trust. While the loan is in place, the trustee holds the title on behalf of the lender, who is the beneficiary of the trust.

7.27 (a) title-theory state.
States that regard the mortgage document as a conveyance of ownership from the mortgagor to the mortgagee are called title-theory states.

7.28 (b) usury.
Many states have laws against usury, which is the charging of excessive interest rates on loans. Such states have a maximum rate that is either a flat rate or a variable rate tied to an index such as the prime lending rate.

7.29 (c) $1,200.
A point is one percentage point of a loan amount. Thus, 2 points on a $60,000 loan equal (.02 x $60,000), or $1,200.

7.30 (a) an amortized loan is paid off over the loan period.
Amortized loans retire the principal balance over the loan period. If a loan does not do this, one must make a balloon payment at the end of the loan term to complete the loan payoff.

7.31 (c) it is a negotiable instrument.
A promissory note is a negotiable instrument, which means the payee may assign it to a third party. The assignee would then have the right to receive the borrower's periodic payments.

7.32 (d) may be required to execute a release of mortgage document.
Lenders may be required to release the mortgage or trust document to the borrower when the borrower has paid off the loan and all other sums secured by the document. The release clause, also known as a defeasance clause, may specify that the mortgagee will execute a satisfaction of mortgage (also known as release of mortgage and mortgage discharge) to the mortgagor.

7.33 (a) an appraisal report.
Loan underwriting is the process of assessing the lender's risk in giving a loan. Mortgage underwriting includes: evaluating the borrower's ability to repay the loan; appraising the value of the property offered as security; and determining the terms of the loan.

7.34 (c) the ability to re-pay, the value of the collateral, and the profitability of the loan.
A lender assesses risks by examining, or qualifying, both borrower and property. In qualifying a borrower, an underwriter weighs the ability of the borrower to repay the loan. In qualifying a property, an underwriter assesses the ability of the property value to cover potential losses. In this evaluation, a lender requires that the appraised value of the property be more than adequate to cover the contemplated loan and costs. Finally, the loan must make money for the lending organization as a basic business precept.

7.35 (b) they want to ensure there is more than enough collateral to cover the loan amount.
Without an ample difference between the property value and the loan amount, a drop in property values could cause the loan balance to exceed the collateral itself. This greatly increases the risk of a loan loss should the borrower default since the balance could not be completely recovered in a foreclosure sale.

7.36 (b) consider the income of a spouse in evaluating a family's creditworthiness.
The Equal Credit Opportunity Act (ECOA) requires a lender to evaluate a loan applicant on the basis of that applicant's own income and credit rating, unless the applicant requests the inclusion of another's income and credit rating in the application. In such a case, a lender may not discount or disregard income from part-time work, a spouse, child support, alimony, or separate maintenance.

7.37 (a) insure the buyer has the earning power to make the loan payments.
Both the income and debt ratios in borrower qualification quantify how much a borrower can safely afford to pay on a mortgage loan. The income ratio focuses on the borrower's earning power.

7.38 (d) debt payments divided by gross income.
The debt ratio formula is (debt obligations) ÷ (income).

7.39 (c) the parties complete all loan origination documents and the loan is funded.
Closing of a mortgage loan normally occurs with the closing of the real estate transaction. At the real estate closing, the lender typically has deposited the funded amount with an escrow agent, along with

instructions for disbursing the funds. The borrower deposits necessary funds with the escrow agent, executes final documents, and receives signed copies of all relevant documents.

7.40 (b) Truth-in-Lending laws and Regulation Z.
Regulation Z, which implements the Truth-in-Lending Act, applies to all loans secured by a residence. It does not apply to commercial loans or to agricultural loans over $25,000. It prescribes requirements to lenders regarding the disclosure of costs, the right to rescind the credit transaction, advertising credit offers, and penalties for non-compliance with the Truth-in-Lending Act.

7.41 (a) The Equal Credit Opportunity Act.
ECOA prohibits discrimination in extending credit based on race, color, religion, national origin, sex, marital status, age, or dependency upon public assistance.

7.42 (c) the Real Estate Settlement and Procedures Act.
RESPA is a federal law which aims to standardize settlement practices and ensure that buyers understand settlement costs. RESPA applies to purchases of residential real estate (one- to four-family homes) to be financed by "federally related" first mortgage loans. In addition to imposing settlement procedures, RESPA provisions prohibit lenders from paying kickbacks and unearned fees to parties who may have helped the lender obtain the borrower's business.

7.43 (b) Buying securities, changing the discount rate, and controlling banking reserves.
The Federal Reserve System regulates the money supply by means of three methods: selling or re-purchasing government securities, primarily Treasury bills, changing the reserve requirement for member banks; changing the interest rate, or discount rate, the system charges member institutions for borrowing funds from the Federal Reserve System.

7.44 (a) It cycles funds back to primary lenders so they can make more loans.
Secondary mortgage market organizations buy pools of mortgages from primary lenders and sell securities backed by these pooled mortgages to investors. By purchasing loans from primary lenders, the secondary market returns funds to the primary lenders, thereby enabling the primary lender to originate more mortgage loans.

7.45 (a) Fannie Mae, Freddie Mac, and Ginnie Mae.
As major players in the secondary market, the Federal National Mortgage Association (FNMA, "Fannie Mae"), Government National Mortgage Association (GNMA, "Ginnie Mae), and Federal Home Loan Mortgage Corporation (FHLMC, "Freddie Mac") tend to set the standards for the primary market. FHA, VA, and the Federal Reserve are not organizations in the secondary mortgage market.

7.46 (c) It purchases FHA-backed and VA-backed loans.
Fannie Mae buys conventional, FHA-backed and VA-backed loans; gives banks mortgage-backed securities in exchange for blocks of mortgages; and sells bonds and mortgage-backed securities. It does not guarantee, insure, or originate loans.

7.47 (b) It insures loans made by approved lenders.
The Federal Housing Administration (FHA) does not lend money, but insures permanent long-term loans made by others. The lender must be approved by the FHA, and the borrower must meet certain FHA qualifications.

7.48 (a) It guarantees loans made by approved lenders.
The Veterans Administration (VA) offers loan guarantees to qualified veterans. The VA partially guarantees permanent long-term loans originated by VA-approved lenders on properties that meet VA standards. The VA's guarantee enables lenders to issue loans with higher loan-to-value ratios than would otherwise be possible.

7.49 (c) the loan payments gradually increase.
Graduated payment mortgages allow for smaller initial monthly payments which gradually increase. The interest rate remains fixed as does the loan term.

7.50 (b) the borrower pays additional interest at the onset in order to obtain a lower interest rate.
A buydown loan entails a prepayment of interest on a loan. The prepayment effectively lowers the interest

rate and the periodic payments for the borrower. Buydowns typically occur in a circumstance where a builder wants to market a new development to a buyer who cannot quite qualify for the necessary loan at market rates.

NATIONAL TEST 8: Investments; Taxation; Ethics

8.1 (b) negative leverage.
Leveraging is borrowing funds in order to make an investment that is larger than your own resource permits you to do directly. In negative leverage situations, your cost of borrowing funds to make the investment becomes greater than the income the investment returns to you.

8.2 (b) income properties.
Cost recovery, or depreciation, allows the owner of income property to deduct a portion of the property's value from gross income each year over the life of the asset. Principal residences cannot be depreciated (unless portions are treated as a home office.) Further, land cannot be depreciated.

8.3 (c) 19.5 %.
Appreciation amount is the current value of the property minus the original cost. The total appreciation rate is derived by dividing the appreciation amount by the original cost. Subtract the estimated current market value from the price originally paid (239,000 - 200,000 = 39,000) and then divide the result by the original price (39,000 / 200,000 = . 195 or 19.5%).

8.4 (d) a deduction for mortgage interest.
Deducting mortgage interest is a significant tax advantage of owning one's residence. Depreciation and cost-deductions do not apply to a non-income producing residence. Appreciation is a benefit, but not a tax benefit.

8.5 (d) $232,900.
The figure for net proceeds from sale is expressed by the formula: sale price - costs of sale = net proceeds. Thus $250,000 - (6% x 250,000) – 600 – 1,500 = $232,900.

8.6 (b) $157,000.
The beginning basis is the cost of acquiring a property. Basis is increased by capital improvements and decreased by depreciation. The basic formula for adjusted basis is Beginning basis ($150,000) + capital improvements ($3,000 + $4,000) - depreciation ($0) = adjusted basis ($157,000).

8.7 (c) $34,000.
The gain on sale (capital gain) of a primary residence is represented by the basic formula: amount realized (net sales proceeds, $210,000) - adjusted basis ($176,000) = gain on sale ($34,000).   Note the purchase price of the second house is irrelevant.

8.8 (a) There is no taxable gain.
There is no taxable gain because the gain falls under the exclusion limit of $250,000. As of August 5, 1997, tax law provides an exclusion of $250,000 for an individual taxpayer and $500,000 for married taxpayers filing jointly on the gain from sale of a principal residence. The seller must have owned the property for at least two years during the five years preceding the date of sale; used the property as principal residence for a total of two years during that five-year period; and have waited two years since the last use of the exclusion for any sale.

8.9 (c) direct investment.
Individuals, corporations, or other investor entities may invest as active investors in a property by buying it directly and taking responsibility for managing and operating the property. This investment mode is called direct investment.

8.10 (a) $2,100.
Annual gross operating income ($1,500 x 12 = $18,000) - annual operating expenses ($500 x 12 = $6,000) = annual net operating income ($12,000); annual net operating income ($12,000) - cost recovery expense ($5,000) = taxable income ($7,000); taxable income ($7,000) x tax rate (30%) = tax liability ($2,100).

8.11 (b) the more the investor stands to gain, the greater the risk that the investor may lose.
The general rule in investments is that the safer the investment, the more slowly it gains in value. The more you want it to gain, and the more quickly, the more you must risk losing it. Reward in investing corresponds directly to the degree of risk.

8.12 (a) income and tax benefits.
The basic financial rewards of an investment include income, appreciation in asset value, positive borrowing leverage, and tax benefits.

8.13 (d) relatively illiquid.
Real estate is by nature more difficult to convert to cash than many other types of investment. Compare the selling of a home with the ease of drawing money out of a bank account or selling a stock.

8.14 (b) a more management-intensive investment.
Real estate tends to require a high degree of investor involvement in management of the investment. Even raw land requires some degree of maintenance to preserve its value. Improved properties often require extensive management, including repairs, maintenance, onsite leasing, tenant relations, security, and fiscal management.

8.15 (a) a general partnership.
A general partnership is a syndicate in which all members participate equally in managing the investment and in the profits or losses it generates.

8.16 (d) gross income minus expenses minus building depreciation.
Taxable income from investment real estate is the gross income received minus any expenses, deductions or exclusions that current tax law allows. Depreciation of land is not allowed.

8.17 (c) deduct interest payments from income.
Taxable income is net operating income minus all allowable deductions. The interest portion of debt service is allowed and is deducted from Net Operating Income as interest expense. Principal repayment is not an allowable deduction on investment properties. Capital gain derivation does not involve interest or principal payments.

8.18 (d) The owner may be able to avoid capital gain tax when the property is sold.
Provided the owner meets certain ownership and use tests, there is no capital gain tax on sale of the property unless the gain exceeds $250,000 for a single taxpayer or $500,000 for married taxpayers who file jointly. Since the property is not used for business, deductions for expenses against income are not allowed.

8.19 (c) may be deducted from the sale price for gains tax purposes.
Selling costs include such expenses as brokerage commissions, relevant advertising, legal fees, seller-paid points and other closing costs. These costs are deducted from the selling price to get the amount realized, which is reduced by the adjusted basis to calculate gain on sale for gains tax purposes.

8.20 (b) the difference between amount realized and adjusted basis.
The formula for gain tax is Taxable Gain on Sale x the owner's marginal tax bracket. The formula for gain on sale is: Amount Realized - Adjusted Basis = Gain on Sale. The formula for Amount Realized is: Selling Price - Selling costs = Amount Realized. Therefore, the gain tax = (Amount Realized - Adjusted Basis) x tax rate.

8.21 (c) A tax district.
Real estate property taxes are imposed by "taxing entities" or "taxing districts" at county and local levels of government. States may legally levy taxes on real property, but most delegate this power to counties, cities, townships and local taxing districts. The federal government does, however, tax income derived from real property and gains realized on the sale of real property.

8.22 (b) properties owned by a government agency.
Certain types of property are exempt from property taxes. Certain classes of property owner may also be

exempted or have a reduced liability. Exemptions include government-owned properties, real properties owned by churches, and properties owned by other non-profit organizations.

8.23 (c) It adjusts assessments in a locality to make them more consistent with an average level for the state or other higher level jurisdiction.
Equalization factors level out the unevenness of valuations for groups of properties. For instance, if assessed values of properties in one county are consistently ten percent below the average for other counties, an equalization board may multiply each assessed value in that county by a factor of 110% to raise them to the average level for the state.

8.24 (c) $2,000,000,000.
The mill rate = (tax requirement / the tax base). A mill is one one-thousandth of a dollar ($.001). To solve for the tax base, reconfigure this formula to be: Base = Tax Requirement / Mill Rate. Thus the Base = $20,000,000 / .010, or $2,000,000,000.

8.25 (d) $441.
The library tax is ($1.00 x 147) and the fire district tax is ($2.00 x 147). Thus the tax is $441.

8.26 (b) $5,700.
Special assessments are based on the cost of the improvement and apportioned on a pro rata basis among benefiting properties according to the value that each parcel will receive from the improvement. Here, Mary's share is 38 / 200, or 19%. 19% x $30,000 = $5,700.

8.27 (a) A conveyance instrument for a property that is sold to enforce a tax lien.
A tax deed is a legal instrument for conveying title when a property is sold for non-payment of taxes. The application for a tax deed causes the taxing agency to institute a tax sale or tax foreclosure.

8.28 (d) a statutory right of redemption.
If the taxpayer can redeem the property after the tax sale, this right is known as a statutory right of redemption. In this case, the taxpayer must pay the amount paid by the winning bidder at the tax sale, plus any charges, additional taxes, or interest that may have accumulated.

8.29 (b) the total of all assessed values of properties minus exemptions.
The tax base of an area is the total of the appraised or assessed values of all real property within the area's boundaries, excluding partially or totally exempt properties such as those owned by the government or non-profit organizations.

8.30 (c) multiplying each district's tax rate times the taxable value of the property.
Each property owner's tax bill is determined by multiplying the tax rate for each taxing district times the taxable value of the property. Taxable value is the assessed value after all exemptions and adjustments have been taken into account.

8.31 (a) Civil Rights Act of 1866.
The original fair housing statute, the Civil Rights Act of 1866, prohibits discrimination in housing based on race. The prohibition relates to selling, renting, inheriting, and conveying real estate.

8.32 (c) race, color, religion, and national origin.
Title VIII of the Civil Rights Act of 1968, known today as the Fair Housing Act, prohibits discrimination in housing based on race, color, religion, or national origin.

8.33 (c) Advertising a property as available to individuals of a particular race. The prohibition against discriminatory advertising states that an agent may not advertise residential properties in such a way as to restrict their availability to any prospective buyer or tenant.

8.34 (c) An agent persuades a family to put their house on the market because ethnic minority families are beginning to move into the neighborhood.
Blockbusting, a prohibited activity, is the practice of inducing owners in an area to sell or rent to avoid an impending change in the ethnic or social makeup of the neighborhood that will cause values to go down.

8.35 (a) The Home Mortgage Disclosure Act.
The Home Mortgage Disclosure Act requires lenders involved with federally guaranteed or insured loans to exercise impartiality and non-discrimination in the geographical distribution of their loan portfolio. In other words, the act is designed to prohibit redlining, the practice of restricting loans by geographical are(a)

8.36 (c) privately owned single-family residences listed with a broker.
Among the circumstances where the Fair Housing Act might allow for an exemption is: a privately owned single-family home where no broker is used, with certain additional conditions. In other words, as soon as a broker is used in the sale, the law applies.

8.37 (a) illegal, because the agent changed the terms of the sale to discourage this particular couple.
The Fair Housing Act prohibition against discriminatory misrepresentation states that an agent may not conceal available properties, represent that they are not for sale or rent, or change the sale terms for the purpose of discriminating.

8.38 (d) The owner of a duplex who resides in one of the units refuses to rent the other unit to a non-Christian.
The Fair Housing Act would exempt the owner in this situation because it involves rental of an apartment in a 1-4 unit building where the owner is also an occupant and there is no discriminatory advertising.

8.39 (b) File a complaint with HUD and/or file suit against the offending parties in a state or federal court within the prescribed time period.
The Fair Housing Amendments Act of 1988 prohibits discrimination based on sex. If May feels she has been discriminated against in this way, she may file a complaint with the Office of Fair Housing and Equal Opportunity (OFHEO) in HUD within one year or file suit in a federal or state court within two years of the alleged violation.

8.40 (a) Inform Scott that the condition is illegal and that she cannot comply with it.
Scott is not allowed to discriminate based on race, color, religion, national origin, sex, family status, or handicap. If an agent goes along with a client's discriminatory act, the agent is equally liable for violation of fair housing laws. It is thus imperative to avoid complicity with client discrimination. Further, an agent should withdraw from any relationship where client discrimination occurs.

8.41 (c) require families without children to pay the same security deposit that families with children must pay.
Fair housing laws prohibit discriminatory advertising, discrimination on the basis of national origin, discrimination based on age in dwellings of more than four units, and discrimination against families with children. The fact that the owner is requiring the same deposit from tenants with and without children does not discriminate against families with children but actually favors them.

8.42 (d) It is a single-family house, and the owner owns only one other rental home in addition to his own residence.
Federal fair housing laws do not prohibit age and family status discrimination in residential dwellings of four units or less and in single family houses if sold or rented by owners who have no more than three houses.

8.43 (c) the Fair Housing Amendments Act of 1988.
The Fair Housing Amendments Act of 1988 prohibited discrimination based on sex and discrimination against handicapped persons and families with children. Executive Order 11063 concerned racial discrimination in housing where federal funding was involved; the Civil Rights Act of 1968 concerned discrimination based on race, color, religion, and national origin; Jones v Mayer concerned racial discrimination.

8.44 (c) steering.
Steering is the illegal practice of limiting customers' choices by encouraging or discouraging them about the suitability of an area and directing them only to areas the agent deems suitable for them.

8.45 (a) providing unequal services.
The agent may be illegally providing unequal services by altering the nature or quality of brokerage services to a party based on race, color, sex, national origin, or religion.

8.46 (a) discriminatory misrepresentation by omission.
Discriminatory misrepresentation is the concealing of available properties, representing that they are not for sale or rent, or changing the sale terms for the purpose of discriminating.

NATIONAL TEST 9: Closings; Risk Management; Property Management

9.1 (c) returns funds to the buyer.
If for any reason the transaction cannot be completed, the escrow instructions usually provide a mechanism for reconveying title to the seller and funds to the buyer. In such a case, both parties return to their original status as if no sale had occurred.

9.2 (d) disclose in writing any business relationships they have with other parties involved in the transaction.
Business relationships and affiliations among real estate firms, mortgage brokers, title insurance firms and other such companies that are involved in a transaction are permitted, provided the relationships are disclosed in writing to the consumer, the consumer is free to go elsewhere for the relevant service, and the companies do not exchange fees for referrals.

9.3 (a) The item must be prorated and recorded as a debit to one party and a credit to the other party for the same amount.
An income or expense item that affects both parties is apportioned, or prorated, to each party to reflect the proper amount that each owes or should receive. A prorated item is treated as a debit to one party and a credit to the other party for the same amount.

9.4 (b) at some time after the expense is incurred.
Items paid in arrears are paid after the expense has been incurred.

9.5 (d) A debit to the seller and credit to the buyer for $580.
For income the seller received in advance, the buyer receives a credit and the seller receives a debit. In effect, the seller has received some of the buyer's income, and the seller must pay this share to the buyer. Therefore the seller is debited and the buyer is credited the $580 the buyer is entitled to earn as the new owner.

9.6 (b) A debit to the seller and credit to the buyer for $43.
For an item the buyer will pay in arrears, the buyer receives a credit and the seller receives a debit. In effect, the seller has incurred some of the expenses that the buyer will be paying for after closing. Thus the seller must pay the buyer the used portion of the expense, or $43.

9.7 (b) $546.00.
The daily tax expense, first, is ($2,190 ÷ 365) or $6.00. Since the buyer will pay the taxes after closing, the seller will owe the buyer his or her portion of the tax bill, which is the 91 days from the beginning of the year through closing. Therefore, credit the buyer and debit the seller ($6.00 x 91), or $546.00.

9.8 (d) $191.67.
This method assumes all months are 30 days and the year is 360 days. The daily proration is therefore $375 ÷ 360, or $1.04. The closing occurs on the 184th day of the year. Thus, ($1.04 x 184) = $191.67. Note that if the day of closing is the buyer's, there would be 183 day's worth of prorated expense.

9.9 (d) $735.34.
Assuming a 365 day year, the daily tax expense is ($1,100 ÷ 365), or $3.013. As taxes are paid in arrears, the buyer will be paying the annual bill. Thus, he will be owed a credit for the seller's share of the bill, which is $3.013 x 244 days, or $735.34.

9.10 (a) $116.03.
The buyer's share is the unused portion, or (365 days − 244 days), or 121 days. The daily expense is ($350 ÷ 365), or $.9589. ($.9589 x 121) = $116.03. The seller receives this amount as a credit and the buyer a debit.

9.11 (a) $507.50.
If the buyer pays $525 interest for 30 days, the daily expense is ($525 ÷ 30), or $17.50. If there are 29 days of pre-paid expense, the buyer's charge is ($17.50 x 29), or $507.50.

9.12 (c) $1,775.
$88,750 x .02 = $1,775. Remember, one point = 1% of the loan amount.

9.13 (d) $11,250.
$187,500 x 6% = $187,500 x .06 = $11,250.

9.14 (d) the buyer must pay the expense.
Explicit agreements in the sale contract supercede traditional expense-payment responsibilities which can vary from state to state.

9.15 (a) the excess of the buyer's debits over the buyer's credits.
To determine how much money the buyer owes at closing, the buyer's debits are totaled and compared with the total of the buyer's credits. The excess of debits over credits is the amount the buyer must bring to the closing.

9.16 (d) negligence, error or omission in carrying out professional services.
A standard E&O policy provides coverage for "damages resulting from any negligent act, error or omission arising out of Professional Services." It does not cover dishonest or illegal acts, including environmental violations and mishandling of funds.

9.17 (a) Failing to inform and disclose properly.
Agency risks commonly concern the requirement to inform and disclose. Most states require agency relationships to be in writing and to be disclosed to all parties to a transaction. In states that do not use agency, there is still the obligation to explain and disclose the nature of the relationship.

9.18 (b) failing to disclose known adverse facts.
Depending on the state, the licensee may have no further duty to disclose property condition after properly informing parties of their rights and obligations. However, the licensee may still be subject to legal action for failing to disclose adverse facts the licensee knew about or should have known about.

9.19 (d) avoid creating a false impression that the licensee is a certified appraiser.
Misuse of such terms as "appraisal" and "value" could lead to a charge of misrepresenting oneself as an appraiser.

9.20 (b) exceeding the authority of the agreement.
Licensees must stay within the bounds of the authority granted by the agency agreement and avoid doing anything requiring permission without first getting that permission in writing.

9.21 (a) use a checklist of all items, contingencies, dates and responsibilities that must be met.
One way to reduce risk in the contracting process is to use a checklist that covers all the contract items, such as inclusions and exclusions, contingency periods, documents, forms, data checking, and milestone dates.

9.22 (d) the principals may make changes as long as they sign or initial each change.
Real estate professionals who are not attorneys are usually limited to filling in blanks or making deletions on a preprinted contract form prepared by a lawyer. While a licensee may make deletions, additions to a form should be drafted by an attorney. The principals themselves can make changes as long as each change is signed or initialed by all signers.

9.23 (b) obtain education in the content and intent of the laws.
The risk of violating fair housing laws can be minimized through ongoing education that addresses both the intent of the laws and their current content..

9.24 (a) being present at a conversation where the setting of commission rates is discussed.
Antitrust laws forbid brokers to band together to set a price on their services in listing and selling property.

Even being overheard discussing commission rates or being present at such a conversation can lead to charges of *price fixing*.

9.25 (a) License discipline, fines, and possible incarceration.
Intentional misrepresentation, as a type of fraud, is a criminal act that may result in fines and incarceration, in addition to discipline from state regulators and professional organizations.

9.26 (c) stating that a client should seek legal counsel.
Unintentional misrepresentation occurs when a licensee *unknowingly* gives a consumer inaccurate information concerning a property, financing or agency service. Information that the licensee, as a professional, should have known to be false or inaccurate may be included in the definition. Telling a client that legal counsel would be advisable is not misrepresentation and, in fact, is often an important risk management technique.

9.27 (d) avoid speculative statements in all reports.
Progress reports should be accurate, timely, in writing, and free of speculation. Speculation may encourage the consumer to believe the agent has expertise that in fact is non-existent. If a consumer has a question about the meaning of something in an inspection report, the licensee should refer the consumer to the person who wrote the report rather than trying to explain it.

9.28 (b) It reduces the chance of presenting an offer from an unqualified buyer.
Using a lender to qualify the buyer protects the agent against leading a seller to believe a purchaser is fully qualified when this may not be the case. Also, lenders and loan agents are better able to look into the buyer's qualifications than a real estate licensee is. If it is necessary to show a property to a potential buyer who has not been qualified by a lender, the licensee can gain some protection by performing an informal qualification and documenting the fact that it was based on the information provided by the buyer.

9.29 (c) the agency relationship.
Maintaining the confidentiality of any information that would harm the client's interests or bargaining position or anything else the client wishes to keep secret, unless the law requires disclosure, is one of the primary duties of agency. The duty to maintain confidentiality generally survives the termination of a listing agreement into perpetuity.

9.30 (a) performing a comparative market analysis.
In preparing a Comparative Market Analysis, licensees should guard against using the terms "appraisal" and "value," which are reserved for the use of certified appraisers. Misuse of these terms could lead to a charge of misrepresenting oneself as an appraiser.

9.31 (d) make a substantial misrepresentation.
The license laws of most states list as illegal advertising activities subject to discipline such actions as making any substantial and intentional misrepresentation, making false promises, and making misleading or untruthful statements in any advertising.

9.32 (c) fiduciary
The management agreement creates an agency relationship between the manager and the principal. This is a fiduciary relationship and, in general, the agent is charged with producing the greatest possible net return on the owner's investment while safeguarding the value of the investment for the owner/investor.

9.33 (b) financial reporting to the principal.
Financial reporting to the principal is a fundamental responsibility of the property manager. Reports may be required monthly, quarterly, and annually. Required reports typically include operating budget, cash flow, profit and loss, and budget comparison statements.

9.34 (d) revenue from all sources minus losses from uncollected rents, vacancies, and evictions.
The total of scheduled rents plus revenues from such sources as vending services, storage charges, late fees, utilities, and contracts is the potential gross income. Subtracting losses caused by uncollected rents, vacancies and evictions gives effective gross income.

9.35 (a) cost per tenant prospect generated per lease.

The efficiency of marketing activities can be judged in terms of how many prospects per completed lease they generate. The lower the cost per prospect per lease, the more effective and efficient the program.

9.36 (b) raise rental rates.

Vacancy rates are directly related to demand and competitive supply in the market. If vacancy rates in the managed property are too high, the manager may have to lower rates or identify problems in the property or its management that are contributing to vacancy level. On the other hand, if the property's vacancy rate is significantly lower than market rates, the manager may conclude that higher rental rates are called for.

9.37 (b) Routine, preventive, and corrective

The foremost maintenance objective is generally to preserve the value of the physical asset for the owner over the long term. Three general types of maintenance are required to keep a property in serviceable condition: routine (day-to-day), preventive (scheduled), and corrective (repairs and replacements).

9.38 (a) ensure that disabled employees have the same level of access to facilities that all employees have.

Employers with at least fifteen employees must follow nondiscriminatory employment and hiring practices and make reasonable accommodations to enable disabled employees to perform essential functions of their jobs. Modifications to the physical components of the building may be necessary to provide the required access to tenants and their customers. Existing barriers must be removed when the removal is "readily achievable," that is, when cost is not prohibitive.

9.39 (a) replacement value.

The amount of coverage provided by certain types of policies may be based on whether the property is insured at depreciated value or current replacement value. Depreciated value is original value minus the loss in value over time. Current replacement value, which is more expensive, is the amount it would cost to rebuild or replace the property at current rates. Commercial policies include coinsurance clauses requiring the insured to bear a portion of the loss. Fire and hazard policies usually require the coverage to be in an amount equal to at least 80 percent of the replacement value.

9.40 (b) cash for the management firm's operating expenses.

Managers are responsible for proper handling of monies belonging to other parties (trust funds) that come into the manager's hands in the course of doing business. For property managers, such trust funds include rents collected from tenants, security deposits, and capital contributions from the property owner. Funds belonging to the management firm must not be commingled with those of the client

9.41 (c) General

Property managers are usually considered to be general agents empowered to perform some or all of the ongoing tasks and duties of operating the property, including the authority to enter into contracts.

9.42 (b) The tenant pays a fixed rent, and the landlord pays all operating expenses.

In a gross lease, the tenant pays an established, fixed rent, and the landlord pays all property operating expenses, such as taxes, insurance, utilities, and other services. This is the arrangement commonly used in residential leases. If the tenant pays some of the operating expenses, the lease is a form of net lease.

9.43 (d) the property manager does not have to maintain it.

The lease should set forth items that are excluded or included in the leased property. For instance, a residential lease may include built-in appliances such as dishwashers but exclude freestanding ones, such as refrigerators. At issue for the landlord is the cost of maintenance. If a refrigerator is not included, it does not have to be maintained by the property manager.

9.44 (b) deliver a habitable property.

The landlord (by way of the property manager), is expected to deliver a property that is habitable. This means keeping heating, plumbing, cooling, and electrical systems in good repair as well as maintaining serviceability of floors, stairways, railings, roofs, and windows.

9.45 (c) A tenant declares a landlord in default and vacates the leased premises.

A constructive eviction occurs when a tenant vacates the leased premises and declares the lease void, claiming that the landlord's actions have made the premises unfit for the purpose described in the lease. The tenant must prove that it was the landlord's actions that were responsible and may be able to recover damages.

9.46 (a) the competitive market for the property.
In preparing a management plan, a manager must consider the owner's objectives, including financial goals; the competitive market for the property, both local and regional, depending on the property type; and the features of the particular property. The plan will also include a budget and indications of what the manager intends to do with the property to meet the owner's objectives.

NATIONAL TEST 10: Real Estate Math

10.1 (a) $.023 / SF
5/6ths of an acre = (5 x 43,560 SF) / 6, or 36,300 SF. Her commission was (.06 x $28,000) x .50, or $840. $840 / 36,300 SF = $.023 / SF.

10.2 (b) $370,170
The land costs $.50 x 43,560 SF/ac. x 1.5 ac, or $32,670. The home will cost $135 / SF x 2,500, or $337,500. The total property will cost $370,170.

10.3 (a)   12%
The lot measures 43,560 / 4, or 10,890 SF. The tennis court will take up 9,600 SF, leaving 1,290 SF. This amount is 11.8% of the total lot area.

10.4 (c)   40
The total area available for lots is 11.2 acres (16 acres x 70% for houses), or 487,872 SF (11.2 x 43,560). Dividing this area by 12,000 SF / lot = 40.66. Thus he can have a 40-lot subdivision.

10.5 (a)   6
First, the requirement = 2(13'x 9') +2 (18'x 9') =558 SF. Each roll is 2'x 50', or 100 SF. Thus she will need 6 rolls.

10.6 (d)   1,376 SF
First figure the area to be mulched. If the home is 40 x 30, the flower area adds 8' to each side of the house. Thus the outside perimeter of the flowered area is (40+8+8) by (30+8+8), or 46' by 56'. The area of the flowered area is (46' x 56') minus the house area of 1,200 SF. This is 1,376 SF.

10.7 (b)   40 acres
First, remember that a section contains 640 acres. The area in question is a forth of a half of a half of the total section. So divide 640 by (4 x 2 x 2). 4 x 2 x 2 is 16 and 640/16= 40 acres.

10.8 (c)   10 acres
This key to this question is to recall that a section has 640 acres. Theresa's property only is a ¼ of a ¼ of a ¼ of the entire section. Multiply 4 x 4 x 4 which equals 64. Savannah owns 1/64 of the section. Divide 640 by 64 and you get the answer of 10 acres.

10.9 (a) $38,955
Their fixed rent is (1,800 SF x $1.40/SF) x 12 months, or $30,240. The percentage rent is ($41,500 x .0175) x 12, or $8,715. Total rent is ($30,240 + 8,715), or $38,955.

10.10 (a)   5.04%
First, convert to decimals: 2 2/3 % = 2.67%; 5 1/5% = 5.2%; 7 1/4% = 7.25%. Thus total appreciation = (2.67% + 5.2% + 7.25%), or 15.12%. Divide by 3 to derive the average: 15.12% / 3 = 5.04%

10.11 (c)   29 %.
Appreciation as a per cent can be estimated by (1) subtracting the estimated current market value from the price originally paid (239,000 - 185,000 = 54,000) and (2) dividing the result by the original price (54,000 / 185,000 = . 29 or 29%).

10.12 (c)   94%

To find the percent of listing price the offer is, divide the offer by the listing price. In this question the offer is $290,000 and the listing price is $308,000. $\dfrac{\$290,000}{\$308,000} = 94\%$

10.13 (a) $206,000.

Remember the formula V = I / R where V is value, I is annual income, and R is the cap rate. Variations of this are: R = I / V in solving for the cap rate, and I = V x R in solving for income. Here, first identify net income by subtracting out vacancy and expenses. Then divide by the capitalization rate. Thus, ($30,000 – 1,500 – 10,000) / 9% = $205,555, or $206,000 rounded.

10.14 (b) $375,000.

Value = Income / Cap rate. Thus, V= $30,000 / .08 = $375,000.

10.15 (b) $13,600.

First derive the annual depreciation which is the cost divided by the economic life. Then multiply annual depreciation times the number of years to identify total depreciation. Remember to subtract depreciation from the original cost if the question asks for the ending value. Thus, ($16,000 / 20 years x 3 years) = $2,400 total depreciation. The ending value is $16,000 –2,400, or $13,600.

10.16 (a) $1,077

First, Lee's depreciable basis, without the land, is $280,000 x 75%, or $210,000. The annual depreciation for the entire home is ($210,000 / 39 years), or $5,384.61. Second, his office is 20% of the house (500 sf / 2,500 sf). Therefore Lee can take annual depreciation of ($5,384.61 x 20%), or $1,076.92.

10.17 (d) $188,000.

Cost Approach formula: Land + (Cost of Improvements + Capital Additions – Depreciation) = Value. Thus you have $40,000 + ($175,000 - 27,000), or $188,000.

10.18 (c) $475,000

Use the same Cost Approach formula: Land + (Cost of Improvements + Capital Additions – Depreciation) = Value. The land is worth (100,000 x 125%), or $125,000. Remember, you cannot depreciate the land, only the cost of the improvements. Therefore, annual depreciation is ($400,000 / 40), or $10,000. Total depreciation is ($10,000 x 5 years), or $50,000. Thus the value is ($125,000 + 400,000 – 50,000), or $475,000.

10.19 (d)   125.

Use the formula: GRM = Price / Monthly Rent. Thus, $400,000 / $3,200 = 125.

10.20 (c) $194,000.

Use the formula: GIM = Price / Annual Income. To solve for price convert the formula to Price = GIM x Annual Income. Thus, ($1,100 x 12) equals $13,200 annual income. ($13,200 x 14.7 GIM) = $194,040, or $194,000 rounded.

10.21 (d) $750

The loan amount is $200,000 x .75, or $150,000. The first month interest equals ($150,000 x 6%) / 12 months, or $750.

10.22 (b) $179,000.

The equation for the loan amount is (annual interest divided by the interest rate) = loan amount. Thus, ($790 x 12) / .053 = $178,868 or $179,000 rounded.

10.23 (a)   4.82%.

The equation for the interest rate is (annual payment / loan amount) = interest rate. Thus ($1,000 x 12) / $249,000 = 4.82%.

10.24 (b) $1,456.95
In the first month they pay interest of ($280,000 x 6.25%) / 12, or $1,458. If their fixed payment is $1,724, they paid down the principal by $266 ($1,724 - 1,458). Now they must pay 6.25% interest on the new principal balance of $279,734. This equals (279,734 x .0625) / 12, or $1,456.95.

10.25 (b) The second option, by 150.
The first option's interest total is (6.5% x $60,000) x 5 years, or $19,500. The second option will charge (6.25% x $60,000) x 5 years, plus $600, or a total of $19,350. The 2nd option is $150 cheaper.

10.26 (b) 1.67 points
A discount point is one percent of the loan amount. Jose's loan is ($410,000 x 90%), or $369,000. If he paid $6,150, he paid 1.67% of the loan amount ($6,150 / 369,000), or 1.67 points.

10.27 (c) $4,875.
$325,000 x .015 = $4,875. Remember, one point = 1% of the loan amount.

10.28 (c) $162,500
Use the formula: Price x LTV Ratio = Loan. Then plug in the figures and calculate: Price x .80 = $130,000. Therefore, Price = $130,000 / .80 = $162,500.

10.29 (c) $379,259
First, the annual interest paid is $1,600 x 12, or $19,200. The interest rate is 6.75%. Using the formula (Loan = Interest / Rate), the loan amount is $19,200 / 6.75%, or $284,444. As this is 75% of the price, the price is ($284,444 / .75), or $379,259.

10.30 (b) $1,900.
Monthly income qualification is derived by multiplying monthly income by the income ratio. Thus (76,000 / 12) x .30 = $1,900. Remember to first derive the monthly income.

10.31 (a) $253,846
Total depreciation on this property = ($600,000 / 39 years) x 10 years, or $153,846. His adjusted basis is therefore ($680,000 original price – 153,846 depreciation taken), or $526,154. The gain is then ($780,000 – 526,154), or $253,846.

10.32 (b) $257,000.
Adjusted basis = beginning basis ($250,000) + capital improvements ($2,000 + $5,000) – depreciation (0) = adjusted basis ($257,000).

10.33 (c) $34,000.
Capital gain = amount realized (net sales proceeds, $265,000) - adjusted basis ($231,000) = ($34,000).

10.34 (d) $125,000.
The basic formula for adjusted basis is: Beginning Basis + Capital Improvements - Exclusions and Credits = Adjusted Basis. Debra's adjusted basis is therefore $120.000 + $5,000 = $125,000. The financing terms and subsequent selling price are not relevant.

10.35 (c) $15,000 overpriced.
Use the same formula V = I / R where V is the price and R is the rate of return. Then plug in the numbers to solve for V. The NOI of this property is ($60,000 - $22,000), or $38,000. The return is 11%. Therefore, the value to get this return must be $38,000 / .11, or $345,455. Since the price is $360,000, the price exceeds the amount needed for an 11% return by approximately $15,000 ($360,000 - $345,455 = $14,545).

10.36 (b) Yes, since he will yield 8.375%
Use the same formula R = I / V where V is the $2 million price, and R is the cap rate or rate of return. To identify income: (25,000 SF x $10/SF) = $250,000 gross income, minus 5% vacancy (.05 x $250,000), or $12,500, minus expenses of $70,000 = $167,500 net income. ($250,000 – 12,500 – 70,000) Now divide net income of $167,500 by $2,000,000 to derive the return of 8.375%.

10.37 (a) $1,680.
Annual gross operating income ($1,650 x 12 = $19,800) - annual operating expenses ($600 x 12 = $7,200) = annual net operating income ($12,600); annual net operating income ($12,600) - cost recovery expense ($7,000) = taxable income ($5,600); taxable income ($5,600) x tax rate (30%) = tax liability ($1,680).

10.38 (c) $10,640
The basic formula for tax liability is: Taxable Income x Tax Rate = Tax Liability. Taxable Income is Net Operating Income - Interest Expense - Cost Recovery Expense. Therefore, the annual tax is $150,000 (NOI) - $105,000 (Interest Expense) - $7,000 (Cost Recovery Expense) x 28% = $10,640. Note that the principal payment is not deductible in calculating taxable income.

10.39 (d) 31.4%
The formula for profit % is (profit / initial investment). The profit made was ($23,000 x 4) – 70,000 initial investment, or $22,000. Dividing this by the amount invested derives a profit percent of 31.4%.

10.40 (c) $1,000,000,000.
The mill rate = (tax requirement / the tax base). A mill is one one-thousandth of a dollar ($.001). To solve for the tax base, reconfigure this formula to be: Base = Tax Requirement / Mill Rate. Thus the Base = $10,000,000 / .010, or $1,000,000,000.

10.41 (a) $1,495
First, always use the assessed valuation, not the market value. Subtract out the homestead exemption to derive taxable value, or $140,000 – 25,000 = $115,000. As a shortcut to calculating the tax bill, simply add up all the mills, multiply them times .001 to convert mills to decimals, then multiply this number times the taxable value. Thus (7 + 3 + 2 + 1) x .001 x $115,000 = $1,495.

10.42 (b) 2.13%
The rate = budget / tax base. Thus, $8,000,000 / (400,000,000 – 25,000,000) = 2.13%

10.43 (d) $1,778.
First calculate the total commission, then the co-brokerage splits, then the agent-broker split. Thus: $127,000 x 7% = $8,890 total commission. ($8,890 x 50%) = $4,445 total listing broker share. ($4,445 x 40% = $1,778 agent's share.

10.44 (a) $6,866
Figure the total commission, then the co-brokerage splits, then the broker-agent splits. Thus, ($325,000 x 6.5%) = $21,125. ($21,125 x 50%) = $10,563. ($10,563 x .65) = $6,866.

10.45 (c) A credit to the buyer and debit to the seller for $785.34.
The daily tax expense, first, is ($3,150 / 365) or $8.63. Since the buyer will pay the taxes after closing, the seller must pay the buyer his or her portion of the tax bill at closing, which is the 91 days from the beginning of the year through closing. Therefore, credit the buyer and debit the seller ($8.63 x 91), or $785.34.

10.46 (a) $507.50.
If the buyer pays $525 interest for 30 days, the daily expense is ($525 / 30), or $17.50. If there are 29 days of pre-paid expense, the buyer's charge is ($17.50 x 29), or $507.50.

10.47 (d) Credit buyer $712.26.
For the monthly proration using the 365-day method, solve first for the daily rent amount: ($1,380 / 31), or $44.52. Since the landlord received the rent and owes the buyer portions of the rent, the buyer will be credited. The owed amount is for the 16th through the 31st, or 16 days, since the closing day belongs to the buyer. Therefore, credit the buyer and debit the seller ($44.52 x 16),or $712.26.

10.48 (d) $86,372
First calculate the transfer tax: ($322,600 / 500) = 645.2 units of $500. Round this up to 646, then multiply times $1.00 to get $646 transfer tax cost. Next figure the commission @ ($322,600 x .07), or $22,582. Next, the seller's real estate tax proration charge will be $2,000. Then, add up the expenses: ($646 transfer tax + 450 title + 550 attorney + 22,582 commission + 210,000 loan payoff + 2,000 tax proration) = $236,228. Subtracting this from the sale price = $86,372.

10.49 (d) $5,848.
Be careful here. Since the net price is $5,000, the taking price (TP) minus the commission must equal the net price. In other words, the net price is 90% of the taking price. Since TP x 90% = Net, TP = Net / 90%. So the taking price is $5,556 ($5,000 / .9). Apply the same logic to deriving the asking price: the taking price is 95% of the list price, therefore the list price = (taking price / 95%), or $5,848. Now work backwards to prove your answer: (5,848 x 95% margin x .90 net of commission) = $5,000

10.50 (d) $468,750
Use the formula: (Percent of insurable property value carried / 80% replacement cost) x claim = recovery, where the insurable property value variable excludes the land value and is valued at replacement cost. Here, the insurable portion of the property is ($740,000 - 25% land value), or $555,000. The Wildes are carrying insurance to cover 75% of the replacement cost of the entire property. Their recovery amount is therefore (75% / 80%) x $500,000, or $468,750.

10.51 (c) $140,000
Use the formula: (Percent of insurable property value carried / 80% replacement cost) x claim = recovery. Thus, (75% / 80% x $150,000) = $140,625. However, the face value of the policy is the maximum they can receive, which is $140,000

STATE TEST 11: Arizona Law; Arizona Licensing Laws; Easements, Encumbrances, Ownership; Conveyances

11.1 (b) prepare any and all documents incidental to a real estate transaction.
Article XXVI (26) of the Arizona State Constitution authorizes real estate licensees to engage in the limited practice of law by preparing any and all documents for clients incidental to a real estate transaction. Licensee may not charge for this service and must represent one of both parties in the transaction.

11.2 (c) common law.
Statutory law is law which begins is legislative committees, is passed by one or both houses of congress, and signed into law by the governor. Administrative law is where agencies of government are given the authority to draft rules and regulations and the power to enforce them. Civil law concerns person-to-person or entity-to-entity conflicts. Common law is based on customs and traditions that have emerged from court challenges over the years.

11.3 (d) is appointed by the governor.
The current governor appoints the Arizona Real Estate Commissioner and serves at the governor's pleasure.

11.4 (c) 9
The real estate advisory board consists of nine members, two with Arizona brokerage experience, two with residential brokerage experience within the past five years before appointment, two developers/subdividers, and three not closely related to an Arizona licensee.

11.5 (b) a person selling or renting her or his own property
A person selling his or her own property is often known as an "unrepresented seller" and the transaction called "for sale by owner." Arizona citizens can sell or rent an unlimited number of properties for compensation without holding a real estate license as long as they own the property.

11.6 (a) 18 years of age and meet no state residency requirement.
The minimum age for obtaining a salesperson or broker's license in Arizona is 18 years of age. Arizona licensees can live in any state and are not required to live in Arizona or to have lived in Arizona.

11.7 (b) have three years of full time real estate experience in the past five years.
Successful candidates for a broker's license in Arizona must have previous real estate experience. That experience must be full-time, can be in any state, and is verified by information from current or past employing brokers and income tax records.

11.8 (b) Fair Housing
Fair housing concepts, rules, regulations, and actions are so vital to today's licensed real estate practitioner that a fair housing course is required for license renewal every two years. Many state and federal fair housing laws are applicable only to persons legally licensed. Penalties for violations can be severe.

11.9 (c) With the employing broker's designated broker
An Arizona licensee never has possession of the official copy of her or his license. When first activated, the license is in a file at ADRE in Phoenix. Upon employment the license is held by the employing broker. At severance, the license is returned to ADRE in Phoenix until the licensee is employed by a new broker. A licensee can download an unofficial copy of his or her license from the ADRE website.

11.10 (d) temporary cemetery salesperson license.
A temporary cemetery salesperson license can be issued to a person who has applied for and otherwise qualifies for a cemetery salesperson license. It is valid for only 90 days after issuance.

11.11 (a) do not call it an appraisal.
Arizona law allows for real estate licensees to generate broker price opinions (BPOs) as long as they are not referred to as appraisals. Only people holding active appraiser's licenses can perform appraisals.

11.12 (b) adjudication of the lawsuit.
In order for a citizen to apply for relief from the ADRE recovery fund, her or his complaint must be already adjudicated through lawsuit and judgment. ADRE will move forward if it determines the complaint did not receive enough damages to make him or her "whole" again. Then, the recovery fund may provide additional financial relief.

11.13 (c) an easement in gross.
An appurtenant easement is said to benefit the land whereas an easement in gross benefits the corporation or individual holding it. Easements in gross are often called personal easements or corporate easements in gross.

11.14 (a) community property
Community property is the default method of holding an interest in real property in Arizona. That means if a married couple does not specify otherwise, the state will assign real property as the method of holding by law. Married couples often prefer community property with right of survivorship or joint tenancy because of their automatic survivorship rights but must specifically ask for them prior to closing

11.15 (c) a community property state.
Dower and curtsey, and tenancies in the entireties, are names for husband and wife methods of holding real property, but not in Arizona. Along with many other Southwestern U.S. states, Arizona is a community property state because it models its land law after early Spanish Land Grant law.

11.16 (c) is personal property.
A manufactured home on land owned by the owner of the manufactured home is considered real property but one on a rental pad is personal property. As personal property, a manufactured home transfers like an automobile with a bill of sale. A manufactured home considered real property transfers with a deed and requires a licensee to represent it in a sale.

11.17 (b) leasehold estates.
Cooperatives are rentals and thus leaseholds. While tenants receive stock in the company which owns the building, their individual apartment is not a freehold because it isn't purchased. The stock they receive is personal property, not real property.

11.18 (b) statutory law.
Like other statutory laws, the code of real estate was approved by one or both houses of the Arizona legislature and signed into law by the governor. The collection of laws regarding real estate in the state is A.R.S. Title 32, Chapter 20. A.R.S. stands for Arizona Revised Statutes, and the codification in its designation indicates it is statutory law as well.

11.19 (c)   Article 26 of the state constitution.
Article XXVI (26) does not allow licensees to write contractual and other conveyance and related documents on a freelance fee basis. Licensee rights are granted only when incidental to a real estate transaction where the licensee represents one or both principals in a transaction.

11.20 (c)   Community property with right of survivorship
Community property with right of survivorship is specific to the state of Arizona. It was passed and authorized by the state legislature in 1994-95. Other states may have similar opportunities for married couples.

11.21 (b)   Cooperatives
Cooperatives are very popular in New York City and almost unheard of in Arizona and the rest of the west. Also called proprietary leases, they are sought after in central-city urban areas where apartment living is more common that single family dwellings.

11.22 (c)   Profit a prende.
Profit *a prende* is a form of Arizona easement that gives a person other than the land owner the right to remove natural products from the land. These products include soil, timber, and fruit.

11.23 (a)   summary suspension
A summary suspension requires immediate stoppage of all licensed activities. It does not allow for the due process – evidence, hearings, testimony - found in other license procedures because the licensee's actions are considered an immediate danger to public health, safety, and welfare.

11.24 (c)   The Office of the Arizona Attorney General
The Arizona Office of the Arizona Attorney General has the authority to seek remedies of the state's consumer fraud act. It is charged with protecting the public from consumer fraud as well as anti-competitive behavior. Its primary emphasis is on fraud and abuse.

11.25 (b)   Article 26 of the State Constitution
Transactional brokerages are ones which provide paperwork service to clients but do not represent them as agents. Transactional brokerages are allowed by law and many states but not in Arizona. To use the authority granted by Article 26, an Arizona licensee must represent one of both parties in a transaction. Because transactional brokers do not represent either side in a transaction, they cannot advocate for their clients, aid in negotiations, or promote the best interests of principals.

11.26 (a)   suspended.
A licensed salesperson or broker in Arizona who misses his or her due date for renewal is immediately suspended. The real estate practitioner may not participate in activities requiring a license or earn and collect commissions. They have a grace period in which to reinstate but must complete a state questionnaire and pay late fees.

11.27 (a)   The certified general appraiser.
To become a certified general appraiser, a candidate must complete 300 hours of classroom education, exam passage, and 3,000 hours of appraisal experience in no less than 30 hours. The successful candidate must also hold a bachelor's degree or higher from an accredited institution. The classification of appraiser is qualified to appraise all types of property.

11.28 (b)   laches.
A delay in homeowners taking action against violations of homeowner usage rules is called laches.

11.29 (b)   A mortgage lien
Almost all equitable or financial liens are voluntary. Home buyers voluntarily accept them as a way of obtaining the financing required to complete a purchase. A specific lien liens only against the property encumbered, in this case, against the specific property financed.

11.30 (c)   7 years
Arizona takes the property of a decedent who dies intestate (without a will) or without apparent heirs and sells it in order to reduce the number of abandoned properties across the state. This is called escheat, and it

requires the state to search for legitimate heirs for seven years. If found, the state will repay the heirs using a special appropriation to obtain the money for repayment.

11.31(a)   common forms of nuisances.
Light, smell, and noise are non-monetary encumbrances in real estate. They prevent property owners from full enjoyment of their property and can potentially have a material effect on transfer of title.

11.32 (b)   automatically void unless the minor is emancipated.
A minor does not have the legal capacity to sign a contract in Arizona, thus any contract signed by a minor is automatically void. An exception is a minor who has been emancipated from parents or guardians by a court of law. The age of majority in Arizona is 18 years of age.

11.33 (a)   a warranty deed.
The Arizona Association of Realtors® purchase agreement contract form calls for title to pass in a voluntary sale of real property via a warranty deed.

11.34 (c)   a treasurer's deed
A treasurer's deed is proof of title transfer from a property tax sale. Property being seized and sold to pay tax debts is a form of involuntary alienation. To alienate is to separate; to have one's property taken for tax debt is involuntary.

11.35 (b)   grantee.
A person transferring real property to another is called a grantor, and the receiver of the property is a grantee. An "or" ending on a word indicates a doer or giver or something and "ee" is the receiver.

11.36 (c)   nominal consideration.
Most U.S. deeds include a statement of nominal consideration to be received in return for transferring title to a property. On Arizona warranty deeds, the nominal amount is "…$10 or more…" This nominal amount is combined with "…& other valuable consideration…" to describe the payment made in exchange for title. "Nominal" can be described as a token amount of payment to strengthen a contract.

11.37 (d)   disclaimer deed.
A disclaimer deed or spousal disclaimer is used to allow one spouse in community property to allow the other spouse to hold an interest is real property as tenancy in severalty or as sole and separate. A spouse must disclaim interest in the property at close of escrow.

11.38 (c)   A lien
CC&Rs, deed restrictions, and trespass are non-monetary encumbrances; a lien is an example of a monetary or equitable lien. Encumbrances are claims, liens, charges or liabilities attached to or binding on real property. They may lessen the value of property or burden, obstruct, or impair its use. An encumbrance is a right or interest in property by someone other than its owner. They affect title. Other monetary encumbrances include mechanics liens and escheat.

11.39 (c)   a detached garage.
A garage that is not attached to the main dwelling structure in any way is called a detached garage.

11.40 (a)   A gift
Good consideration is often described as payment via "love and affection." In real estate, the gift of real property is a good example of payment resulting from love and affection. Valuable consideration, a second type of contract consideration in Arizona is generally money payment such as down payment or earnest money.

11.41 (b)   of quiet enjoyment.
Five covenants or promises are made by grantors to grantees in Arizona warranty deeds. These assure protection of the grantee's title and are generally enforced via title insurance. The covenant of quiet enjoyment promises the grantor will defend title against claims of third parties.

11.42 (a)   they are pre-paid vacations in real estate.
The federal Internal Revenue Service regards timeshares as prepaid vacations in real estate and as a result, most expenses of timeshare ownership and use are not tax deductible. The major federal tax deduction is on loan interest just like any other freehold real property purchase involving lending.

11.43 (d)   administrative law.
Arizona has many administrative law agencies. These include the ADEQ, ADWR, Corporation Commission, and office of the attorney general. The Arizona Department of Real Estate is the primary administrative law regulating real estate in the state.

STATE TEST 12: Land; Environmental Law; Disclosure & Consumer Protection; Regulated Activity and Relationships

12.1 (c)   hazardous waste.
These classifications are determined by the federal government but adopted by Arizona to define potentially dangerous or destructive materials.

12.2 (b)   asbestos.
Asbestos is a construction material used often for insulation. It can cause serious health issues when released into the air in commercial or residential buildings and dwellings. It is often found in older homes with "popcorn" ceilings and wrapped around pipes in commercial buildings. It requires professional remediation when found.

12.3 (a)   G&SRBM.
G&SRBM stands for Gila and Salt River Baseline and Meridian, which is the initial point from which townships are designated in Arizona. Located near Phoenix, it identifies the confluence of the Gila and Salt Rivers. All government rectangular survey land descriptions in Arizona end with G&SRBM, identifying a parcel as one in Arizona.

12.4 (c)   lot, block, and tract.
Lot, block and tract is a method of land description used to identify small home site parcels in Arizona subdivisions. These descriptions generally begin with the trade name of the subdivision followed by lot, block and tract numbers. The numbers match pages where the parcel is recorded with the county assessor, but assessor's parcel numbers are not, in themselves, considered a complete legal land description.

12.5 (b)   2
There are two principal baselines and meridians in Arizona. In 1869, a small portion of the northeast corner of the state was changed to the Navajo Meridian and Base Line to describe part of the Navajo reservation. The part of the original designation in New Mexico has disappeared but Arizona retains its. The Navajo Meridian and Base Line designation is not used in land description as is the G&SRBM.

12.6 (a)   beams.
In construction, a framing term for headers which provide extra support above doors and windows is beams.

12.7 (d)   size of homes to be built
While the ADRE subdivided land questionnaire requires detailed information regarding a proposed subdivision, the state does not require information on proposed housing for consideration of subdivision approval and issuance of a CPA.

12.8 (c)   disclosure law.
As the result of abuses in subdivision development and marketing in the late 1940s and 1950s, Arizona requires full disclosure on subdivisions to potential and actual buyers. This allows buyers to make informed buying decisions and rescind contracts if buyers disagree with subdivision characteristics.

12.9 (c) Purchasers have seven days after signing the contract; six months if the buyers haven't seen the property; and up to three years of promised access isn't delivered.
The rescission rights of subdivision buyers are generous by state law. Purchase contracts may be cancelled up to seven days after signing and as long as up to three years for access.

12.10 (b) more than 36 acres but less than 160.
Suddivided land consists of parcels less than 36 acres, while unsubdivided land is described as more than 36 acres or more but less than 160 acres. Parcels larger than 160 acres are not regulated under Arizona unsubdivided land law.

12.11 (a) When the same licensee or brokerage is representing both the buyer and seller in a transaction
Dual agency, where a licensee or brokerage represents both principals in a transaction, requires the informed consent of both parties. Both parties must understand the potential conflicts with dual agency, so disclosure to both is required. Consent is granted by both sides signing a document agreeing to the arrangement.

12.12 (c) actual notice.
Constructive notice generally means written or verbal intent to do something, whereas actual notice means something will actually be done. Buyer due diligence by contract requires the buyer to personally and physically inspect the property subject to purchase. This is to make certain the property is not occupied by someone other than the seller. Actual notice means a physical inspection.

12.13 (a) They are examples of consumer protection laws.
Subdivision disclosure laws are designed to protect the public. Many Arizona real estate laws are specifically designed to encourage consumer protection.

12.14 (d) excessive watering of plants can cause mold, and growers often reroute water and electricity to growing areas in violation of building codes and structural safety.
While not necessarily as damaging to structures as the dangerous chemicals used in meth labs, damage from illegal marijuana growing can be severe. Rerouting electricity can result in structure fires, and excessive moisture in interior areas leads to mold.

12.15 (a) determine if a Phase II is needed.
A Phase I environmental study is conducted primarily on commercial and industrial properties. It is a visual inspection or verbal questioning to determine if there is a likelihood of potential environmental problems. No actual testing is generally done in a Phase I study. If environmental problems may exist, a Phase II study – with extensive testing – may be ordered. Phase III is remediation.

12.16 (a) ADRE.
The ADRE is charged with the responsibility for regulating subdivision creation, which includes the application.

12.17 (d) discloses how a client will be represented by a brokerage.
Arizona mandates clients understand how they are to be represented by a brokerage. They can be represented as buyers in buyer brokerage, sellers by seller brokers, or both in dual agency. The real estate disclosure and election form is a document which discloses representation and confirms, but does not create agency.

12.18 (d) Wetlands
The Arizona Department of Environmental Quality has three specific areas of responsibility: water quality, air quality, and waste. Wetland regulation and monitoring is shared by the state and the federal government, generally under water laws.

12.19 (a) they are broker-to-broker payments.
ADRE prohibits licensees from sharing commissions with unlicensed people. It feels that if anyone can earn a commission, there is little incentive to get a real estate license. Referral fees are negotiated, earned and paid between licensed entities. A finder's fee is one paid to an unlicensed person for new business leads and is prohibited

12.20 (b)   the doctrine of prior appropriation.
The doctrine of prior appropriation is common in arid states like Arizona. The doctrine is based on "first in time, first in use." That means historic rights are granted priory rights for water usage in the state over new potential users.

12.21 (a)   overdraft.
The 1980 Groundwater Management Code was adopted to control severe overdraft occurring in many parts of Arizona. Overdraft occurs when water is pumped out of the ground in greater quantities than what is replenished by natural recharge.

12.22 (c)   the Colorado River.
The U.S. Army Corps of Engineers designates navigable waterways throughout the U.S. Whether or not the waterway can be used for commerce is one factor considered. Approximately 30% of Arizona's water comes from the Colorado River, and neighboring states are always seeking to reduce Arizona's allocation and increase theirs.

12.23 (a)   withdrawal permits.
Withdrawal permits allow for new withdrawals for non-irrigation uses in AMA. There are eight different withdrawal permits covering various groundwater usage which are subject to different requirements.

12.24 (a)   first in time, first in use.
First in time, first in use is the basis for the doctrine of prior appropriation used in Arizona.

12.25 (b)   the designated broker
Arizona administrative law, Commissioner's Standards, requires designated brokers to provide reasonable supervision to licensees under the brokerage's direct control. That includes responsibility for all advertising and promotion. No matter how modest the advertising effort, the broker should review and approve it.

12.26 (b)   an area of land representing 43,560 square feet.
Most land in real estate is quoted in miles, feet, or acres. ADRE commissioner's standards require the term acre to refer to a parcel of 43,560 square feet to prevent misunderstandings and misrepresentations regarding parcel sizes.

12.27 (a)   There is no exception.
ADRE wants to make certain all licensee advertising includes the name of the brokerage in a clear and prominent manner. The brokerage name can be in addition to the name of the salesperson or broker, but it must be in and on all ads including websites and small space classified print ads. It is also a violation to publish or air any advertising suggesting a brokerage is not part of the sale.

12.28 (d)   The Arizona Association of Realtors®
ADRE pursues law violations, and the Arizona Association of Realtors® deals with violations of civil matters, practice issues, and code of ethics violations. ADRE can impose license penalties and AAR uses fines, suspensions of association benefits, and required education to enforce their findings.

12.29 (d)   in the main brokerage office.
Transaction files mandated by ADRE must be stored in the brokerage's main office. They may be stored off-site with ADRE approval. The files must be presented for ADRE inspection upon demand. ADRE mandates their content and filing system. Most required documents must be kept for a minimum of five years.

12.30 (b)   courtesy
Courtesy toward clients and the public is a very effective practice but it is not required by Arizona agency law.

12.31 (c) $3,000
A brokerage may keep up to $3,000 of brokerage funds in a broker trust account. A trust account is for holding money belonging to others such as some forms of earnest money and returnable rental deposits. Brokers must be cautious to avoid comingling money, and fully accurate in trust account bookkeeping.

12.32 (c) a property reputed to be haunted.
Due to the controversial nature of whether ghosts exist, the possibility of a property being haunted does not need to be disclosed. Most property disclosure focuses on material facts.

12.33 (c) The Arizona Corporation Commission
Most HOAs are organized as legal entities through the Arizona Corporation Commission. As a result, the corporation commission is a source of redress regarding HOA complaints.

12.34 (a) A listing agreement
A listing agreement is also an employment contract. It employs a brokerage to aid a principal in the marketing and sale of real property. The listing agreement includes a start and stop date for the employment agreement, commission compensation, and responsibilities of both parties to the agreement.

12.35 (d) law.
Agency is a personal relationship between a broker and client which is governed by law. Delegation of authority by a client to an agent and acceptance of that authority by the agent is all that is required to create agency. Legal requirements of a licensee/agent include confidentiality, loyalty, obedience, and accountability among others.

12.36 (a) brokerage versus licensee telephone numbers in ads.
Commissioner's standards have no guidelines or restrictions on broker versus licensee telephone numbers in ads. ADRE does require a brokerage identity to be clear and prominent, but the brokerage telephone number does not need to be included if the individual licensee wants to highlight contact information.

12.37 (b) renegotiate all listings on behalf of the brokerage.
Employment agreements are made between real estate principals and designated brokers. Upon the death of a designated broker, all contracts would need to be renegotiated. Clients are not willed by designated brokers.

STATE TEST 13: Arizona Finance & Taxation; Leasing & Property Management; Other Arizona Practices & Laws

13.1 (b) evidence of debt, promise to repay, and terms of repayment.
A promissory note is a financial instrument only. It is one of two instruments required in a loan for real property. The other instrument is a security instrument which hypothecates the property being financed as collateral for the loan. Two common security instruments are a mortgage or deed of trust. The promissory note is evidence of debt, promise to repay, and terms and conditions of the loan.

13.2 (a) There is no redemption period but a reinstatement period instead.
There is a six-month statutory redemption period in a mortgage foreclosure that allows the original borrower an opportunity to buy back the foreclosed property. In a deed of trust foreclosure, there is a 90-day reinstatement period in which a borrower may reinstate a loan by paying back all missed payments and fees.

13.3 (a) a mortgage foreclosure.
In a mortgage foreclosure, the lender must get a court order to sell the property in default. It is a judicial procedure. A deed of trust foreclosure is non-judicial because the borrower has already given a trustee the power of sale in case of default.

13.4 (c) must pay in full on October 1 of each year.
A property tax payer in Arizona who owes less than $100 must pay on or before October 1 each year.

13.5 (c) to protect landlords and tenants.
The purpose of the Arizona Landlord and Tenant Act is to protect both the landlord and tenant by specifying the rights and responsibilities of both.

13.6 (a) Industrial and commercial rentals
The ARLTA only guides residential rental arrangements. Arizona has a separate landlord and tenant act for industrial and commercial rentals.

13.7 (b) allows commercial tenants to be locked out of their units and their property confiscated in case of default.
Commercial tenants may be locked out and their property confiscated. This is called a distraint clause and is allowed in Arizona. Residential tenants may not be locked out of units, and their property may only be seized after a rigorous process.

13.8 (b) 150%
If a landlord requires a deposit equal to one and one-half times the monthly rent amounts as a security deposit and then collects the last month's rent in advance, the landlord is in violation of the ARLTA. That's because the last month's rent is considered security deposit to assure the last month's payment. As a result, the landlord has collected more than the 150% maximum amount allowed.

13.9 (d) the lessee and lessor.
A valid lease must be signed by both the lessee and lessor. In general good real estate practice and contract law everyone who signs a lease or other real estate document should receive a copy of it as quickly as possible.

13.10 (d) The building housing the business
If the building in which is business is housed is transferred with the business in a sale, the transaction is commercial rather than a business opportunity sale. This transfer assumes the land on which the building sits is also conveyed. Together they are real property whereas a business opportunity sale includes personal property such as supplies, fixtures, and equipment. Business opportunity sales are generally of businesses in leased facilities.

13.11 (a) deed
Because a business in a commercial transaction includes real property, its title will transfer with a deed. Personal property which is exclusively acquired in a business opportunity sale transfers with a bill of sale.

13.12 (a) deal primarily with personal property conveyed in commercial or business opportunity sales.
The Uniform Commercial Code (UCC) and bulk sales laws are designed to protect vendors of personal property which might be encumbered in the sale of a business. Owners of encumbered inventory, supplies, equipment, etc. must be notified of an upcoming sale to guarantee payment. These laws also help govern the use of personal property intended to be used as collateral for a business loan.

13.13 (b) for anything unlawful.
The ARLTA prohibits rental units from being used for any unlawful purpose. It also requires residential rental units to be used as rental dwellings only. In Arizona, it also unlawful for anyone to contract to do anything illegal, and a lease is an Arizona contract.

13.14 (d) A commercial or business opportunity sale
Letters of intent are normally found in commercial or business opportunity sales and transactions. These intents to buy may be specified as binding or non-binding.

13.15 (b) Automatic renewal provisions
An automatic renewal provision is an optional clause in an Arizona property management agreement. A mutually agreed upon cancellation policy, agreement start and stop date, and management company compensation are all required in a property management agreement.

13.16 (c) a computerized listing of local and regional real estate inventory for sale or lease.
At present, a statewide MLS does not exist in Arizona. Local and regional boards and associations all provide MLS services for their members. As a result, they only include properties for sale or lease in the areas served by the board or association.

13.17 (d)   not in violation of anti-trust laws.
Designated brokers have the legal right to set commission amounts and standards within their own brokerage. It would be a serious anti-trust violation if designated brokers from several different brokerages agreed on set commissions for their market areas.

13.18 (b)   landlords do not have to accept partial payments.
The ARLTA does not require landlords to accept partial rent payments from tenants but landlords may elect to do so.

13.19 (b)   deliver notice of the failure and intent to terminate the lease within 5 days of the event.
In cases of issues which may impact tenant health and safety, a tenant in Arizona may give a landlord a five-day notice of the lease violation and tenant's intent to terminate the lease. For less dire problems, the tenant may provide a ten-day notice if a landlord fails to comply with the terms of the lease.

13.20 (c)   buyer or tenant
In Arizona prorations, the day of closing or first day of rent is credited to the buyer or tenant.

ARIZONA LICENSE EXAMINATION SAMPLE TEST

S 1. (b) Trade fixtures that are personal property.
Trade fixtures are items of a tenant's personal property that the tenant has temporarily affixed to a landlord's real property in order to conduct business. Trade fixtures may be detached and removed before or upon surrender of the leased premises. Should the tenant fail to remove a trade fixture, it may become the property of the landlord through accession. Thereafter, the fixture is considered real property.

S 2. (c) Severance and affixing.
Severance is the conversion of real property to personal property by detaching it from the real estate; affixing, or attachment, is the act of converting personal property to real property by attaching it to the real estate, such as by assembling a pile of bricks into a barbecue pit, or constructing a boat dock from wood planks.

S 3. (d) absolute fee simple estate.
The fee simple freehold estate is the highest form of ownership interest one can acquire in real estate. It includes the complete bundle of rights, and the tenancy is unlimited, with certain exceptions. The fee simple absolute estate is a perpetual estate that is not conditioned by stipulated or restricted uses.

S 4. (c) the estate may revert to a grantor or heirs if the prescribed use changes.
The defeasible fee estate is perpetual, provided the usage conforms to stated conditions. Essential characteristics are: the property must be used for a certain purpose or under certain conditions; and, if the use changes or if prohibited conditions are present, the estate reverts to the previous grantor of the estate.

S 5. (a) conventional life estate.
A conventional life estate is a freehold estate that is limited in duration to the life of the owner or other named person. Upon the death of the owner or other named individual, the estate passes to the original owner or another named party. A legal life estate is created by law as opposed to a property owner's choice.

S 6. (a) a condominium owner owns a unit of air space whereas the co-op owner owns a proprietary lease.
The owner of a condominium has a fee-simple ownership interest in his/her unit and its air space. Whereas, a co-op owner has a leasehold, not fee-simple, interest with the property's corporation. Since the corporation owns an undivided interest in the cooperative property, debts and financial obligations apply to the property as a whole, not to individual units as in a condominium.

S 7. (d) Trustor, trustee and beneficiary.
In an estate in trust, a fee owner-- the grantor or trustor-- transfers legal title to a fiduciary-- the trustee-- who holds and manages the estate for the benefit of another party, the beneficiary.

S 8. (c) fee simple ownership of the airspace in a unit and an undivided share of the entire property's common areas.
A condominium is a hybrid form of ownership of multi-unit residential or commercial properties. It combines ownership of a fee simple interest in the airspace within a unit with ownership of an undivided share, as a tenant in common, of the entire property's common elements, such as lobbies, swimming pools, and hallways.

S 9. (a) the date of recordation.
Among junior liens, date of recording determines priority. The rule is: the earlier the recording date of the lien, the higher its priority. For example, if a judgment lien is recorded against a property on Friday, and a mortgage lien is recorded on the following Tuesday, the judgment lien has priority and must be satisfied in a foreclosure ahead of the mortgage lien.

S 10. (b) A state in which a mortgagor retains title to the property when a mortgage lien is created.
In lien-theory states, laws give a lender on a mortgaged property equitable title rather than legal title. The mortgagor in a lien theory state retains legal title.

S 11. (b) transfers with the property.
The term appurtenant means "attaching to." An easement appurtenant attaches to the estate and transfers with it unless specifically stated otherwise in the transaction documents.

S 12. (c) Giving constructive notice of one's rights and interests in the property.
Recorded instruments may include deeds, mortgages, liens, easements, sale contracts, and marriage, probate and tax records. The primary purpose of recording and maintaining records of these instruments is to provide constructive notice of the conditions of a property's title-- who owns it, who maintains claims against it.

S 13. (c) A chronology of successive owners of record of a parcel of real estate.
Chain of title refers to the succession of owners of record dating back to the original grant of title from the state to a private party. It is thus more than a mere list; it is a chronological list as reflected in title records.

S 14. (c) Title insurance.
A title insurance policy indemnifies the policy holder against losses arising from defects in the title and is thus generally accepted as the best evidence of marketability after a Torrens certificate, which is not available in every jurisdiction. A signed deed is no evidence of marketability, only of an intent to convey title. An attorney's opinion and a title certificate, while forms of evidence of marketability, do not guarantee clear title or offer any protection against a defective title.

S 15. (c) percentage lease A percentage lease allows the landlord to share in the income generated from the use of the property. A tenant pays percentage rent, or an amount of rent equal to a percentage of the tenant's periodic gross sales.

S 16. (d) net lease.
A net lease requires a tenant to pay for utilities, internal repairs, and a proportionate share of taxes, insurance, and operating expenses in addition to rent.

S 17. (b) The leased property is foreclosed.
A foreclosure extinguishes all prior interests in a property, including a leasehold.

S 18. (c) the construction conforms with applicable building codes.
Building inspectors inspect a new development or improvement for code compliance. If the work complies, the municipality or county issues a certificate of occupancy which officially clears the property for occupation and use.

S 19. (b) takes title subject to the same restriction.
Deed restrictions attach to the title of the property. Therefore, the restriction passes to the new buyer.

S 20. (a) She has the right to re-possess the property because the grantee has violated the condition.
A deed condition may restrict certain uses of a property, much like a deed restriction. However, violation of a deed condition gives the grantor the right to re-take possession of the property and file suit for legal

title.

S 21. (a) To create a consistent, unchanging standard for identifying a property's unique location.
A legal description of real property is one which accurately locates and identifies the boundaries of the subject parcel to a degree acceptable by courts of law in the state where the property is located. The general criterion for a legal description is that it alone provides sufficient data for a surveyor to locate the parcel. A legal description identifies the property as unique and distinct from all other properties.

S 22. (b) They identify an enclosed area, beginning and ending at the same point.
The metes and bounds description always identifies an enclosed area by starting at an origination point, called point of beginning, or POB, and returning to the POB at the end of the description.

S 23. (a) is void.
By changing any of the terms of an offer, the offeree creates a counteroffer, and the original offer is void. At this point, the offeree becomes the offeror, and the new offeree gains the right of acceptance. If accepted, the counteroffer becomes a valid contract provided all other requirements are met.

S 24. (a) may be assigned.
A real estate contract that is not a personal contract for services can be assigned to another party unless the terms of the agreement specifically prohibit assignment. Listing agreements, for example, are not assignable, since they are personal service agreements between agent and principal. Sales contracts, however, are assignable, because they involve the purchase of real property rather than a personal service.

S 25. (c) A two-year lease.
A contract may be in writing or it may be an oral, or parol, contract. Certain oral contracts are valid and enforceable, others are not enforceable, even if valid. For example, most states require listing agreements, sales contracts, and leases exceeding one year to be in writing to be enforceable.

S 26. (b) a dual agent.
Dual agency occurs whenever a single broker represents both principal parties to a transaction. Here, since Bob and Sue work for Bill, Bill is the dual agent.

S 27. (a) upon first substantive communication.
The agent must provide written notice to all parties or their agents as soon as substantive communication occurs, which can include initial face-to-face contact.

S 28. (d) neither seller nor buyer.
In recent years, the brokerage industry has striven to clear up the question of who works for whom, and who owes fiduciary duties to whom. One solution allows a broker to represent no one in a transaction. That is, the broker acts as a transaction broker, or facilitator, and has no allegiance to buyer or seller.

S 29. (b) the principal has proposed an illegal act, which should not be obeyed.
An agent must comply with the client's directions and instructions, provided they are legal. If the directive is illegal, the agent must also immediately withdraw.

S 30. (b) negotiated with clients.
The amount of a broker's commission is whatever amount the client and broker have agreed to.

S 31. (b) the client may be liable for a commission and marketing expenses.
With an exclusive right-to-sell listing, if the property sells during the term of the revoked listing, the client is liable for the commission. If the property does not sell, the client is liable for the broker's actual costs.

S 32. (b) the agent has a claim to a commission if the owner sells or leases to a party within a certain time following the listing's expiration.
Many listings include a protection clause stating that, for a certain period after expiration, the owner is liable for the commission if the property sells to a party that the broker procured, unless the seller has since listed the property with another broker.

S 33. (c) the advertising must not be deceptive.
Advertising may not be misleading or deceptive in promoting the brokerage or listed properties. Blind ads

are also prohibited without exception. Sales agents, moreover, must identify their employer.

S 34. (a) collusion.
Collusion is the illegal practice of two or more businesses joining forces or making joint decisions which have the effect of putting another business at a competitive disadvantage.

S 35. (b) The brokers have illegally fixed prices.
Price fixing is the practice of two or more brokers agreeing to charge certain commission rates or fees for their services, regardless of market conditions or competitors.

S 36. (a) The seller may cancel the contract, since it can be ruled invalid.
A contingency that is too broad, vague, or excessive in duration may invalidate the entire contract on the grounds of insufficiency of mutual agreement. To avoid problems, the statement of a contingency should be explicit and clear, have an expiration date, and expressly require diligence in the effort to fulfill the requirement.

S 37. (d) claim the deposit as compensated damages for the buyer's failure to perform.
If a buyer fails to perform under the terms of a sale contract, the breach entitles the seller to legal recourse for damages. The usual remedy is forfeiture of the buyer's deposit as liquidated damages, provided the deposit is not grossly in excess of the seller's actual damages.

S 38. (b) The optionor must perform if the optionee takes the option, but the optionee is under no obligation to do so.
An option-to-buy places the optionee under no obligation to purchase the property. However, the seller must perform under the terms of the contract if the buyer exercises the option. An option is thus a unilateral agreement. Exercise of the option creates a bilateral sale contract where both parties are bound to perform.

S 39. (b) a decline in demand for all types of real estate in the real estate market.
Businesses that support the departing company will lay off or fire new employees, causing some to leave town in search of work. Some of these businesses may also have to cease operations. Hence the demand for residential real estate, as well as for commercial and industrial, will decline, and new construction will probably also halt until some other factor increases demand again.

S 40. (b). rental prices in that market will rise
An undersupply of commercial properties in relation to demand will most likely increase prices, as renters have fewer choices and less bargaining power.

S 41. (b) absorption.
Absorption is the amount of available property that becomes occupied over a period of time, usually measured in square feet.

S 42. (b) $17,000.
First derive the annual depreciation, which is the cost divided by the economic life. Then multiply annual depreciation times the number of years to identify total depreciation. Remember to subtract depreciation from the original cost if the question asks for the ending value. Thus, ($20,000 ÷ 20 years x 3 years) = $3,000 total depreciation. The ending value is $20,000 – 3,000, or $17,000.

S 43. (b) Apartment buildings.
The income capitalization approach, or income approach, is used for income properties and sometimes for other properties in a rental market where the appraiser can find rental data. The approach is based on the principle of anticipation: the expected future income stream of a property underlies what an investor will pay for the property.

S 44. (c) estimates net income and applies a capitalization rate to it.
The steps are: estimate potential gross income; estimate effective gross income (potential minus vacancy and credit losses); estimate net operating income (effective minus total operating expenses); select a capitalization rate; and apply the capitalization rate. Use the formula: income ÷ cap rate = value.

S 45. (c) potential gross income minus vacancy and credit loss minus expenses.
Net operating income, or NOI, is always income after vacancy, credit loss and expenses. It does not, however, include debt service.

S 46. (b) $400,000.
Value = Income ÷ Cap rate. Thus, V= $40,000 ÷ .10 = $400,000.

S 47. (a) the interest rate may vary.
Adjustable rate mortgages (ARMs) allow the lender to change the interest rate at specified intervals and by a specified amount. Federal regulations place limits on incremental interest rate increases and on the total amount by which the rate may be increased over the loan term.

S 48. (b) A wraparound lender can profit when the interest rate of the wraparound exceeds that of the underlying mortgage.
In a wraparound loan arrangement, the seller receives a junior mortgage from the buyer, and uses the buyer's payments to make the payments on the original first mortgage. This potentially enables the seller to profit from any difference between a lower interest rate on the senior loan and a higher rate on the wraparound loan.

S 49. (b) a blanket mortgage loan.
A blanket mortgage is secured by more than one property, such as multiple parcels of real estate in a development.

S 50. (b) Payments are not sufficient to retire the loan.
Negative amortization causes the loan balance to increase over the term. This occurs if the borrower's periodic payment is insufficient to cover the interest owed for the period. The lender adds the amount of unpaid interest to the borrower's loan balance.

S 51. (b) the loan amount needs to be less than the property's value.
Lenders must have a margin of borrower equity to protect against falling real estate values which increase the risk of the loan. Without this margin, a lender can incur a loan loss in a foreclosure sale since the proceeds may be less than the loan amount.

S 52. (b) Truth-in-Lending laws
Truth-in-Lending Laws, implemented by the Federal Reserve's Regulation Z, regulate the disclosure of costs, the right to rescind the credit transaction, advertising credit offers, and penalties for non-compliance with the act.

S 53. (d) Participants sell mortgage-backed securities in order to buy pools of loans.
Secondary mortgage market organizations buy pools of mortgages from primary lenders and sell securities backed by these pooled mortgages to investors. By selling securities, the secondary market brings investor money into the mortgage market. By purchasing loans from primary lenders, the secondary market returns funds to the primary lenders, thereby enabling the primary lender to originate more mortgage loans.

S 54. (a) cost recovery expense.
Cash flow is the difference between the amount of actual cash flowing into the investment as revenue and out of the investment for expenses, debt service, and all other items. Cash flow concerns cash items only, and therefore excludes depreciation (cost recovery), which is not a cash expense.

S 55. (c) dividing net income by the price paid for the property.
The investment return measure known as return on investment (ROI) is calculated by dividing net income by the value of the investment. This yields a rate of return on investment.

S 56. (a) Installing a higher capacity air conditioning and purifying system.
Basis is increased by the cost of capital improvements made to the property. Examples of capital improvements are: putting on an addition, paving a driveway, replacing a roof, adding central air conditioning, and rewiring the home. Repairs, maintenance, and redecorating are not generally considered capital improvements.

S 57. (c) There are no federal ad valorem taxes on real property.
There are no federal taxes on real property. The Constitution of the United States specifically prohibits such taxes. The federal government does, however, tax income derived from real property and gains realized on the sale of real property.

S 58. (b) the assessed value of property.
General property taxes are levied on an ad valorem basis, meaning that they are based on the assessed value of the property. Assessed value is determined according to state law, usually by a county or township assessor or appraiser.

S 59. (d) The prohibition may be legal if performed correctly.
The condominium association may be exempt from fair housing prohibitions against age discrimination if it is established as a retirement community in which 80 % of the dwellings have one person who is 55 years of age or older and it has amenities for elderly residents.

S 60. (c) The agent and the owner.
The owner has illegally discriminated, and the agent, by going along with the owner, is equally guilty of violating fair housing laws.

S 61. (b) Inspection fees.
Prorated items are expenses that both parties must share. Non-prorated items are one-time individual charges such as sale commissions, recording fees, and title insurance.

S 62. (d) A lender paying a fee to a broker for referring a borrower to the lender.
RESPA prohibits the payment of fees as part of a real estate settlement when no services are actually rendered. This prohibition includes referral fees for such services as title searches, title insurance, mortgage loans, appraisals, credit reports, inspections, surveys, and legal services.

S 63. (b) Copies of required communications to principals.
Some communications with transaction parties are good and necessary for business. Others are required by law, and records of them must be maintained for a statutory period. Required records typically include listing agreements, offers, contracts, closing statements, agency agreements, disclosure documents, correspondence and other communication records, notes and any other relevant information.

S 64. (a) refuse to use terms that refer to or describe any of the classes of persons protected by the laws.
Before entering into a listing agreement, a licensee should explain that it is necessary to comply with fair housing laws and obtain the potential client's acknowledgment and agreement. The agent should make it clear that the agent will reject the use of terms indicating race, religion, creed, color, national origin, sex, handicap, age or familial status to describe prospective buyers. Such terms should be avoided in conversation as well as in advertising.

S 65. (a) Alterations to a rental space made to fit a particular tenant
Alterations made specifically for certain tenants are called build-outs or tenant improvements. The work may involve merely painting and re-carpeting a rental space, or erecting new walls and installing special electrical or other systems.

S 66. (c) maintain a special trust account in a qualified financial depository.
State laws and real estate commission rules specify how a property manager is to manage trust funds. In general, the agent is to maintain a separate bank account for these funds, with special accounting, in a qualified depository institution. The rules for how long an agent may hold trust funds before depositing them, and how the funds are to be disbursed, are spelled out. The fundamental requirements are that the owners of all funds must be identified, and there must be no commingling or conversion of client funds and agent funds.

S 67. (c) 3
The total area of the living room is (8' x 14' + 8' x 18' + 8' x 16' + 8' x 18') = 528 SF. They will therefore need 528 / 200 SF, or 3 whole gallons.

S 68. (d) 218'
Since the investor paid $100,000 total, and that equals $250 per frontage foot, there are 400 frontage feet (100,000 / 250). If the property is two acres, it totals 87,120 SF. Dividing this by 400 produces a lot depth of 217.8'.

S 69. (c) Yes with $360 left over.
The loan she can get amounts to ($240,000 x 80%), or $192,000. The points charge is ($192,000 x .02), or $3,840. Total closing costs are then $3,840 + 800, or $4640. Thus she has $360 to spare.

S 70. (c) $90,000
First, the sale price is 115% of the appraised value, so the appraised value is $230,000 / 115%, or $200,000. The lender will lend $140,000 (70% of appraised value), so the investor will have to come up with $90,000 ($230,000 – 140,000).

S 71. (c) $96,000.
Since the comparable has an extra half-bath, it is adjusted downward to equalize with the subject. Conversely, since it has no patio, the appraiser adds value to the comparable. Thus, $100,000 minus $5,000 plus $1,000 equals $96,000.

S 72. (c) $508
The total assessed value is ($84,550 + 235,000), or $319,550. The annual tax is based on ($319,550 / 100) = 3195.5 100's. Round up to 3196. To derive the annual tax, multiply 3,196 x 1.91, or $6,104.36. Divide this by 12 for the monthly escrow: ($6,104 / 12) = $508.

S 73. (d) $92,000
The formula for equity is (current value – indebtedness). The current value is ($180,000 + 25% x 180,000), or ($180,000 x 125%), or $225,000. The current debt is ($180,000 x 80%) - $11,000, or $133,000. Their equity is therefore $92,000.

S 74. (b) $166,150
Use the formula: Gain = (Net selling price – adjusted basis) where adjusted basis = (beginning cost – depreciation). The selling price is $240,000 x 5% annual appreciation x 10 years, or ($240,000 + 50% x 240,000), or $360,000. Since land cannot be depreciated, the depreciable basis is ($240,000 total cost – 60,000 land value), or $180,000 (land = 25% total value). Annual depreciation = ($180,000 / 39 years), or $4,615. Thus total depreciation is ($4,615 x 10 years), or $46,150. The adjusted basis is therefore ($240,000 – 46,150), or $193,850. The total gain is therefore ($360,000 – 193,850), or $166,150.

S 75. (c) $80,000
Applying the formula (percent of insurable property value carried / 80% replacement cost) x claim = recovery), divide the amount of coverage carried ($160,000) by 80% of the insurable property value ($250,000) to get the percent of the claim the company will pay (80%). Multiply this percentage by the claim amount to get $80,000, what the company will pay.

S 76. (a) Tom cannot accept the offer because he does not represent the neighbor in the transaction.
Article XXVI of the Arizona State Constitution authorizes licensed real estate people to draft purchase contracts and other documents incidental to the transfer of real property. Article XXVI specifies the licensee must be "…acting in such capacity as broker or salesperson for the parties, of agent for one of the parties…" to a transaction.

S 77. (c) Arizona's Code of Real Estate.
The A.R.S. Title 32, Chapter 20 identifies this as a statute which is part of Arizona Revised Statutes. A.R.S. Title 32, Chapter 20 is a collection of statutory laws governing real estate in Arizona. They are collectively called Arizona's Code of Real Estate.

S 78. (d) Common law
Common law is law based on customs and traditions. Who buys title insurance for whom has emerged over the years resulting in the seller buying title insurance for the buyer and the buyer buying it for the lender.

S 79. (c) engage in the limited practice of law.
Drafting contracts and other legally binding documents is the exclusive right of licensed attorneys in many states. While Arizona real estate licensees may not practice law without a license, they are granted limited right by Article XXVI. Arizona real estate licensees must have a general understanding of contract law but must be very careful to avoid giving what might be considered legal advice on other issues.

S 80. (b) Mary is not legally part of a team because she is unlicensed.
ADRE defines real estate team as made up of licensees working under the same employing broker. Unlicensed support people cannot be named or shown in photographs as part of a real estate team in Arizona.

S 81. (a) A warm smile and hearty "thank you"
Finder's fees – money to unlicensed people for business leads - are prohibited in Arizona with the exception of defrayed rent earned by a tenant who recruits another tenant for her or his same complex. ADRE does not allow non-licensed people to share in a commission earned by a licensee. Thus, no money can be given to Larry for helping Susan find new customers.

S 82. (b) protect the public.
The Arizona Department of Real Estate protects the public through licensing and regulation. By establishing licensing standards for salespeople, brokers, brokerages, and real estate schools and instructors, ADRE makes certain licensees are skilling and responsible. The department also regulates real estate, cemetery and membership camping brokers to protect the public as well. It also regulates the sale of subdivisions, unsubdivided land, timeshares, and condominiums.

S 83. (a) Two
While a total of six members must have real estate experience, two need general experience within the last five years, and two can have subdivision experience. Only two must have specifically residential experience within five years of appointment, and the remaining three may have no close ties with any licensee.

S 84. (a) Despite requiring three years of real estate experience in the last five years for broker candidates, salespeople and brokers must be at least 18 years of age.
According to basic math, if a salesperson must be 18 to get licensed and then must work in real estate for at least three years, the minimum age for a broker should be at least 21. That isn't however, what Arizona state statutes say regarding minimum ages for licensure. Broker candidates as well as salesperson candidates must both be 18 years of age or older to hold an Arizona real estate license.

S 85. (b) No, because only a designated broker can accept money from the public for real estate services in Arizona.
Arizona real estate salespeople and associate brokers may not accept money from the public for real estate services. Only a designated broker may do so. When a brokerage is paid a commission, it receives payment in its name and reissues a new check to the salesperson for his or her share of the commission, minus the brokerage share, and any related fees and expenses. Salespeople and associate brokers are not allowed receive money in their names from clients and customers.

S 86. (d) an associate broker with no additional responsibilities
An associate broker is often thought of as a salesperson who holds a broker's license. He or she may have no additional responsibilities, duties, or liabilities within the brokerage. As a result, an associate broker who may not ever be called on to be a temporary designated broker does not need the additional management skills and practice and legal knowledge covered in the broker management clinics.

S 87. (c) called puffing.
"Puffing" is legal and allowable in Arizona real estate marketing. It is defined as exaggerated or superlative comments not intended as fact. Arizona believes the public can discern the difference between fraudulent and misleading statements and obvious puffing.

S 88. (b) non-possessory rights which are written and recorded.
Easements are real property interests which cannot be possessed by the holder of the easement. They are written and recorded so that they are disclosed in a title search. Appurtenant easements, personal

easements and easements in gross, and easements by necessity (preventing land-locked property) are types of easements but none of these represent all easements in Arizona.

S 89. (a) either the dominant or servient owns both parcels.
An easement created by a dominant on the property of a servient can terminate if either party acquires both parcels. If one person owns both, there is no longer any use for the easement because the property owner is entitled to drive anywhere on her or his own property.

S 90. (a) reservation in deed.
Reservation in deed allows a grantor to retain a limited right to use the property of another after title transfers. It is agreed to by both parties to the transaction and found in the new deed given to the grantee. Farmer Brown reserved access to his fishing hole as part of his agreement with the grantee, and the easement will be recorded.

S 91. (c) Yes, community property is a mode, manner or way of holding interest in property in Arizona allowing a husband or wife in a marriage to will one's share to a third party.
Community property allows one person in a marriage to will his or her share of real property to someone other than the spouse, community property with right of survivorship in Arizona does not. Holding as community property may result in the real property becoming an issue in probate because one share of the property can be willed. Community property with right of survivorship has an automatic survivorship right thus disposition of the real property does not require probate court clearance. A survivorship right also defeats any will.

S 92. (c) Spanish land grant law.
Nineteenth century Spanish property law held that husband and wife were equals in marriage rather than a combination into one entity. That is the basic premise behind community property. Arizona's history with the Spanish led to adopting this idea for modern property law, and other Southwestern states like California, Nevada, New Mexico and Texas are community property states as well.

S 93. (b) leasehold interest.
Popular in New York city, a cooperative is a rental, thus a leasehold. Since the cooperative's apartment unit is rented, it is considered a proprietary lease or leasehold for life. Since it is not a freehold or ownership estate, it cannot be willed. Cooperative tenants own stock in the corporation which owns the apartment building which allows tenants increasing equity but only in the value of the stock as well as an increased voice in building policies and acceptance of new tenants.

S 94. (d) have a "dealer's" license from the Arizona Department of Fire, Building and Safety.
Manufactured homes on rented pads are considered personal property. They have vehicle identification numbers like an automobile and transfer with a bill of sale. Real estate licensees are not allowed to represent sellers and buyers without a dealer's license and this requirement extends to modular homes as well. Manufactured home located on lots owned by the manufactured home owner are considered real property and may be represented by a real estate licensee.

S 95. (c) percolated water.
Alluvion is the natural buildup of land due to wind or water; avulsion is the rapid and sudden natural removal of land; and erosion is the gradual natural wearing away of land. Percolated water filters or seeps through the earth.

S 96. (c) general provisions that apply statewide.
The 1980 Groundwater Management Code established three levels of water management. The lowest level includes general provisions that apply statewide; the next level of management applies to Irrigation Non-Expansion Areas; and the highest and with the most extensive provisions is applied to Active Management Areas where groundwater overdraft is most extensive.

S 97. (d) non-irrigation purposes including industry, livestock watering, and golf courses.
Groundwater withdrawn under a Type 2 right can only be used for non-irrigation purposes. The right is based on historic pumping of ground water for non-irrigation use and equals the maximum amount pumped in any one year between 1975 and 1980.

S 98. (b) 1%
Wetlands are defined as consistently saturated lands which support a variety of plant life. Arizona is an arid state with few rivers, tanks, marshes and rain fall collection areas. As a result, only 1% of land in Arizona is designated as wetlands. Special wetland projects around Tucson and Phoenix help enhance wetland development.

S 99. (b) ADEQ
The ADEQ is the Arizona Department of Environmental Quality. It was created under the state's Environmental Quality Act of 1986. The EPA and Army Corps of Engineers are both federal entities, and the ADWR has a mission centered on water use management.

S 100. (b) She has five days from acknowledging the notice to cancel the contract.
In Arizona, every buyer who signs a contract to buy a property where an illegal remediated methamphetamine (ecstasy or LSD) lab existed must receive notice within five days of the past presence of the lab and owner's arrest. The buyer must acknowledge receipt of the notice and then has five days to elect to cancel the contract. The same notice must be given to a tenant prior to signing a rental agreement.

S 101. (c) twelve months.
Arizona state statutes require the owner of real property where a lab was located to remediate the residual contaminated property within 12 months of date of removal. A registered drug laboratory remediation firm must do the remediation.

S 102. (a) radon.
Radon is a colorless, odorless radioactive gas produced by the natural decay of radioactive substances released in soil and geological formation below the surface on which structures sit. It is a known carcinogen which can enter the building through basements and foundations. It is most dangerous when it builds up in enclosed spaces and if found "out of thin air" in homes throughout the state.

S 103. (a) Surveyors sought natural monuments which wouldn't change in the future.
Early surveyors dividing the west into townships sought characteristics of nature that they felt would not change in years to come. Where two rivers come together had such perceived durability, and in fact, the location of the confluence of the Gila and Salt Rivers south of Phoenix has not changed since the initial point for Arizona was selected.

S 104. (c) It is a second principal baseline and meridian in Arizona.
Unlike many states, Arizona has two principal baselines and meridians. In 1869, a small portion of the northeastern corner of Arizona was changed to the Navajo Meridian and Baseline to describe part of the Navajo Reservation. Part of the original designation in New Mexico has disappeared but Arizona maintains a second baseline and meridian in the state.

S 105. (d) 360
To determine the size in acres of SE4, NW4; E2 multiply 4 (SE4) x 4 (SW4) which equals 16. Divide 640, the number of acres in a section, by 16 to get 40 acres. The semi colon in this land description separates two parcels. The first one is 40 acres, the second is determined by dividing 640 by 2 (E2) for a total of 320 acres. 320 + 40 equals 360 acres for the entire parcel size.

S 106. (a) 320
A rod is an early survey tool used when land was actually measured with physical rods and chains. A rod is 16.5 feet so 5,280 (the number of feet in a mile) divided by 16.5 equals 320, thus there are 320 rods in 5,280 feet.

S 107. (a) A Commissioner's Public Report (CPR)
Arizona subdivision law allows for developers to take lot reservations for unimproved subdivision parcels and conditional sales contracts for lots that include improvements prior to issuance of a CPR. Developers may not, however, close on any sale until CPR is approved. Until that time, lot reservations and conditional sales contracts may be rescinded at any time with full refund of deposit money.

S 108. (c) up to three years

Buyers have seven days after signing a contract, up to six months if buyer(s) have not personally inspected the property, and up to three years if promised access is not delivered on subdivided land. Contracts on unsubdivided land is simply up to three years.

S 109. (c) property taxes.

Property taxing authorities place a property tax lien on all taxable Arizona properties on January 1 of each year. Property taxes are in first priority position always in Arizona.

S 110. (b) involuntary and specific.

Jennifer's mechanic's lien is involuntary because it is statutory (created by law), and she does not voluntarily acquire it. It is specific because it liens only against the property affected, i.e., Jennifer's house on which she failed to pay for the repairs or remodeling.

S 111. (d) unlicensed contractors and handypersons cannot lien.

Only licensed contractors can file mechanic's liens in Arizona when their work goes unpaid.

S 112. (c) return the sales price of the property to John after recovering it via a special appropriation.

When a property owner in Arizona dies without a will or apparent legitimate heirs, the state acquires it via escheat. To reduce the number of abandoned properties, the state sells it, and then must search for legitimate heirs for seven years. If heirs are found, the state goes to the legislature for a special appropriation to get the sales price back and then gives the money to the heirs.

S 113. (a) CC&Rs.

Like CC&Rs, deed restrictions are placed on property before it is developed. Both deed restrictions and CC&Rs can restrict and regulate size and type of improvements, setbacks, operations of home businesses, parking, etc.

S 114. (b) Put a lien on his property

Like most creditors, the HOA can put a lien on Sam's property for collection of payment. It can only foreclose for failure to pay an assessment, not for a violations penalty. The HOA does have legal recourse, but cannot discontinue service such as trash removal because they are generally contracted individually by the homeowner.

S 115. (c) A trustee's deed from deed of trust foreclosure

Bargain and sales deeds are used in cases of involuntary separation from one's property such as foreclosure or tax sale. General and special warranty deeds are used in voluntary alienation such as a purchase. A quit claim deed is not a conveying deed. A trustee's deed is the result of a deed of trust foreclosure.

S 116. (b) It is valid and competes with the new buyer's deed, but has lesser validity because it was never legally delivered.

A valid deed in Arizona must be signed, sealed, and delivered. Grandpa Jones' was signed and sealed but never delivered. Delivery is generally accomplished by putting the new deed physically in the hands of the grantee or via title company registered mail. Deeds in Arizona are not required to be recorded but approximately 95% of them are.

S 117. (b) The homestead exemption is transferred to their new home in Tucson.

Arizona homestead exemptions are provided for primary residences only. They are Arizona's only legal life estate because they are on the life of the primary home owner. They transfer when a citizen buys a new home and the new home becomes his or her primary residence; they are lost to the previous residence. A homestead exemption terminates if a homeowner moves out of Arizona since it is exclusive to Arizona law.

S 118. (a) one which materially impacts the value or desirability of a property.

A real property fact is considered material if it has an impact on the value of the property or which might impact its desirability for a potential owner.

S 119. (d) Jennifer and Sharon have an agency relationship.

Agency is a personal relationship governed by law. To create agency in Arizona, a person only needs to delegate authority to an agent, and the agent accepts that authority. That's what happened between Jennifer and Sharon. Arizona does not require any paperwork between parties for a licensee to represent a principal in a real estate transaction.

S 120. (a) a deed of trust and lien theory state
While there are still some mortgages in Arizona, it is primarily a deed of trust or trust deed state. Lenders prefer deeds of trust, and they offer a better opportunity for borrowers to recover their property than they have in mortgage foreclosure. Lien theory means title to property is transferred at time of sale and a lender's interests are protected via a lien against the property.

S 121. (d) trustor.
A deed of trust is a security instrument which hypothecates the property as collateral in case of default. A deed of trust is a three-party instrument in which the lender is the beneficiary, borrower is the trustor, and third party with power of sale and bare naked title (no right of possession) is held by a neutral party called a trustee. Mortgages are two party instruments made up of the lender, the mortgagee, and borrower, the mortgagor.

S 122. (a) It is on time.
The second half of the current year's property taxes is due on May 1 of the following year. She paid on time

S 123. (a) issue a five-day pay or quit notice or otherwise initiate eviction action.
The Arizona Residential Landlord and Tenant Act gives an Arizona landlord to right to issue a pay or quit (leave the property) after default. Should the tenant not pay in five days, the landlord may take action to reclaim the rental unit.

S 124. (c) They have no rights under the ARLTA because it exempts fraternal and social organization housing.
Whether the sorority house is on or off university property has no bearing. Residential institutions, purchasers under a contract for sale, hotel/motel/recreational lodging, employees of landlords where living in a rental unit is a perk, condos and proprietary leases, and federal government public housing are also exempt. Mobile home rentals, commercial and vacant land rentals, and membership camping each have their own landlord and tenant act and are not covered by the Arizona Residential Landlord and Tenant Act.

S 125. (b) a warranty deed
A warranty deed – the deed used most often in voluntary alienation such as a real property purchase – contains five covenants including the promise that the grantor will defend the grantee against all claims made by third parties, will compensate the grantee if title fails at any time, and will deliver all instruments needed to make title good. These are all liabilities for the grantor and assets for the grantee.

Appendix: Useful Websites

Arizona Real Estate Candidate Handbook
This contains crucial information regarding the Pearson Vue Arizona Real Estate Exam. Make sure to download and read this participant booklet to fully understand the entire test taking process.
https://www.asisvcs.com/publications/pdf/090300.pdf

Key Arizona Contacts

Arizona Department of Real Estate
2910 N 44th Street, Suite 100
Phoenix, AZ 85018
http://www.re.state.az.us/Default.aspx

Pearson Vue Testing Service
5601 Green Valley Drive
Bloomington, MN 55437
952-681-3000
https://home.pearsonvue.com/Home.aspx

Arizona Association of Realtors
255 East Osborn Road, Suite 200
Phoenix, Arizona 85012
602-248-7787
https://www.aaronline.com/

Phoenix Association of Realtors
5033 N. 19th Ave., Suite 119
Phoenix, AZ 85015
602-246-1012
https://paronline.com/

If you liked Arizona Real Estate License Exam Prep, check out the other titles of Performance Programs Company!

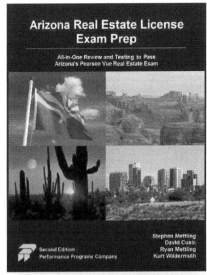

Cramming for your Arizona real estate exam? You need Arizona Real Estate License Exam Prep!

Where can you buy Real Estate License Exam Prep?
Arizona Real Estate License Exam Prep (AZ-RELEP) is available as a printed book or e-book through nearly all online retailers.

Looking for a real estate principles textbook? Get what all the students love -- Principles of Real Estate Practice!

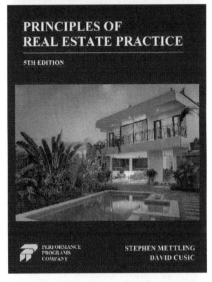

Principles of Real Estate Practice is invaluable reference material for real estate professionals. Its 460-pages contain the essentials of real estate law, principles, and practices taught in real estate schools and colleges across the country.

Where can you buy Principles of Real Estate Practice?
Principles Real Estate Practice is available as a printed book or e-book through nearly all online retailers.
http://www.amazon.com/dp/1500569399/

Struggling with real estate math? The solution to that equation is Real Estate Math Express!

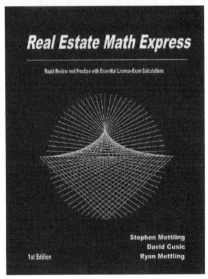

Real Estate Math Express is a concise, easy-to-study test preparation guide to help real estate students improve their real estate math scores to pass the state licensing test. The primary feature of Real Estate Math Express is that it contains all necessary formulas and practice questions in 70+ pages.

Where can you buy Real Estate Math Express?
Real Estate Math Express is available as a printed book or e-book through nearly all online retailers.
http://www.amazon.com/dp/1495255573

Publisher Contact
Ryan Mettling
Performance Programs Company
502 S. Fremont Ave., Ste. 724, Tampa, FL 33606
ryan@performanceprogramscompany.com
www.performanceprogramscompany.com

Made in the USA
Lexington, KY
02 April 2018